REEF & BEEF

Identical Twins
Walking Different Paths

The First Fifty years

BY **JACKI JAMES AND KYLIE FISHER**

Published 2025
Copyright © Reef and Beef Publishing 2025
The moral right of the author has been asserted
All rights reserved. No part of this publication may be reproduced, stored in a retrieval system, or transmitted in any form or by any means, electronic, mechanical, photocopying, recording or otherwise, without the prior written permission from both the copyright owners and publisher.
For permission requests, email: reefandbeef68@gmail.com

Disclaimer
The content in this book, Reef and Beef is intended for informational and educational purposes only and is not a substitute for professional advice or therapy. The author's experiences and those of others shared within these pages aim to offer insight and empowerment. Each individual's experience is unique; readers should seek professional help tailored to their circumstances. The author and publisher disclaim any liability or responsibility for any outcomes related to using this book's information.
Published by Ingram Spark
Publishing Partnership with Change Maker Press Pty Ltd
ISBN 978-1-7640373-0-3 (Paperback)

Please join our social media pages,
we would love to hear your twin stories!
Facebook: Reef and Beef 1968
Instagram: reefandbeef1968

Connect with Jacki James and Kylie Fisher at:
reefandbeef68@gmail.com

CONTENTS

DEDICATION vii

FOREWORD BY THE HUSBANDS ix

AUTHOR'S NOTE xiii

Twins 01

Beach and Bush 15

Double Trouble 33

Free and Easy 59

A Crisis 79

Police Academy 105

Badge and Honour 125

Detectives 171

1000 Kilometres 211

Multitasking 285

Pilgrimage 331

DEDICATION

*To our families, David, Isabella, Harrison and Adelaide,
Scott, Georgia, Sophie, and Grace.*

*To all those members of our extensive family tree
who have shared many of these experiences with us.*

*To the many people who have assisted with the research
and writing of this book.
Thank you!*

To twins all over the world.

FOREWORD BY
THE HUSBANDS

Thank you for taking the time to read this book. I would like to congratulate you in advance for wanting to be enlightened and educated in the unique synergy that twins are fortunate to be blessed with.

My name is David Fisher, and I met my wife, Kylie, twenty-five years ago. I was immediately attracted to her special qualities—and the fact that she had a gun in her handbag.

Within hours of meeting Kylie, I was told about her twin sister Jacki and the 'twin thing' they share. I was not aware that I was about to embark on an advanced diploma in the life experience of twinology, because by getting tangled up with one twin, I automatically got entangled with the other.

It's often said that twins share an unbreakable bond, but the true depth of this connection is something you can only understand when you experience it firsthand. This bond takes on a whole new meaning, a meaning that this book will reveal to you.

Although Kylie and Jacki are twins, they are still two individual people who have lived separate lives, so this book has two authors, and each twin individually tells her own life story at parallel periods in their lives. At first, these stories intertwine, before they reach a fork in the road, one traveling up the coast, and one, inland to the bush. They are Reef and Beef.

While reading the two stories, you will discover it's not a book, but a journey; a journey that once you're on, you will find hard to stop. You will be driven down highways with blue lights flashing, taken down unsealed roads and ushered up dry gullies, only to be washed back down in raging floods. You will be taken above the earth in aeroplanes, and you will walk up planks while boarding seafaring ships, all before you cross a country on foot.

There are twists and turns, the exciting, the sad, the funny, and the unexpected experiences of living a life as a twin.

I'm sure after reading this book, you will conclude how lucky they are to be twins.

Thanks
Dave Fisher

My name is Scott James. I am the husband of the second born twin Jacki, having first met her in at Parramatta in 1987, when we were both working in the New South Wales Police Force. I actually 'rescued' Jacki who had broken down driving a plain clothes police vehicle (she had run out of petrol) in Phillip Street about seventy metres from the entrance to Parramatta Police Station. I displayed my vast array of mechanical skills and saved the day. Over the next few months, I was pursued relentlessly by Jacki (she will say I pursued her), and I was lucky enough to walk down the aisle with her in 1993.

The book is a fascinating read of the life and times of Jacki and Kylie and the unique connection of twins. Jacki maintains she is the reef coastal twin, however I think the country is really ingrained in her, and I would not call upon her for a surf rescue, if she had to venture further than ten metres out at Sawtell Beach

As young women both Jacki and Kylie left the then fairly sleepy country town of Dubbo to embark on a career with the New South Wales Police Force and enjoy the bright lights and changes a life in the big city would bring. They forged their own lives and careers, but throughout have always had a very close connection, and I learnt very early on that I had to 'share' Jacki with her sister. Over the years they have had considerable challenges, but always met those challenges and forged on—even if on numerous times it does take fourteen telephone calls a day to solve a 'problem' that could be solved with one call. I guess that is the 'twin thing'.

Kylie is living an incredible life out in the bush (really out in the bush) and despite this isolation she has also raised a lovely family with three great kids. I love her old man Dave who is a champion and one of the best blokes you could meet. I am not allowed to do a lot of mechanical work on the property for a number of reasons (mostly lack of skill) but assist in other ways.

Congratulations to Jacki and Kylie on your book. To readers, enjoy, it is a delightful read.

Cheers
Scott James

AUTHOR'S NOTE

What is it like to have an identical twin? After being asked this continually throughout our lives, we were inspired to share through our life experiences, what it is truly like to have a twin.

This is a rare dual memoir, which is revealing and personal. Each chapter has two parts, Reef and Beef. We both write separate stories written at parallel periods in our lives, and these stories compare and connect our twin lives.

The unity of twins is complicated and unshakable. We grew up side by side with a deeply woven thread of understanding, and a bond and love that time and separation could not diminish.

As children, we lived through most life events together, but as adults, we have been separated by distance and circumstance, with us individually experiencing vastly different things. We have often considered how nature and nurture has changed two identical people over the first fifty years of our lives.

Our memoir has a little bit of everything: laughter, embarrassing stories, heartbreaking periods, proud moments, and the occasional questionable life choices. Though much of it is light-hearted, we also share stories about challenging and confronting periods in our lives, such as domestic violence, anorexia, and traumatic police incidents. These moments have been written with care, honesty, and respect. But still, with a light touch and at times with humour, as in many instances humour was used as a coping mechanism during some distressing events.

Memory is both a gift and an illusion. We have made every effort to ensure the events and details in this book are written accurately to the best of our recollections. Any errors or omissions are unintentional. We have changed some names to respect the privacy of certain people in our story; however, the heart of the story remains true.

We hope that this memoir will make you think about any twins in your lives, their love, their relationship, and sometimes their struggles for individuality. Grab a wine or a cuppa, find a nice spot by the beach under a palm tree, or perhaps next to your caravan near a gum tree, and please enjoy the read.

Jacki and Kylie, a.k.a Reef and Beef

Twins

Beef

My twin and I have always been exceptionally close, even when distance separates us. 'What is it like being a twin?' is something I have often been asked, but it's all I have ever known from the time the fertilised egg split in my mother's womb! As strange as it may seem, even though I am a twin, I also find the idea of multiple births amazing. People are fascinated by two or more people who look exactly alike, as demonstrated at one Milan fashion show when Gucci had sixty-eight pairs of identical twins model their clothes; unfortunately, we were not asked to participate. Often, people have said to me, 'I wish I had a twin,' but like all things, there are positives and negatives to being a twin. I don't like it if my sister and I are together and people stare; however, I find myself doing that exact thing when I see identical twins. I read articles on twins or watch documentaries, and I wonder why twins or multiple births occur. Of course, I know scientifically why it happens, but the phenomenon still amazes me—having someone who looks, speaks, and has the same mannerisms as yourself is weird.

At times, when I am with my sister, I feel like I am having an out-of-body experience, floating above, watching myself, but actually, I am watching her, with no control. We have similar builds and matching faces with a crop of freckles. There have been occasions in my life where I have felt like I have been given a new identity and placed in witness protection, instinctively answering to a pseudonym Jacki, the name of my identical twin. As any identical twin can testify, there are times when someone unfamiliar approaches you and starts talking to you in a comfortable tone. This is a difficult situation. Have I forgotten who they are, or do they think I am my twin? Sometimes, I have found it is easier to assume my twin's identity and just go with it. Throughout our lives there have been occasions when even our husbands have confused us. Once I travelled to see Jacki after she had given birth to her first baby. I woke early and tiptoed through the hallway before entering their large, open-plan living room. As I entered, I thought, fair dinkum, as I spotted my brother-in-law standing stark naked on the opposite side of the room. Apparently, he had just gotten out of the shower and had run to answer the phone. I was a little shocked at the naked sight in front of me, but I kept walking towards him, expecting him to cover up any second. I got within two meters of him before he recognised, I was not my sister. Twins or not, there are some things only a wife needs to see.

When Jacki phones, sometimes several times a day, my husband never complains and appears to understand our twin connection. He is often heard saying, Metaphorically, 'if you marry one twin, you marry the other.' Once, an episode of Insight on SBS TV featured twins. Jacki and I decided we would watch the show together via the phone. The presenter had a roomful of identical and fraternal twins and asked them their thoughts and opinions about being born a twin. Near the conclusion of the show, she asked the audience of twins, 'If you had to choose between your twin's life or your partner's life, who would you choose?' One twin said something like, 'If I was on the Titanic and there was only one spare life jacket left, I would give it to my twin, and my husband would have to swim.'

This caused laughter amongst all the twins in the audience, with many nodding their heads in agreement. My husband, who was close by and overheard this, thought the reply was very amusing, particularly when both my twin and I agreed we would do the same. A few weeks later, my sister posted my husband a parcel containing some yellow floaties, inscribed with the words SMS Titanic, to keep for future use.

In many family photos, our other two sisters are in the middle, and we are positioned on either end; our family joke is that we are the bookends. Interestingly, when I scour the family photo albums, I find that there are very few individual photos of Jacki and me; we are always together. I love all my sisters dearly, but I do feel exceptionally close to my twin; we are like a family within a family. Maybe this closeness is because we have similar interests, maybe it's because we have experienced many of life's milestones together, or perhaps it's because she knows me better than anyone. Like a long-term married couple, we can communicate with just a glance. Although not always the case, other twins I have spoken to, both identical and fraternal, agree that they have a special bond with their twin. Of course, Jacki and I have had arguments throughout our lives, lots of them, mostly over trivial things, but we always make up and move on. I have read stories about twins who, even in adulthood, dress identically, live and work together and are completely entwined. I love Jacki, but now as an adult, I could not live with her every day.

Since we were young, our lives have been filled with what some would describe as psychic phenomena. I get annoyed when I have a terrible dream in which something frightening is happening to Jacki; instead of brushing it off as just a bad dream, I panic and think, 'Is this a twin telepathy moment?' and I can't relax until I find out she is okay. I have read and watched programs regarding bizarre things happening to twins. Even now, when I live out the back of woop woop, 'twin things' still occur, and I can't explain them. Other twins have had similar experiences. Are 'twin things' coincidental, telepathy, or just a deep emotional connection? There is a well-known story of twin boys separated at birth and raised apart. The famous Jim twins had been adopted by different families at four weeks of age. Both boys were named Jim by their adoptive families; both had sons that they named James Allan, both had a pet dog named Toy, both hated spelling but excelled in maths, and both had the same career. Both men married women named Betty, divorced, and married women called Linda. I'm not sure how that can be explained. Thankfully the brothers were reunited when they were thirty-nine years old.

Just because Jacki and I look incredibly similar and share a birthday does not mean we are one person. We have many differences, even minor ones that most people overlook. Sadly, many people think of twins as two halves of one soul, instead of two separate, individual people. I watched a news item recently in which 100-year-old twins were celebrating their milestone birthday, sitting squashed together, blowing out the candles of one cake. I thought, 'Even after all those fabulous years, they were not given their own individual birthday cake; they had to share.' Perhaps it was just a safety issue, and they were concerned that 200 candles might set off the fire alarm?

I learned from a very young age that if my twin did something, I also did it, and vice versa. 'The twins did it' was a phrase I have been familiar with my entire life. Unfortunately, being compared to your twin is something twins must, but shouldn't have to get used to. Singleton siblings suffer this a little, but twins suffer it to a higher degree. Who is more intelligent? Who is less successful? I believe neither of us is better nor worse at something. Although I hate it when people compare us as twins, I find that I do at times compare my own life to Jacki's. It's hard not to when our lives are like salt and pepper. Interestingly I don't compare my life to our singleton siblings' lives.

I live several hours from the closest town, the small country town of Bourke, or the Back O' Bourke as it is commonly referred to in far-western New South Wales. Bourke sits on the bank of the Darling River and has a population of about 1800 people, which fluctuates according to the seasons. The town's identity is woven with the culture and history of its aboriginal community, with murals telling dreaming stories scattered on the shop walls. Charles Sturt arrived in the area in 1828, but it was not settled by colonists until 1835. The history of the area includes early exploration, paddleboat trade, farmers, stockmen, bush poets, bushrangers, and Afghan cameleers. Many caravanning tourists flock to the area in winter and explore the historical town or enjoy the beauty of the nearby national parks, but all leave before the scorching summers arrive. The winters are cool and short, and the summers are long and desert-hot. The small main street has around twenty buildings, and you never have trouble finding a car park amongst the utes and other four-wheel-drive vehicles. Walking the main street, you are greeted by familiar faces who offer a friendly 'Gidday,' often followed by 'How much rain did you get?' or 'How do things look out your way?'

My husband, Dave, and I own three rural properties that are connected. Despite sharing boundaries, each property has its own unique qualities and environments. Property one is where our home is situated. It is mostly mulga woodlands wrapped around hills and creek systems. Some of the hills are large, and in some areas there are cliff-like drops into ancient gorges. The creek systems all spread out like veins through the rocky country and are mostly dry, but explode with water after rainstorms, creating fast torrents.

Property two is predominately black soil, lignum, and cane grass wetlands. This area is part of a nationally important breeding site for hundreds of waterbirds and unique aquatic animals and has been the subject of many scientific studies.

Property three is generally Napunya Creek country, with a mixture of black soil floodplains and semi-permanent water holes—a carefully controlled number of cattle mix in harmony with the plant, animal, and birdlife. Combined, the three properties cover

100,000 acres, and their diversity supports our family along with a wide range of plant and animal species.

Although I was born in a country town, I was not raised on an isolated cattle station in outback Australia. I certainly cannot throw a sheep and shear it, but I do feel like a wild bush flower that over the past twenty-odd years has slowly adapted to my remote environment.

Reef

My older sister, my younger sister, my twin—this is how I have always described my three sisters. Throughout my life, it was easier to describe each sister this way to identify which particular sister I was talking about. I'm sure I would have referred to her as just 'my sister' if there had been only my twin and me.

What is it like being a twin? How much has nature and nurture influenced our personalities? How much have genetics and the environment influenced our child rearing, fashion, medical history, house styles, and faith? What part has our DNA played in these outcomes?

There have not been many days in my life when I have not spoken to my twin sister Kylie, and this can be challenging as she lives fourteen hours away from me. But somehow, we always manage, and I even sneak a quick call in if I'm travelling overseas, which can be difficult when navigating different time zones. When I'm not thinking of my twin, I am often reminded of her. My neighbour is also named Kylie, and like all suburban blocks, our homes are relatively close. When I hear the neighbours, family call out her name, I always turn. Kylie hasn't lived near me for over twenty-five years, but this distance has not diminished the closeness that we have felt throughout our lives. However, our relationship has not always been like that of two characters in the novel Little Women, where the sisters walk the streets, arms locked together in complete contentment. As family and friends can testify, we have had our fair share of fights over the years. Overall, most of my arguments with Kylie are sorted quickly with one of us backing down, defeated, exhausted by the tension. Most women will defend their children like a seagull protecting its greasy chips, and that protective behaviour is similar to that extended to your twin. It's fair game that I criticise my twin sister, but if anyone else does so, I will actively defend her. We have strong personalities and were raised to have an opinion that we often express to each other. I do give my opinion to my twin sister far more readily than I would dare express to my other sisters. Although we might bicker occasionally, at least we are communicating, and we rarely hold a grudge.

The bond of twins, in most cases, is very strong. We have a good relationship with our other sisters, but Kylie and I have a stronger connection. I'm sure my other sisters are aware of this, and I often wonder if they get frustrated by the fact that we are twins. Would our relationship with them have been different if Kylie and I were born as singletons?

Being a twin is the most natural thing to me, and when I'm with Kylie, I feel whole; I feel complete. I have never lived NOT being a twin, so I don't know what living as a singleton would feel like, but I would be lonely without my twin sister. However, that doesn't mean I haven't pondered what it would be like to have my own unique identity. Facebook tags me in my twin sister's photos, and she can unlock my iPhone with camera recognition security. I am not used to having to make a decision entirely on my own. I have discussed most significant decisions in my life with her. I guess she is my unqualified therapist or life coach, not that this has always turned out so well.

We have always received more attention because there are two of us. As time has progressed, twins have become much more common due to women giving birth later in life and the introduction of fertility treatments. With so many twins about, I now secretly fear we have been upstaged by triplets and quadruplets. Walking around today without my twin, I blend into the environment as if I'm in camouflage amid all the other ordinary people living life.

I live by the ocean, in a little seaside village on the north coast of New South Wales, situated between the Great Dividing Range and the Pacific Ocean. I don't live right on the beach, but close enough to hear the pounding waves on a still night and smell the aromatic sea air. Our house is nestled in the middle of the Bongil Bongil National Park in a gated community. The houses and its residents are securely locked behind gates in the estate between 6pm and 6am. Well, we are not locked inside, but the gates close, and it makes me feel a little safer during the night. The close-knit privacy resulting from living in a small community association does not always have a 'kumbaya' atmosphere, especially given the inevitability of a few alpha residents who elect to be on the executive committee. They relish the once-in-a-lifetime chance to dominate the remaining residents and take full advantage, making the Big Brother house look like a kindergarten.

However, the fact that we can literally step out our backdoor and walk straight into a lush tropical rainforest is a win as far as we are concerned. An estuary about twenty metres from our backdoor snakes its way to the Pacific Ocean. It provides an excellent location for paddle boarding or kayaking, and the tranquil national park is great for bushwalking. When we first moved here, we often saw koalas in the trees. We don't see many these days. The increase in housing developments and household pets has driven them further into the bush. The green vegetation consists of tropical plants like ferns and tall eucalyptus trees. I love that our house is swaddled in green, the colour of life, nature and energy. In the early mornings, lying in bed and looking out my bedroom window, I can see the tops of the tall trees swaying in the gentle breeze. This movement is not only peaceful to watch but, as an added bonus, acts as a weather forecast; if the treetops sway too much, I know that the local beach will not be pleasant that morning, and the north-easterly breeze will provide resistance on my morning walk or run.

My husband and I were lucky enough to be transferred to the pretty seaside village of Sawtell through work twenty-five years ago. The millennials have taken to calling it 'The Village'. The axis of our village is a shopping strip about 200 metres long. A wide, well-kept mowed lawn is up the centre, lined with heavily branched Morton Bay figs. The majestic trees are illuminated at night by intense spotlights to highlight their beauty and strength. Our little strip is the beating heart of our community, providing the perfect place to eat fish and chips and Indian or organic Dorrigo bacon with avo accompanied by a soy mocha latte. At night, festoon lights decorate the restaurants, creating an ambience to the street. There is an R.S.L, bowling club and pub all within easy walking distance, and my husband somehow has to donate to the Salvation Army at all three of the licenced premises when they do their weekly donation drive, as he is known to wander between all three on the one night. He calls it networking. We have festivals throughout the year, and once a month, the street is closed to vehicles to allow families and friends to gather and enjoy an evening outside. The mid-north coast has a very moderate temperature all year long, making thongs and swimwear our indigenous apparel.

The two-kilometre beach, with a headland at either end, is only a short distance from the main street and is manned by volunteer lifeguards. Both headlands have walking paths and lookouts to appreciate views of the coastline. I walk or run along the beach almost daily and enjoy the salty air. If I am lucky enough, I will see whales during their annual migration, where they perform like large wet acrobats throwing themselves in the air, playing in the freedom of our protected ocean. I often sit and watch the sea, which gives me a sense of calm. The beach is a great place to think; sunshine is my vitamin, and serotonin gives me happy hormones. The beach is well-maintained, and an offshore island shelters our position on the coast. This creates a very safe beach for families, and during the school holidays, the area explodes in population, with many tourists also enjoying the beauty and serenity of our quaint seaside village.

Beach and Bush

Beef

Life on the land is unique, a constant cycle of boom and bust, struggles and triumphs, laughter and tears, freedoms and restraints. At this time of my life, we were nearing the end of years of unforgiving drought, a bust cycle. This one was declared in the Murray Darling Basin area of New South Wales to be the worst drought on record, exceeding the Federation Drought, The World War One Drought, and the Millennium drought. When droughts are named, they are a concern.

Fortunately for us, property two had recently flooded, thanks to floodwaters that had travelled over 700 kilometres from Queensland, winding down into the Warrego River and arriving at an area on our land called The Cuttaburra Basin. In more significant flows, the water continues through the basin and links up with the Darling River. A large volume of water had arrived, and over the past weeks, some had subsided and soaked into the thirsty black soil, leaving hundreds of water channels that were yet to dry up, which were surrounded by large lignum bushes and lush grasses. The environment on properties one and three regrettably looked vastly different from the now rejuvenated ecosystem of property two.

The winter brought a flood and a nasty influenza bug that spread rapidly throughout the country. I had been miserably sick with the flu for three lingering weeks, and for several days, I genuinely felt like I was about to die. I am confident I should have sought medical help, but this is difficult when I live in a remote location, and the thought of bouncing in a vehicle on a very bumpy, unsealed road to seek help was not appealing. That season, my family had all suffered the effects of the flu; unfortunately, I had it the worst, which was confirmed when I unexpectedly fainted while sitting on a chair, only coming to at the panicked sound of my husband's voice yelling at our little rescue dog, who was savagely trying to protect my limp body. It took over twenty minutes for me to feel fully aware of my surroundings again, discovering that when I collapsed, I had bruised my sternum, shoulder, and knee, and peed my pants, all adding to my miserable state. I am unsure how we got the flu so far from town. I imagined we would be safe when we were so isolated from other people. The flu needles we received six weeks earlier had not protected us either. I did consider phoning the Royal Flying Doctor Service (RFDS) as we have a Flying Doctor medical chest at the homestead. This is stocked with medicines for emergencies, that can be prescribed via phone by an 'on-call' doctor at the Flying Doctor base. Instead, not wishing to take up their precious time, I settled for the ample supply of over-the-counter medicines we always had.

Three weeks later, I had not died and woke feeling a little better. Usually, I would phone my twin to tell her I had recovered;

however, she was travelling overseas. I was still weak, but the warm winter sun shone, luring me outdoors. I have a small photography business, so I decided to venture off to property two and take some photos of something green, of precious water, of something alive. Who knew how long the sight of green grass would last? After a flood, the basin area comes to life; the bronzed lignum turns olive, the crusty brown soil sprouts green grass shoots, and the choir-echoing noise from the masses of birdlife migrating to this area to nest is deafening. If I was lucky, I would get a photo that even David Attenborough would be proud of.

Before I left, my husband offered to chaperone me, as I don't have a good track record when I venture off alone to take photos. The previous year, the summer heat was starting to creep in when I decided to treat myself to a few hours off to take some photos. As I twisted and turned, relishing the opportunity to explore the vast property, where few people have walked, I somehow managed to get lost! Looking in the direction of the sun was no help as that day, there was a thick, fluffy covering of clouds, much like a luxurious quilt. The more I tried to work out where I was, the more lost and confused I became. When my husband finally, and I emphasise the word *finally*, found me, I was hungry, wind burnt, and sunburnt. Wearily, I asked him why it had taken so long to come looking for me. I had been due back at the homestead hours earlier. His casual response was, 'If you were a Swedish backpacker, I would have come looking earlier.' I have blond hair and would have happily pretended to be Swedish if it meant him rescuing me sooner.

On yet another occasion, isolated dry storms were creeping in from the western horizon, so with the camera in hand, I left the homestead to explore, and see what I could capture through my lens. There are areas with unique names, such as Bills Bore, Stallion Island and Camp Oven, and I have often wondered how these areas received their names, particularly one spot named Hells Gorge. I remember sitting happily on the motorbike, looking across an open, desert-like claypan, fringed in the distance with large gum trees congregating along a creek bed. I was savouring my afternoon of freedom, peacefully resting in the open paddock, watching isolated storms slowly build as they floated along the distant sky. One particular cloud mass caught my attention as there were many lightning strikes periodically shooting from it. I was amazed that this 'scud' was sitting stationary for such a long time, but stupidly, I didn't recognise that it was actually moving straight towards me, therefore giving the impression of sitting still. Suddenly, the trees in the distance started violently dancing, and the claypan dirt lifted, hindering my vision. Before I knew it, the storm was almost upon me, hitting quickly and with a vengeance. With the powerful storm chasing my tail, I sped the five kilometres home along the bumpy dirt track, going much too fast for my limited motorbike skills. I almost collided with two kangaroos, and one startled cow along the way. I arrived at the homestead with literally minutes to spare.

But on this particular day, I reassured my husband that I did not require a chaperone, telling him I would be fine. The sky was scattered with only a few cotton puffs of cloud, and I had no intention of getting lost. With that, he decided to go to property three so he could 'walk', meaning drive, the heavy, tank-like bulldozer back to the house. This meant he would be gone most of the day. I prepared for my outing, packing supplies for the day, including a handheld UHF radio for communication, a camera, a drone, and my version of some bush tucker, before confidently heading in the opposite direction.

I am sure I jinxed myself, as not an hour later, I found myself hanging on tight as the wheels on the four-wheel motorbike spun ferociously, trying to gain some grip. Oh shit! I was bogged. Just before my predicament, I had been trying to get some drone photos of ducks—that incidentally were now circling above my head, quacking, I'm sure, with laughter—when the battery alarm on my drone control had sounded. When I looked at the little drone hovering about 600 metres away I did not trust the return-to-home button to bring it safely back. Being cautious, I decided to simply land the drone where it was and ride on the motorbike to its landing site to collect it. Looking ahead of me and not down resulted in the motorbike getting bogged. Now, my drone was sitting hundreds of meters away in a paddock surrounded by grazing cattle, with several deep, snake-like water channels blocking my path.

Although expensive, the drone is a valuable and satisfying addition to my still camera photos. Thanks to the drone, I take images from a unique perspective. This drone was relatively new, and as the Civil Aviation Safety Authority (CASA) rules required, I registered it with them. Like all aircraft, my little drone was issued with its very own Aircraft Identification Number (AIN), so technically, I own a plane. I feel that now that I am an aircraft owner and pilot, I should be entitled to sit in the pilot's lounge at Sydney Kingsford Smith Airport.

The bogged motorbike was not going anywhere, so my priority was to retrieve my precious drone before curious grazing cows stomped on it. Unfortunately, the only way to get my drone safely back in my hands was to walk to it, which meant paddling my way through the winter's icy cold channels. I searched for a water channel that didn't appear deep and poked a stick into it to check the water level. Hesitantly, I entered the freezing water; I began to slip and sink in the mud as I slugged my way across through the thigh-high muddy water, exiting the channel with an inch of black dirt super glued to my boots and ankles. I staggered along the uneven black soil and repeated this process three more times before I finally had my drone safely back in my hands. I retraced my steps, holding my drone above me, and finally, I returned wet, cold, and muddy to the bogged motorbike, where I fell to the ground exhausted.

I was a long distance from the homestead and bogged in a pretty remote area. If the worst-case scenario happened, and it was dark when my husband discovered I was missing, he might find it difficult to locate me. There was no landmark or way to explain my position over the UHF radio. The area is known for feral pigs, wild dogs, and deadly snakes. I was not sitting out there all night alone, so I did exactly what you're not supposed to do and decided to pack up my belongings and start walking. As I plodded along with my heavy, mud-caked boots and cold, wet clothes, I saw hundreds of water birds, but I was so angry with myself and the thousand annoying flies accompanying me that I could not be bothered to stop and photograph them. Eight exhausting kilometres later, the effects of my recent flu and chest infection caught up with me. I was now out of the black soil country, into red soil land, and I knew exactly where I was, which was a bonus. I stopped and set up a little bush camp.

I impatiently started a fire, and the radiating heat quickly dried my wet clothes and thankfully warmed me to the core. The rising smoke also helped to keep the thick swarm of pesky flies away. I drank a sweet black tea from my thermos and waited and waited. Occasionally, I'd pick up the UHF radio: 'Dave, are you on channel?' There was silence on the other end. The hours ticked by slowly, very slowly. After gazing into the glowing embers, I fell back heavily, resting on the red soil, my camera bag making a hard pillow. I watched the few puffed clouds float in the sky above. I began spotting shapes in the clouds like I remembered doing for an activity in primary school. I am sure I saw a woman resembling the Virgin Mary.

My warm fire started to die, so I wearily collected more firewood to feed it and rested some more. After eating out of boredom, I re-assumed my position lying in the dirt. Staring upwards, I spotted a fellow pilot flying a commercial jet high in the sky, the plane leaving a white jet stream behind it. I wondered where the aircraft was headed—America, Ireland, France, Dubai, Italy, Germany? That's how the other half live, I jealously pondered.

I thought of my twin sister, who was currently in Milos, a small island in Greece. She was the other half. After living such parallel lives in our youths, our lives now could not be more contrasting.

I live in the bush, married to a grazier, and she lives on the coast, and is married to a solicitor. I am a country girl surrounded by beef and gum trees, while she is a coastal girl surrounded by reefs. My daily outfits consist of denim jeans, a work shirt and dusty work boots, which are accessorised with an Akubra; hers are a flowing summer dress and sandals. My twin goes to a beautician regularly; I must buy razors. She gets to eat out at beautiful restaurants; I must cook every meal. That day, I wished I was living her life. We are reef and beef.

The sun slowly set, creating identical colours in the sky to the flames of my secure fire. The darkness crept in, and night noises echoed around me. I stoked my fire and sat protectively close to its warmth, staring at the hypnotising flames. The thought crossed my mind that my husband might also be in some predicament, and I might have to sit here all night. This was not an appealing prospect. I did not wish to be a meal to a feral pig, toyed with by wild dogs, or bitten by a snake. I admire our indigenous people and early settlers, who would laugh if they knew I was nervous at the thought of a sleepover in the bush.

I regretfully drank my last cuppa and moved closer to the warmth of the fire. Thankfully, the pesky flies had gone to bed. The choir of frogs broke the silence as my eyes were drawn to the heavens. In the outback, the evening stars are like magic, igniting the heart; they have a safe and calming presence. Without the pollution of the city lights, I sometimes feel like I can reach up and take hold of one. The bright Southern Cross is always visible and is a comforting reminder that I am an Aussie. I wondered what my twin was doing right at that moment. Was she still out exploring the beauty of Greece, or would she be in bed? I wasn't sure of the time difference.

Suddenly, my thoughts were interrupted. 'Kylie, are you on channel?' My husband's voice echoed in my ears.

I grabbed the radio, 'Dave, can you hear me? I need help. I'm near that white bag tied to the fence north of the cattle yards.' I was immensely relieved to speak to him and ready to end my day's adventures. The minutes seemed to tick by slower than before, but finally, I heard the distant sound of a vehicle. I spotted the small headlights in the darkness and was relieved as they grew.

My husband stopped his ute and stepped out laughing. 'What happened?'

I got bogged out there somewhere; 'I walked here,' I replied wearily.

'Come on, jump in; we'll find the bike tomorrow.' He gave me a loving hug, and I felt like I had been wrapped in a secure blanket. After putting out my fire, we collected my belongings and headed home to the protection of my sanctuary.

A few days later, my very own vehicle emergency retrieval service went to remove the bogged motorbike from its resting place. As my husband left the homestead, I apologised for giving him another job. As he was walking off, he casually replied, 'It could have happened to anyone.' He paused and then continued, 'It probably wouldn't have though.'

Reef

On a sunny day, it is difficult to feel lonely in Sawtell as I see many people outside enjoying the sun's warmth. There are surfers watching the ocean to find a good wave, and trust me, if there is a good swell, I know where to find a tradie. Their vans are often seen patrolling the beach, and they keep their surfboards close just in case the swell increases throughout the day. Families congregate in one of the many parks or headlands, and there is rarely a day I don't run into someone I know for a chat, offload, or gossip, as often occurs in small communities. In the early mornings, as the sun is about to rise, I see the regulars out running and bike riding, sometimes accompanied by an excited dog. The coffee shops provide a regular meeting place where some locals have such a routine that I could almost set my watch by their arrival.

Living in an idyllic holiday location doesn't stop us from getting away and exploring other parts of the world. We are at the stage in our lives where overseas travel is becoming a regular occurrence, and this still amazes me as it is something I never expected I would be able to do when growing up in country New South Wales. I love roaming old cities and running my hand along the walls of narrow stairwells in old castles. I let my imagination wander, who before me, has used their hand on the wall to steady themselves, who turned the door handles on an ancient building, that has stood for centuries. I still believe travel is a luxury, and the realisation that I get to travel rarely escapes me. My twin sister will surely remind me if I forget how lucky I am. Somehow, all our holidays have a significant component dedicated to an area near an ocean. The sea has a seductive atmosphere that draws us to it wherever we are.

My husband and I had been holidaying around Europe for five weeks and had travelled to Santorini, Greece, to help celebrate a special 'O' birthday for a friend. Our holiday was spent yachting the Mediterranean, hiking the many elevated peaks like mountain goats, shopping, wining and dining. After four days, we left our entertaining friends and decided to de-stress and relax on one of the quieter Greek islands.

We caught a ferry to the beautiful island of Milos and attempted to explore in a hire car, but before long, we started to argue. I have always measured a person's driving skill by my ability to sleep as a passenger, as I am usually the first person to nod off.

My husband's current driving was not giving me any confidence (or any sleep). He was having trouble positioning the car in the middle of our lane. Winding the narrow roadway, I saw oncoming cars veer sharply out of our way, so I closed my eyes tightly. We had a short reprieve with no other vehicles in sight, so I snuck a glance to my right and saw a steep 100-foot drop. However, I had little opportunity to admire the beautiful blue ocean glistening below. The road had no guardrail, which added to my fear. Suddenly, the unthinkable happened! A road worker was standing in the middle of the road holding a traffic sign, and at the same time, cars approached us head-on. There was little to no conversation taking place between us at this point as Scott was concentrating, and I was sitting ashen-faced, looking directly at the road ahead. My heart was racing, and Scott appeared to be racing! I clung to the seat in a vain attempt to feel secure. I could sense the wheels on my side of the car were now off the tarred road and on the gravel verge. Thankfully, the agile, beefily-built Greek road worker jumped out of the way while clearly thinking, 'Bloody tourists.' Why my husband failed to remember that the vehicle he was driving had a brake shocked me and took my breath away.

Somehow, we grazed past the oncoming vehicles without hitting anyone. I can't say I saw much, as my eyes were tightly closed. My knuckles were white as my right hand was now clenched to the Jesus Bar, a term I had heard while working years ago. The Jesus Bar, or grab handle, is the handle affixed to the roof of a car to provide 'stability' to the passenger; in this case, while I was screaming with increased frequency, the very Australian term, 'Oh, shit'. We continued down the road, rounded a corner and pulled over, the wheels on the vehicle rubbing against the concrete gutter and making a loud, screeching sound.

By this point, the local residents were staring at us with curiosity. Scott turned the engine off, and I breathed. We then had a 'discussion' and decided to return the hire car. I must admit, I was too scared even to attempt driving in Europe on the opposite side of the road to Australia. My husband has proved his excellent driving ability over the many years we have been married, but these three hours of driving were and will be, our one and only experience driving ourselves in Europe. I guess I have to say goodbye to my dream of driving in a 1950 Cadillac around European coastlines, with my hair blazing in the wind, Thelma and Louise style. I will have to settle for a tourist bus.

After discovering that driving was not achieving our goal to relax, we returned the hire car and headed to our beautiful island resort. Holidaying on the Greek islands allowed us to indulge in our love for swimming. We soaked up the golden heat of the sun and spent the afternoon by the water. Between swimming and snorkelling, we relaxed on the sunbeds, devouring our novels. We both love the ocean, and in this particular area, the waveless water was so clear that I could easily see fish fourteen feet below. We were now in our happy place. Scott is a really strong swimmer, and although I am a Pisces, and I am supposed to belong to the water element of the zodiac, I don't have the confidence he has when swimming and snorkelling 500 metres from shore. I feel safer when he is beside me, especially far out.

On many European beaches, you have to pay for a place to lie down on a sunbed. The European beaches don't enjoy the luxury of our beautiful, white Australian sand but are covered in pebbles, so it's a good investment. Whilst lying in our allotted sunbeds, we noticed that the front row of sunbeds, situated closest to the water and the main thoroughfare for beach walkers, was reserved for the 'pretty people'. To be fair, in our younger years, we 'may' have been placed in this row, but as we were approaching our fifties, we had been relegated to the third row. On reflection, we thought this row wasn't too bad. We could have been placed further back! The view from our row was good for people watching, a favourite pastime of mine on holidays, trying to work out who's who in the zoo. The ripped young people in their less than modest swimwear does provide me with a bit of a perv as well. The afternoon finished with a few cocktails and a lovely meal, accompanied by a few giggles about the driving 'experience' we had endured earlier that day.

Later that night, we settled into our beautiful, elevated hotel room decorated in typical Greek style with rendered concrete white walls, floors, ceiling, and furniture. During the night, I started to feel sick. That lovely meal may not have been so 'lovely' after all. The sickness became severe, creating a tsunami of vomit that decorated the beautiful white bathroom. My husband, exhausted after all that driving and with the help of a 'few' cocktails, slept blissfully unaware of my sudden exploding sickness. I knew there was no point waking him. What could he do? At least one of us would get a good night's sleep. Once I was sure my stomach could not possibly contain any further contents, I went outside onto the balcony and lay on the curtain-lined, four-poster sunbed. My cramping stomach reminded me that sleep would not come, although I was delirious from lack of sleep.

The air was warm, as expected on a Greek summer night. I lay on the sunbed, looked up at the clear sky, and listened to the ocean lapping the rocky beach. The sky was free from clouds, and I could clearly see the vibrant diamonds of the night sky. Lying on my back, I stared upwards to see if I could find the Southern

Cross but realised I was in the wrong hemisphere and too far from the equator to see the beacon of an Australian sky. Unbeknown to me, on the same weekend, Kylie participated in some unplanned stargazing herself. I started to hum the song Down Under by Men at Work. I didn't sing the whole song as the only words I can ever remember are, 'I come from a land down under'. My health predicament was not helping the situation. As I hummed the song, I started to think about Australia. I have been to many countries and there are some fantastic places to visit in the world, but no country exerts such a strong pull to return to our beautiful Australia. Lying on the sunbed and looking up at the Greek night sky, I thought of home and my twin sister. The stars on her remote outback property are as beautiful as any you will see, giving the impression that there is no line between the horizon and the sky.

Daydreaming was providing me with a good distraction, but my head started to pound from lack of water, and I knew I was dehydrated from all the vomiting. I didn't dare drink any water as my stomach was still petulant, and the grumbling feelings inside had not lessened. I slowly got up and sat on the side of the sunbed, steadied myself, and tried to walk to our room, the dizziness I felt giving the impression that I was intoxicated. I was feeling fevered and restless at the same time. I parted the sheer curtain blowing in the elegant doorway of our hotel room and glanced at my husband, sleeping soundly in the bed. He didn't appear to have noticed that I wasn't there, as he had spread himself in the centre of the bed and looked like a huge starfish.

I walked back outside and collapsed on the sunbed. I tried to do the maths in my head to work out what time it was in Australia and wondered what my unqualified life coach/therapist was doing at that moment. Kylie lives on a large property in far north-western New South Wales. I have a 530 square metre block of land, and if I reach out really far from the windows, I think I could quite possibly touch the neighbour's house. We get to know the neighbours well living that close to them, sometimes too well. As most urban living residents can testify, we are so close to them that we can often hear their private conversations. Especially if that conversation is alcohol-induced and all inhibitions are forgotten. If they play music or have the radio on, I have no choice but to listen to it as well. She has peace and quiet unless a poddy calf is mooing at the back fence. I use the incoming planes as a clock, as we live under a flight path and sleep with many urban noises comforting us at night.

Kylie lives a very different life from mine, and our daily routines are at the opposite ends of the spectrum. I have a very structured life as my day revolves around a schedule of set work times, and when my children were younger, I had to drop them off at daycare, pre-school and school before my work day even commenced. The morning rush with children was not something Kylie had to endure, and I thought her life was much more flexible than mine. I see people daily, but she only has contact with her family most days.

Living these very different lives was never part of our life plan. I never thought I would live so far from my twin sister. While love kept us together for a long time, it was love that eventually separated us. Finding our husbands is ultimately what has kept us from living near each other. Not all twins magically fall in love with another set of twins and live happily ever after, as is often portrayed in the movies. Thankfully, we both like each other's husbands, but they're oceans apart. They are very different men with contrasting lives, to say the least.

Being a twin means learning to share from the very beginning. Sharing the womb, sharing a newborn cuddle, sharing birthdays and birthday cakes. Sharing toys. Sharing achievements and milestones. Don't get me wrong; being a twin has plenty of advantages. In a crowd setting, we are often the centre of attention. Later in life, we also learned that assuming your twin's identity can be advantageous and get you out of tricky situations. When we first left home, I didn't have to find someone to live with, as Kylie and I left home simultaneously, and we moved in together. This was both familiar and comforting at the same time. Our wardrobe is double the size because we can share clothes. But I guess the most significant advantage is knowing I have a walking, talking, living organ donor, with one twin having the spare parts for the other. As I laid on the sunbed like sluggish seal, suffering the after effects of food poisoning, I thought, the way I felt I might actually need an organ donor soon.

The sun started to creep into the morning, and the new day presented itself to the world, so I staggered back into our hotel room. In the light of the day, the white translucent walled bathroom was not so white. It now resembled something like a Pro Hart painting, as my 'lovely' dinner was splattered all over those white bathroom walls. Arghhh! After cleaning the walls, I collapsed on the bed. When I drifted off to sleep, I remember thinking, 'Is it bad to leave my new art exhibition for the cleaners?'

… Double Trouble …

Beef

Out in the bush, there are times when I feel like I am the only person in the entire world. When I study the land, I do not think of it as my land or our land; I believe we are temporary custodians. I feel our job is to care for the environment, improve the land, and pass it on to the next custodian. Living on this property, I have had periods where I have not seen another person apart from my husband for months. The early Australian outback settlers could go years without seeing another person or receiving a precious letter. How my twin and I came to be thanks to our extensive family tree, all of whom came from rural backgrounds. Twins are common, particularly on one branch.

Our first set of great-grandparents were Samuel Condon and Hilda Woodley. Hilda had twin brothers, Harold and Horace, born in 1887. Looking at black and white photos, the brothers look identical, although one brother is slightly taller than the other. As young men, they often wore matching clothing but different coloured ties. and enjoyed swapping them to confuse family and friends. All but one of Hilda's sisters have twin descendants.

Sam and Hilda had four girls, two of whom were non-identical twins, Doris and Grace, born in Dubbo in 1924. Both girls were around eight pounds when they were born, which is a healthy weight for twins. They also had two boys, Harry and our maternal grandfather, Neil Condon.

Our second great-grandparents were James Ney and Alice Deihm. They lived on a small holding near the town of Gollan and had nine children. The youngest child was our maternal grandmother, Rita. During the war, Rita, a young woman, worked on a farm owned by her sister, Ella, and her brother-in-law, Clive. While working at Allambie, she met our grandfather Neil, who was Clive's first cousin.

Neil and Rita married in 1944; soon after, our grandfather was discharged from the army. They had three daughters: our mother, Narelle, followed by Dale and Joy. Our grandfather was a skilled carpenter and moved where the work was, often erecting buildings such as shearing quarters on remote rural properties. As a result, my mother was frequently enrolled in school by correspondence through Blackfriars Correspondence School, Sydney. Blackfriars was established in 1916 to enable education for children living in rural and remote areas. Our mother completed school workbooks before posting them back in the mail to be marked. In 1991, Blackfriars closed and was replaced by seventeen Distance Education Centres. After finishing high school, she trained as a nurse, working for four years at both Wellington and Moree Hospitals.

Our father's branch begins with our third great Grandfather, John Dickerson. John was born in Ophir, a gold mining town near Orange, NSW. As a young man, he met Minnie Barker, and they married in 1891. They lived on a property called Woodlands near Stuart Town. They had ten children; our grandfather, Valentine, was the fourth youngest.

Our fourth great-grandfather was Tottenham Richardson. He married Ethel Wilson from Bathurst, and they settled on land in the Nyngan are, before having eight children, including our grandmother Ena. Valentine and Ena married in July 1935. They bought a small farm, Allambie, at Stuart Town, just down the road from Woodlands, the home of our great-grandfather. Coincidentally, my maternal grandparents met at a property with the same name, although that property was pronounced differently.

Soon, Valentine and Ena celebrated the arrival of their firstborn, a little boy, Bryan Malcom. Tragically, Bryan became ill with pneumonia and died at only four weeks of age. Four daughters followed: Raynor, Enid (Bubby to all), Valma, and Wendy and then our father, Graeme. Dad was born with a hole in his heart and was a sickly child, regularly having convulsions, but despite this, as the only living son, he was adored by his parents and sisters.

In 1956, our grandparents were at Allambie in the middle of their shearing when my grandmother discovered a lump in her breast; however, she refused to seek medical attention until the shearing was finished, when breast cancer was confirmed. She had a mastectomy, but by then, it was too late; the cancer had spread.

Devastatingly, just over twelve months later, she died at only forty-seven years of age. Her last words to our dad were, "Have you got a freshly ironed shirt on?" He was only thirteen years old, and after being told of his mother's death, was sent to school for the day. Our grandmother was buried at Stuart Town. However, our grandfather refused to allow Dad to attend his mother's funeral as he felt he was too young. After the funeral, a wake was held at Allambie. Here, our father was found by an aunt sitting alone, distressed because he did not get to say goodbye to his mother. When she consoled him, he vomited in grief. The following day, two aunts sympathetically drove our dad to his mother's grave, giving him a chance to say goodbye. Three weeks after his mother's death, our father was sent to boarding school at Kinross Wolaroi in Orange. There were only twenty-nine students in the year. Our father was still deeply grieving for his mother, missed the farm, and hated boarding school.

In December 1960, our father was home for the holidays when our grandfather Valentine visited his recently widowed sister-in-law at the neighbouring farm. During the visit, Valentine, who was just fifty-two years old, suffered a fatal heart attack. Our dad, now only fifteen years old, had lost both his parents within two and a half years and was an orphan. He once said that he helped to carry his father's body from the home. I can't begin to imagine the gut-wrenching grief he would have felt. Our grandfather was buried on Christmas Eve. Our father did not return to boarding school and inherited the family farm, Allambie.

While coping with his unimaginable loss, he worked the farm single-handedly, under the guidance and care of guardians, who were relatives that lived not too far away. I believe the loss of both his parents at a young age affected our father his whole life.

In 1964, a Country Women's Association (CWA) Younger Set Dance was held in Wellington, and both our mother and father attended. Our dad once told us that he had had two previous relationships with redheaded women, so when he spotted our mother at the dance, a brunette, he thought he might have better luck. They had several dances together, and at the end of the evening, our father asked our mother out on a date. Date night came around, and when our father arrived at our mother's home in Wellington, a redheaded woman answered the door. He initially thought he had the wrong house. Unbeknown to our father, our mother had been wearing a brown wig at the dance, as was typical for women back then, so he was obviously destined to be with a redhead. After a courtship, our father decided he wanted to propose, and as he was an excellent horseman, he broke in horses to pay for the engagement ring. Our parents were married just twelve months later, in Wellington, before settling on our father's farm.

Our parents decided they only wanted two children, close in age. Our older sister started a new branch of the family tree late in 1966. Only a few months later, our mother fell pregnant again, perhaps a little quicker than she had planned, and my parents were excited about the impending birth of their second and last child. Unlike her first pregnancy, the second time around, our mum said she felt a lot more movement and had a very sizeable baby belly. She told us she was pregnant from her front, all the way around to the middle of her back, and at just over five-foot-tall, she would have looked like a ball.

Early in 1968, our mother went to a scheduled obstetrician appointment. She said to the doctor, 'I feel like I have a bag of worms inside me.'

After the examination, the doctor said, 'I think you have more than one baby in there,' and sent her for an x-ray, which was how things were done back then. Our mother knew the radiologist from when she was nursing at Wellington, so she asked him if she was carrying twins. He secretly confirmed that it was not worms after all but a multiple pregnancy. Despite looking like a ball and carrying two babies, Mum had a straightforward pregnancy with no complications. Our mother commented that she had always felt that she would be a mother to twins one day. I have always had a feeling that I am going to win the lotto, so I hope it comes true. The obstetrician overseeing our mum's pregnancy was the nephew of Sir Edward 'Weary' Dunlop. He told our mum that he came from a medical family and happened to be an identical twin himself; his twin was also a doctor.

We arrived early and undercooked and would never win any baby beauty competitions as our mother described us as resembling skinned rabbits. I was the first one born and only had a short time as a singleton, as my twin was on her way. Some studies have shown that the firstborn of twins is often the leader or more dominant sibling. After my twin was delivered, she was placed next to me, and our mother jokes that perhaps we were mixed up just after birth as my twin prefers to take the role of the leader.

When we were in our tween years, our mother visited a clairvoyant who told her that her second-born child would live by the water and be the wealthiest of her daughters. Perhaps the clairvoyant meant underground water, as I do live above the Great Artesian Basin, and maybe the riches she referred to were not monetary.

In Yoruba, a small tribe in Nigeria, twins are born at a rate of fifty sets of twins to every 1,000 births, and they are seen as gifts from God, dual entities protected by spirits who possess magical powers. Twins are given special names, either Taiwo for the firstborn or Kehinde for the second, but the second twin is considered the elder twin, as their customs believe that Kehinde sends Taiwo to judge if the world is fit and beautiful before he/she descends. All I know is my birth certificate reads, 'elder born of twins'.

We remained in the hospital to complete our incubation period, and our mother returned to the farm. Luckily, I had my twin to keep me company. My twin has known me longer than anyone else, even our parents. We spent forty weeks, or in our case, thirty-four weeks, cramped in the womb together and were destined to become friends. We are identical twins or monochorionic twins in medical terms. There would have been many times when my twin kicked me in the head or stretched herself out, taking up a bit more than her share of the womb, but that's okay; she is my twin, after all. Babies pass urine at about ten weeks of development, which is released into the amniotic fluid, which babies then drink. Most identical twins have one placenta and can have a shared or separate inner sac. Having a shared internal sac means not only did I swallow my own pee, which is bad enough, but I also swallowed my twin's! Some things should not be shared, even with your twin.

I watch in fascination as animals identify their offspring by sound and smell, such as a cow who identifies her calf by the moo sound it makes. When we arrived home from the hospital, our mother said she could easily identify slight physical differences between us, although she did have 'backup' bracelets to assist our father. It makes me wonder how many identical twins have been accidentally confused at some point in their early life and now have their twin's birth name. There was a story about newborn twins who looked so identical their parent's put bracelets on the babies to identify them. One twin wrote, 'My mother left my father home alone with me and my twin sister when we were infants. Our father decided to help by bathing us. She came home during the bathing process, took one look at the bracelets lying next to the baby bath, and asked if he knew which twin was which; he took a stab in the dark.'

Our mother was very busy; however, our father pitched in when he could. Often, if the task allowed, he took our older baby sister with him when he went out to work in the paddocks. She was a very young Jillaroo. With three babies under sixteen months, there was an enormous amount of washing. Our mother only had cloth nappies and no running hot water. Without a modern Hills Hoist clothesline, she only had the 'old fashioned' type, two long wires strung between wooden poles, with sticks propped in the middle to keep the washing off the ground. The clothesline was visible from the quiet country road that bypassed our house, and when the few neighbours drove past, for entertainment, they played a game, guessing how many nappies would be hanging on the line.

Sometimes, we were taken to the small village of Stuart Town for errands, and occasionally, our mum would venture further and travel the thirty-five kilometres to the country town of Wellington. In those days, we travelled in sizeable white cane bassinettes that had carry handles on the top. These large bassinettes were common for families with new babies, but most only had to fit one bassinet in the car at a time. Our parents had to fit two bassinettes and our elder sister on the backseat, so they came up with the ingenious idea to squash a mattress on the back seat and push the excess down behind the front seats, effectively making one big flatbed. Our bassinettes were then placed on top of the mattress, wedged at an angle so they would both fit, and our sister was squeezed into an uncomfortable gap between the bassinettes. There were no baby car seats, seatbelts or safety devices.

Our bedroom was basic with two cots, not matching, a simple chest of drawers, a cupboard, and a small two-bar electric heater that sat on the floor between the cots to help warm the cold room. It wasn't long before our mischievous personalities started to shine. Sometimes, when my sister and I woke, our parents would put us together in one cot, and we would babysit each other. During one of these 'babysitting sessions', we explored our artistic skills. One or both of us had soiled our nappies, and after helping each other remove them, we used the contents to create an abstract and chaotic artwork, our canvas being each other, our cot, bedding, and the walls within our reach. Our mother did not appreciate our creative flare, and after boiling the copper to get hot water, she removed all traces of the artwork.

Once, we were sleeping peacefully in our room; well, we were assumed to be sleeping. Our parents were inside the house when one of them thought they could smell smoke. They entered our bedroom and were alarmed to see a small but blazing fire burning between our occupied cots. Our mother rushed us to safety while our father extinguished the fire. It appeared we had woken from our sleep, become bored and decided to have a little fun throwing pillows back and forth from one cot to the other. One of the pillows missed its mark and landed on top of the ancient bar heater, where the radiating heat caused the resting pillow to combust. Our relieved parents were very fortunate to discover the fire early. After that incident, the heater was put on top of the wardrobe, out of our reach and throwing distance.

A fence surrounded our little farmhouse, but only the walls of Alcatraz would have kept us locked in. We were very active kids and could achieve a lot with our two little brains working together. Our relatives once described us as resembling two little white mice busily scampering around. I suppose this is a step up from our skinned rabbit birth phase. On many occasions, our mother would watch from a distance as we planned another great escape and would intervene, but sometimes we caught her off-guard. We would slip outside the house and run to the locked gate; one of us would get on the ground on all fours, and the other one would climb on her back, reach the gate latch and unlock it. According to the Chinese zodiac, we are born in the year of the monkey, so climbing was natural.

Our father was a horseman and treasured his horse. The mare had recently foaled, so during the day, he would lock the foal up in the stockyards while he worked. Our father returned to the homestead for smoko, tying the horse up just outside the house fence. Jacki and I ran outside 'to play' and decided it was a good time for another breakout. Sometime later, my twin walked into the kitchen alone, crying and complaining that she had a sore foot. As I was not with her, and we were inseparable, our parents decided they better check on me. Leaving the house, they spotted my motionless body on the ground at the horse's feet; Mum's first thought was that I was dead. There were visible injuries to my face, and it was clear, due to the branding of the horse's hoof, that the horse had kicked me in the head. Picking up my limp body, they rushed me to the car, and after quickly dropping my sisters off at neighbours, they raced to Wellington Hospital. I laid motionless on our mother's lap. I was still unconscious when they arrived, and I only came to about an hour after first being knocked out. Our parents presume the accident occurred when the young foal whinnied from the yards to its mother, unsettling the usually quiet horse. My twin's injury happened when she bravely tried to drag me away to safety, and the horse trod on her foot.

In Nigeria, all children are named *Nwa ora,* which means child of the community. This is where the phrase 'It takes a village to raise a child' is believed to have originated from. We were, at times, children of our community. Our father's sisters, particularly Valma and Raynor, were very involved in our lives, along with our mother's sisters, Dale and Joy. My twin and I are similar in many ways to our mum's sister Dale, and we have often joked that we believe she was our true birth mother, and she gave us to our mother to raise. Dale would often come to the farm and help our parents. On one visit, there was a ghastly rat plague, and the rats had no problems getting inside the old farmhouse. Both our mother and Dale spent some time trying to seal our bedroom before they took turns sitting up through the night to protect us from being bitten by the intrusive rodents while we slept. Biting was familiar to my twin and me—we did it to each other often! If anyone was brave enough to intervene, we would instantly stop biting each other and immediately launch ourselves and our teeth at the unsuspecting person's legs. Basically, we could hurt each other, but no one else could!

Our relatives Kelly and Marie lived in Sydney with their daughters Lyn and Joan, and they assumed the role of surrogate paternal grandparents. Occasionally, our parents were brave enough to take us to Sydney to visit. On one visit, Mum and Dad had been provided with a bedroom to sleep in, and their travelling suitcases were on the floor. My twin and I were put on a bed in this room for a nap. With the bedroom door firmly closed, we soon got bored, so we quietly explored our new surroundings. Bingo! Some lollies. Well, they weren't actually lollies, they were medicine in tablet form prescribed for our mum, but we enjoyed them. We were discovered after our delicious feast and rushed to the closest hospital for medical treatment. After our stomachs were pumped and our condition was stable, the doctor gave our mother a lecture on supervision, and he made her feel like a neglectful mother. Interestingly, in keeping with the times, our father did not get the same lecture. Our mother was told that we would have to stay in the hospital overnight for observation, so despondently, she returned to our relatives' home and our waiting elder sister. A few hours later, our mother received a phone call from the hospital asking her to come and collect us early. When she arrived, the doctor, who had lectured her previously, apologised to her for the way he had spoken to her earlier and asked that she take us home. Apparently, we had been quite playful, okay, naughty, during our sleepover at the hospital, and the nurses couldn't control us. With my partner in crime, I was taken back to our relatives and closely watched by all.

Our parents were expecting a surprise fourth child, and soon, we had a new member of our little gang. Soon our parents had four daughters under five. Having four small daughters confused our father, and he would often call us the wrong name, or say all four of our names in a row before matching the correct name to the right daughter, so he adopted the name 'sissy' for all of us. It was easier to just say, 'Sissy, come here' than to have to identify the child in question.

Our mother was busy with a newborn baby and endless house chores, but we delighted in having plenty of space to play and explore and always found something to do. One place on the farm that was strictly off-limits was the farm dam, situated on the side of a hill, sandwiched between the house and shearing shed. The dam had a shallow entrance and, after a few metres, a cliff-like drop into a bottomless pool of muddy water. One day, our father was working up in the shearing shed and just happened to glance down the hill towards the dam when he spotted Jacki, me, and our elder sister wallowing like three little pigs in the dam in waist-deep water, inches from the deep, murky dam drop. Although very young, we were having a wonderful time washing our pure blond hair in the mud, ignorant of our danger. Our father sprinted and stumbled down the hill from the shearing shed, rushing to get us all out of the water to safety before one or all of us took a few more steps forward and drowned. To make matters worse, our father was never taught to swim. He managed to get his three wet, muddy daughters all out to safety. Our mother said we were never intentionally naughty, just mischievous, always chatting like cockatoos and were as busy as bees.

Some believe in ghosts; some do not. The current owners of our childhood farm, Allambie, have talked of regularly seeing a middle-aged man's ghostly figure standing near the front doorway, the figure resembling our grandfather, who had been known to them. Our great-grandfather and grandfather worked this land, and their souls were connected to it. For our father, 'Allambie' was his childhood home, the place where he first walked, rode a horse, and drove a car. The place where he first drafted sheep and learned to fix a fence. The farm was his connection to his parents, and memories of a happy childhood suddenly taken from him. For us kids, the house was much more than cladding and wood; it was our security, where we were loved and felt safe, and we were oblivious to our very basic living conditions. We were country kids; life was free and easy. However, life on the little farm was very tough for our parents. Our father worked hard in the paddocks for little financial return; droughts took their toll, and each day was a struggle. With four young daughters to raise, our parents discussed the possibility of selling the farm. I'm sure this decision was much harder for our father than for our mother. If there was a problem in our family, our father had a saying that we all became familiar with, 'Let's pull together girls.' I am sure he was thinking this at the time.

Reef

Kylie and I were raised in the central west of New South Wales and spent our entire childhood surrounded by a dependable and resilient farming community, some of the ancestors of the pioneers of Australia, good country people. These are people generally acknowledged to possess common sense and look out for each other through the good and bad. We were born in early March at Orange Base Hospital at 11.05 am and 11.30am. I weighed 4lb3oz (1.950kg), and my twin sister weighed 4lb1oz (1.899kg). I have been known as the 'bigger' twin my entire life. It's a wonder I don't have an eating disorder with this term still referenced regularly today. As the saying goes, I have always looked like I was put in the better paddock.

We have a DNA match of 99.9999998%. We are identical twins who came from one fertilised egg that had split. Just because twins look the same does not necessarily mean they are identical twins. Fraternal twins result from two eggs fertilised around the same time, and they are as genetically different as any pair of siblings.

The pregnancy (well, one child) was planned while our parents lived on a property called Allambie, located about three kilometres from an unremarkable village called Stuart Town; the town consists of one long main road with a few auxiliary roads diverting from it. Coming from the Wellington side of Stuart Town, drivers first pass a small, cladded school established in 1858 and comprised of two classrooms in my day. This was the school where Kylie and I started kindergarten, just shy of our fifth birthdays. From memory, kindergarten to year four were in one class, and years five and six were in the other class. I'm sure this arrangement was fluid, as the ages of the kids coming would vary from year to year.

The town cemetery is located behind the school on an arterial road. Walking around the cemetery, I noticed a few consistent surnames on the headstones, including our maiden name, Dickerson. The unmarked grave of my father's baby brother rests peacefully there, surrounded by my ancestors, including my father's parents.

Driving out to the property, we wound our way past farms shaded by mature gum trees that hug the dirt roadway. In times past, the families living on these farms were our parents' relatives, friends and support network. Visitors to Allambie would have seen a small fibro house with a tin roof built on a slightly inclined slope. Our bathroom and laundry were situated outside on the veranda. The house didn't have a hot water service, so the hot water had to be boiled in a copper and bucketed in before we could bath. Usually us kids bathed first, followed by Mum and Dad. The water would not have been very clean after all of us girls had bathed, mixed with dirt and probably the odd wee. The precious tank water, once cooled, would then be poured onto the veggie gardens or the

Reef

Kylie and I were raised in the central west of New South Wales and spent our entire childhood surrounded by a dependable and resilient farming community, some of the ancestors of the pioneers of Australia, good country people. These are people generally acknowledged to possess common sense and look out for each other through the good and bad. We were born in early March at Orange Base Hospital at 11.05 am and 11.30am. I weighed 4lb3oz (1.950kg), and my twin sister weighed 4lb1oz (1.899kg). I have been known as the 'bigger' twin my entire life. It's a wonder I don't have an eating disorder with this term still referenced regularly today. As the saying goes, I have always looked like I was put in the better paddock.

We have a DNA match of 99.9999998%. We are identical twins who came from one fertilised egg that had split. Just because twins look the same does not necessarily mean they are identical twins. Fraternal twins result from two eggs fertilised around the same time, and they are as genetically different as any pair of siblings.

The pregnancy (well, one child) was planned while our parents lived on a property called Allambie, located about three kilometres from an unremarkable village called Stuart Town; the town consists of one long main road with a few auxiliary roads diverting from it. Coming from the Wellington side of Stuart Town, drivers first pass a small, cladded school established in 1858 and comprised of two classrooms in my day. This was the school where Kylie and I started kindergarten, just shy of our fifth birthdays. From memory, kindergarten to year four were in one class, and years five and six were in the other class. I'm sure this arrangement was fluid, as the ages of the kids coming would vary from year to year.

The town cemetery is located behind the school on an arterial road. Walking around the cemetery, I noticed a few consistent surnames on the headstones, including our maiden name, Dickerson. The unmarked grave of my father's baby brother rests peacefully there, surrounded by my ancestors, including my father's parents.

Driving out to the property, we wound our way past farms shaded by mature gum trees that hug the dirt roadway. In times past, the families living on these farms were our parents' relatives, friends and support network. Visitors to Allambie would have seen a small fibro house with a tin roof built on a slightly inclined slope. Our bathroom and laundry were situated outside on the veranda. The house didn't have a hot water service, so the hot water had to be boiled in a copper and bucketed in before we could bath. Usually us kids bathed first, followed by Mum and Dad. The water would not have been very clean after all of us girls had bathed, mixed with dirt and probably the odd wee. The precious tank water, once cooled, would then be poured onto the veggie gardens or the odd pot plant around the house. The house yard was fenced for the joint purpose of keeping stock and feral animals out and an optimistic attempt to keep the kids, particularly my twin and I, in. This arrangement proved relatively ineffective.

Out the backdoor and up a small hill is a large, deep dam built by our father. Perched proudly on top of the hill is a shearing shed built by our grandfather. The sun streaming through the windows highlights the golden hues of the shearing shed and emphasises the stalls with wooden poles, which are fashioned from young trees that were felled on the property and handcrafted to use as dividers. They aren't perfectly straight but are still as sturdy today as the first day they were fixed into place. There is a solid beam across the internal roof with the stencilled date of 1953 painted on it, to commemorate the official year my grandfather completed the project. There is a typical smell of lanolin diffusing from the old wood in the shearing shed, and for some reason, this smell still makes me smile today.

In early March 1968, our heavily pregnant mother, who had only four weeks earlier discovered she was having twins, was hanging washing on the clothesline when she felt her first contraction. Having endured labour only sixteen months earlier with our eldest sister, Mum was quite sure her labour had begun six weeks before her due date. Our father, who was doing cattle work in the yards, was close to the house. They drove from Stuart Town to Orange, leaving our older sister with relatives. Most of the babies in our area were born in Orange Base Hospital if the mothers made it. This was the biggest town in the area, and the hospital had the best facilities. The old dirt roads back then would have made for an uncomfortable ride for our mother, with the drive taking about one and a half to two hours. It was only just starting to be fashionable for fathers to be present in the delivery room, but Mum's obstetrician, Doctor Dunlop, didn't believe in it at all. So, Dad had the difficult job of going to the pub for a few drinks and settling down to a pleasant night's sleep.

The hospital didn't seem concerned that we were so premature as multiple births in those days were often preemie, and still are today. Our mother's pregnancy was straightforward with no complications. In the birthing room, the only people present were Doctor Dunlop and the sister in charge of the maternity ward. The twenty-four-hour labour was long but not arduous, and Mum believes it was because we were so tiny. She felt that the delivery of our other two sisters was much more excruciating. Mum has always said that we fought for twenty-four hours before Kylie was delivered first, then I stubbornly refused to come out. The doctor thought he would have to give Mum a caesarean to deliver me, and they started to prepare her for surgery. He said to Mum, 'You will feel one more contraction.' After Mum gave me one final push, I decided I would enter the world and joined my twin sister twenty-five minutes after her.

Because of our low birth weight, the medical team told our mother we would have to stay in the hospital for quite a few weeks. Our mother's precious breast milk was dried up as we lived too far from the hospital for her to feed us. We were fed via tubes from other breastfeeding mothers in the hospital. Our mother, who had no trouble lactating, had supplied her breast milk to other babies when our elder sister was born.

For the next six weeks, Kylie and I remained in the hospital, where we were put into humidicribs that were much larger and bulkier than they are today. During our hospital stay, there was a shortage of humidicribs, so we were placed in the same one for a short time. I often wonder if this was more beneficial for us, as it is now widely known that twins often settle and relax when they are side by side as newborn infants. It is believed that twins are aware of each other in the womb from as early as fourteen weeks gestation. After Mum had recuperated from the birth, she had to return to Allambie and leave her two newborn babies at the hospital. Mum and Dad drove the long distance on the bumpy roads once a week to visit us.

Six weeks later, Kylie and Jacqueline were brought home from the hospital, and that was the last rest our mother had for many years to come, and the last time our sister had Mum and Dad all to herself. When Mum and Dad decided on our names, they didn't want to give us matching names, like Trudy and Judy, and they also didn't want us to have names that started with the same letter, like our great-uncles Harold and Horace. A lot of parents did just that, and some still do today. Mum has since said that she didn't consider at the time that when my name was shortened to Jacki, both our names end in the same vowels. Mum didn't need to agonise over it, as it wasn't long before we were simply referred to as Jack & Kyl.

Soon after we arrived home, a birthmark appeared on the left side of my face near my hairline. The birthmark is called strawberry hemangiomas. The birthmark is raised and has a strawberry colour, hence the name. These types of birthmarks usually appear at around one to four weeks of age, often get big quite quickly, and usually stop growing between six to twelve months. If it was hard for Mum and Dad to tell us apart before, my birthmark now provided the perfect identification characteristic. They consulted a doctor, who advised that the birthmark would most likely disappear of its own accord. But the doctor was concerned by its location and said if I fell on the birthmark and it ruptured it while I was learning to walk, it might be damaged and scar. Mum and Dad decided to drive me once a month for six months to Sydney for a quarter of a second laser treatment to remove the birthmark. This must have been difficult for them, as they had two other very small children. It was a long distance to travel and also would have cost money that they didn't have to spare. Mum was determined to remove the birthmark as people who knew us were identifying which twin it was by the birthmark. It was often the first thing people reacted to when they met us, and this upset our mother. The laser treatment was effective, and there was little evidence of the birthmark after the treatment.

Twins were not as common back then as they are today. Births, Death and Marriages recorded that in New South Wales, in 1968, there were 81978 children born, of whom 1660 were multiple births, compared to in 2018 when 86211 children were born, of whom 2649 were multiple births. When our mother travelled to Wellington to go shopping, she learned very quickly that it was much easier to leave Kylie and me with our aunt. Shopping was far more successful and quicker without having both of us with her, as too many people would try to stop her and want to look at us and talk to Mum about the twins. We were a little travelling circus. The only twin pram back then was designed to carry the babies side by side. As we got older, Mum quickly worked out that the pram was the perfect width for Kylie and me to reach out on both sides and grab things from the shelves in the supermarket. We would leave a trail of cans and packets of food behind us along the aisles like Hensel and Gretel, so yet another reason it was better to leave us with our aunt.

Kylie and I never dress the same these days unless it's an accident, and that's rare. I believe our different geographical environments have definitely influenced our fashion styles. Well, let's face it, a strappy summer dress and birks aren't very practical in the stockyards. When we were little, we were always dressed the same. We asked our mother why she dressed us this way; she said that's just what you did with twins back then. In fact, during our childhood, many families dressed their children in similar clothing whether they were multiples or not. We were very lucky that our Aunty Marie, who worked in a factory as a seamstress in Sydney, would make us clothes out of offcuts and send them to my mother. Now and then, a box would arrive with new matching garments for us, together with outfits made out of the same material but with a slightly different design for our older sister. I have visions of us walking around like the Von Trapp children from the movie The Sound of Music in their curtain-made matching outfits. Our younger sister was 'lucky' enough to receive two lots of identical hand-me-down clothing!

Kylie and I were mischievous and sometimes just plain naughty. Mum said she got through each day by crossing a mark on the calendar. She had got through another day. Early on, we had our own secret language to conspire with, which didn't help. We would babble away, listening to each other and laughing. The term is called Cryptophasia. 'Crypto' meaning secret and 'phasia' meaning speech. It's thought that when young twins are learning to vocalise, they mimic each other's speech and sounds. We had very little opportunity to interact with other people living on a farm, apart from our very young older sister, who was also developing her own speech. We couldn't attend any sort of mother's group or preschool, as Stuart Town didn't have one. Preemie babies and babies with low birth weights sometimes have language delays, and one school of thought is that this twin language is most likely just sounds that amuse them. However, there have been examples of twins who create what appears to be their own private language. We don't know if we understood each other's sounds or not, but Mum and Dad would watch us fascinated as we listened and laughed at each other. While discovering our voices, we also became fascinated with ourselves and started to recognise that we looked the same. Mum once walked past the bedroom and saw us standing next to each other, looking in her mirror. We were looking in the mirror and then back at each other and touching each other's faces. I think this was the first time we wondered who the prettier twin was.

We were best friends and entertained each other for ages, taking it in turns to push each other around in a walker. One of us would sit in the walker and the other did the pushing around the house. This at least kept one of us secure, as we couldn't get out of the walker once were strapped in.

Our father was involved in our lives, but, as was customary in those days, the men worked outside the house, and the women worked inside the home, rearing the children and doing all the housework. Dad was an excellent horseman and thought it was time he taught us to ride a horse. We were aged about three or four, and Dad would put us on his horse one at a time and leave the horse at the top of a hill. Then, he would walk to the bottom of the hill and whistle for the horse to come to him. Our horse-riding lessons consisted of hanging on, and if we did, we were riding the horse. Not much to it really!

Of course, this didn't always end well, and there were many times our mother had to use tweezers to get burrs out of our bottoms after we had fallen off. This didn't deter us from wanting a horse. One Christmas, we were lucky enough to have Santa bring us a white Shetland pony, whom we named Snowy. Santa was very thoughtful and tied Snowy up to the fence next to a beautiful bush that Mum had been painstakingly watering by bucket to keep it alive. On Christmas morning, we awoke to a new pony, and Mum woke up to no bush. The horse had eaten it during the night. We didn't get to ride Snowy very much because Snowy was a very lazy horse. When we wanted a ride, we would get on his back by using the fence to climb on. He would walk around the house yard once, and only once, and refuse to go any further. It's fair to say I'm not the best horsewoman today.

One day, after yet another successful escape from our yard, we discovered an unlocked car that had been parked in the laneway out the front of the house. The laneway was on a slight hill. Kylie and I climbed into the car, and we decided to take the car for a drive. At the time, we were only about two or three years of age, and while 'playing' in the car, one of us 'knocked' the car into neutral. Somehow, we also released the handbrake, and we were off, the car's momentum our only form of power. We only managed to get fifty metres down the road as our steering wasn't that great, and a big old gum tree ended the short drive pretty abruptly. We were fortunate, as that strong tree was on the edge of a deep gully. Kylie and I somehow were not hurt, but the car didn't fare as well. We were living a simple, sheltered existence filled with freedom and security.

Free and Easy

Beef

Nineteen Seventy-three was the year the World Trade Centre officially opened, Elton John released the song, Goodbye Yellow Brick Road, and our family sold 'Allambie' and moved to Dubbo, a friendly country town situated along the Macquarie River in the Central West of the state. Soon, our father secured a job with a carting company, Thompson Trucks, and I am sure he enjoyed the connection to his rural background. At times, our father would briefly, and possibly illegally, park the stock truck outside our house, and as the offensive stock odour wafted from the truck, I was pleasantly reminded of the farm.

Throughout the day, my twin and I were tremendously active, so at night, exhausted, we would happily take ourselves off to bed without being told. We would climb into separate beds, but every morning, our mother would find us together, nestled like two Kelpie puppies on one bed. Maybe we were reminiscing about our womb days? Our mother, concerned, once discussed this with a doctor who assured her it was just a phase, and we would grow out of it. At some point, we did. We went through a brief period where we would wake up very early, set the breakfast table, and then jump back into bed and pretend to be still sleeping. Later, when we emerged from our bedroom, we would tell our parents and sisters that the fairies had set the table. I wish I had some fairies! Besides having a fondness for sleep, we boarded on obsessive-compulsive disorder (OCD), and our bedroom was always immaculate and orderly. After school, we would neatly hang our school uniforms on the bedroom door, with our socks, shoes, and underwear laid down next to our packed school bags, prepared for the next day.

I thoroughly enjoyed being at a bigger school. In the early days, my teacher telephoned our mother and invited her to the school to secretly watch me rehearse for the Christmas play. I played a leading role as Mary, and the teacher was impressed with my overly dramatic acting skills. These skills would help me later in life!

In the seventies, kindergarten children finished school before the older students. One afternoon, our mother had collected my twin and me from school, and once at home, we went straight to the backyard to play. Later, we ran back inside, around the corner into the kitchen, where we both collided with our mother, who was moving a pot of hot liquid from the stove. The force of us crashing into our mother caused her to tip the contents of the boiling pot straight down my shoulder and back. Somehow, my sister escaped unscathed. In those days, the remedy for burns was putting butter on the skin, but due to our mother's nursing knowledge, she quickly put me in a cold shower. After the burn had cooled, she wrapped me in a cotton sheet. By this time, our older sister had finished school and was somewhere on the bus route on her way home. Our father was at work, so our mother drove my twin, younger sister, and me, still wrapped in the sheet, around the bus route until she located the school bus, removed our older sister, before finally rushing me to the hospital. Thankfully, due to my mother's quick and correct first aid treatment, I did not scar.

When I was five years old, I was once incredibly ill, suffering from vomiting and diarrhoea, which resulted in severe dehydration. Our mother had medication, but my symptoms were not improving. Later, Aunty Joy discovered that our mother had accidentally been giving my twin the medicine instead of me. I was admitted to the hospital and put in an isolation room next to the nurse's station. After a few days, I became very anxious as I was separated from Jacki, so the nurses were forced to break strict visiting rules and contacted our parents, allowing them to bring my twin up to the hospital. The nurse wheeled me to the inside gauzed veranda, and Jacki was brought to the outdoor side, allowing us to see each other. According to our mother, we were both very distressed at being separated and when we sighted each other, we started clawing at the gauze-like wild animals. This is the closeness between twins that some people struggle to understand. Not long after I was discharged, Jacki was admitted, and the whole ordeal started again.

Our mother attended church, and she would take us girls along. We would go to Sunday School in a room attached to the Presbyterian church. This is the first memory I have of our parents arguing. Our father objected to church and eventually refused to let us continue attending Sunday School. I think after the early death of his parents, he struggled to believe there was a God. Around this time, our father secured a new job as a salesman selling farm equipment, and our parents decided to build a new two-storey home in a quiet cul-de-sac in South Dubbo. Although my parents designed the house, my twin and I still had to share a bedroom, while our older and younger sisters had separate rooms. Was this at our request, or was the decision made for us?

We changed schools to Dubbo South Primary, made friends, and soon became involved in sports. We were often allowed to go to the movies for the Saturday afternoon matinee. Grease, the musical, was a favourite, and for years, I dreamt of being Sandy.

On Sundays, we had to go for boring 'family' drives, during which our parents looked at new houses or other developments around Dubbo, and if we were good, we received an ice cream. The usual position in the back of the family car was that our older and younger sisters sat next to the windows, and my twin and I were squashed together in the centre. As seatbelts were now enforced, we had to have the one centre lap seatbelt wrapped across both of us. On longer trips, if we were tired, Jacki and I would curl up on the car floor, one behind each parent, while our older and younger sisters shared the much more comfortable back seat. I'm not sure if the police ever stopped our father while we were in our illegal floor travelling positions, but he did have us convinced that he had magical powers and could predict if there was a highway patrol car in the area. When we were much older, we discovered oncoming cars were flashing their headlights to warn our father of a police presence, and he would illegally do the same in return. Whenever we travelled with our father, he played Charlie Pride,

Kenny Rogers, or Slim Dusty cassettes. To keep us quiet, he would make us listen to the song, and when it ended, he would pause the cassette tape, and we had to tell him the song's meaning. If we were with our mother, we listened to John Denver or The Seekers.

Our dad was very family-oriented and wanted us with him all the time. He would wake up very early and then wake us. This ritual also occurred during the school holidays, and our mother would defend our protests of wanting an occasional sleep-in. We were the sons our father never had. He loved hunting and fishing and made sure his daughters knew basic survival techniques and could skilfully and accurately shoot a firearm. Our grandfather, who we called Pa, was also a keen fisherman, and he spent many hours with our dad in the tinny on a western river. When we were not out shooting, one or all of us girls were usually recruited to go fishing. Pa was frightened of snakes, so when our dad spotted a snake swimming along the top of the water, he would intentionally steer the boat towards it. He was also known to put dead snakes along the riverbank near fishing lines to scare our poor grandfather.

One winter, there had been a flood or rise in the river, and my twin and I were talked into a day out fishing with our father and Pa. Our tinny was not very big, but it felt like the Titanic to me. On this day, Dad was at the stern in charge of the motor, our grandfather was at the bow, and my twin and I were seated in the middle or third class. Our father steered the boat under the canopy of a large willow tree; he continued through its cave and blindly began to exit through the thick cascading leaves. Suddenly, there was a scraping sound, and the boat's bow launched high in the air. We had not hit an iceberg but a large dead tree. The boat tipped to the left, throwing the four of us and some of the boat's contents into the cold, fast-flowing river. The boat stopped, wedged at an awkward angle on the log. Dad, Pa and my twin surfaced, but I did not. Dad and Pa frantically searched the water for me. Pa looked directly down into the chocolate-coloured water and could just see the top of my snowy white hair shimmering with the sun's light, as I was semi-trapped under part of the boat. He reached deep into the water, grabbed a handful of my hair, and ungracefully pulled me to the surface. Gasping for air, I tightly gripped the boat next to my twin. Our father diverted his attention to the boat and desperately tried to hold the motor out of the water. While clinging to the boat, I discovered that somehow, like a Murray cod, I was attached to a fishing line; a large metal fishing hook was embedded in my knee. Dad gave up on saving the boat motor and searched the water for the fishing line I was attached to. He found the line and bit into it with his teeth, breaking the line but leaving the hook in my knee.

We were only about eight meters from the riverbank, but as a small child in a flooded river, that distance felt like the other side of the Pacific Ocean. To add to our distress, we were not wearing life jackets. Our father tried to coax Jacki and I to let go of our Titanic, float down with the fast current, not fight it, and gently swim at an angle towards the riverbank. Nope, we were not having a bar of that. Dad, who was a very poor swimmer, was forced to hold Jackie, float down with the current, reach the bank, deposit her to safety, walk back up the bank past the boat, get back in the water, float down to the boat, collect me and float down again until I was safely on the riverbank. Our grandfather got himself in using similar tactics. Safely on the bank, we stood huddled, wet and freezing in the cool winter air. Our father instructed us all to remove our outer clothes and stand in our underwear. I have never forgotten the shocked sight of our grandfather standing wet and cold in stark white and now semitransparent old-fashioned long johns.

Somehow, Dad started a fire, and as we warmed our freezing bodies, he used some pliers from his pocketknife to cut the fishing hook out of my knee. It bled, but I did not feel any pain. I think I was still in shock at the sight of our grandfather. Eventually, some strangers came along and helped us back to our vehicle some distance further up the river. We were still in our underwear. I am sure after they left us, our rescuers had a laugh at our expense. I don't know what happened to our boat.

I was very thankful that both my twin and I survived the sinking. I once read about one of the oldest living survivors of the Titanic disaster, Lillian Gertrude Asplund. Lillian was only five years old and was on board the Titanic with her parents and siblings, including her twin brother, when the ship struck the iceberg. During the sinking, Lillian, along with her mother and younger brother, were put in lifeboat fifteen. As the lifeboat descended, she watched the faces of her father, who was cradling her twin, standing on the deck with her two elder brothers. They all died, and she said in a rare interview that 'these memories haunted me most of my life'.

Our father lost his salesman job. However, he occasionally found casual part-time work doing a variety of things. Our mother quickly found full-time work and was temporarily the sole financial provider. Around this time, our parents sold our big house and moved to a much smaller home, and our father started a swimming pool business. The advantage of the pool business was that he had an inground pool installed in our backyard so he could show it to potential customers. Swimming was glorious during the long, hot Dubbo summers, and Jacki and I were usually found in the pool, along with our friends and neighbours' kids. Some of our time on Saturday was allocated to listening to the top 40 music charts played on the commercial radio station. We would grab our shared tape recorder and blank cassette tapes, sit next to the radio, and record our favourite songs. Afterwards, we spent hours rewinding, playing and rewinding the cassette tape in an attempt to write down the lyrics to the music. Two sets of ears were better than one!

Our new friends all lived in the South Dubbo area, and we would see each other before, during and after school. We discovered hockey, and it became a huge part of our lives. In our younger years, one or both of our parents were always at the hockey field, supporting our team. Our father would join the team pep talks and offer a bag of twenty-cent lollies to each player for every goal we scored. As hockey was a winter sport, spectators had to wear warm clothing. Our mum had a treasured and much-loved fur coat that she always wore. My twin and I, and our sisters, were so embarrassed by 'the fur'. We joked with our mother that when she died, we planned to stake the fur atop a massive bonfire and watch it burn while we toasted her. Years later, knowing we were serious, our mother ruined our private wake plan by secretly having the fur made into four distinguished teddy bears, which she presented to each of us.

Our mother's sister, Dale, who had been away living in Papua New Guinea, returned to Dubbo to live. Aunty Dale joined the NSW Police in 1969 when my twin and I were only one year old. At the time, less than 200 women had ever joined the NSW Police, and there were only seventy female policewomen serving in the entire state. Up until 1961, women police were called 'Special Police' and had to leave the police force if they married. In 1965, fifty-eight special women police of various ranks were sworn into the New South Wales Police Force as regular officers, with identical police powers and entitlements to males, and were then called policewomen. However, they were given separate police registration numbers and had their own seniority system. When Aunty Dale trained, there were only two women in her academy class. Police training was held at the Police Academy in Bourke Street, Redfern, a suburb of Sydney. Although policewomen did identical training to the men they were not issued with a firearm, only a handbag. The female uniform was a skirt, shirt, stockings, blazer, gloves and hat.

After graduating, Dale was posted to the school lecturing section at Roseberry, where policewomen had their own separate offices. Women police would present lectures on road safety, stranger danger, fire drills, and driver safety for older students. After some time, Dale transferred to the Women's Police Unit, which was based in the same building as the Criminal Investigation Branch (C.I.B) at Surry Hills. Here women police duties involved neglected children, sex offences, incest, and family violence. The male

C.I.B. police would call on the women to assist with interviewing women and children. Another duty for the policewomen was to transport juvenile prisoners to court around the state. This was often done on public transport, mostly trains, but occasionally in a police vehicle. Women police were not allowed to handcuff juvenile prisoners.

I loved hearing Dale's police stories. Being a policewoman sounded exciting. I decided to be a policewoman when I grew up. I entered a competition designing a police poster and received a commendable certificate. Obviously, that little certificate meant a lot to me, as I still have it.

The distance from Dubbo to Sydney was only a five-and-a-half-hour drive at the time, so in country terms, it was not too far to travel for extended weekend trips. In April 1979, our parents took us to the Royal Easter Show and spent a couple of days with our father's sister Raynor, before they headed home. We remained to have a few fun days with our aunt. On the day our parents left, Raynor took us to Luna Park, an amusement park just near the northern side of the Sydney Harbour Bridge. Walking through the entrance, of the mouth of a nine-meter-wide clown face felt amazing. We were having a brilliant time, enjoying the rides. We decided to go on the big dipper, the rollercoaster ride that was 800 meters long and reached speeds of eighty-four kilometres per hour. I loved the twisting and turning as we all hung on for dear life, but our three-minute ride was over before I knew it. We jumped off and ran to the next ride. As that ride ended, we heard many emergency sirens and saw panicked people running past us. We soon found out that just after we exited our rollercoaster ride, there had been an accident on the big dipper. Emergency personnel arrived and, in the chaos, assisted the injured. The park was immediately closed, disappointingly ending our night at Luna Park.

Meanwhile, our parents, who were travelling through the Blue Mountains, enjoying some rare peace, heard about the accident on the car radio. They were desperate to find out if we had been involved. There were no mobiles back then. They stopped at several police stations, but they were closed. Finally, they located an open station, and a policeman made a few phone calls. They somehow found out that none of their daughters were among the thirteen injured. Apparently, one of the steel runners on the roller coaster track had come loose, which stopped one of the trains in the middle of the ride. The following train caught up and rammed into the rear of the stationary train. We were fortunate to have exited the ride when we did. The following holidays, there was a deadly ghost train fire at Luna Park that killed seven people, six of whom were children, and the park was closed again.

My twin was my best friend. We shared a bedroom, went to school together, had the same friends, played the same sport, and finished each other's sentences. We really were as close as two people could be. I loved her dearly and felt lucky to have her to share all life's experiences with, but we were always known as a pair, the twins. In upper primary school, we started to crave our own distinct identities. I parted my hair in the centre, secured by two silver clips; this was not a good look. My twin parted hers to the side with one silver clip, which was also not a good look. We had identical school bags with the words' ABBA" on the side; however, my bag was yellow, and hers was red. Frequently, we chose to wear the same clothes but in different colours; we innocently felt that this gave us uniqueness.

We were not spoilt kids, but life was comfortable. We attended a good public school. We lived on an ordinary residential street, and our home was basic but nice. We were served meat and three veg for dinner and roasts on Sundays. We knew all the neighbours and had extended family close by. We went on holidays and had the occasional weekend treat. This period of our lives was happy and carefree; however, we were not aware of the dust storm that was fast approaching.

Reef

Moving to the 'big' country town of Dubbo at five years of age changed our lives dramatically. We now had access to many facilities and the ability to mix with other children and our extended family. We were brought up to believe that the meaning of Dubbo in the Aboriginal Wiradjuri language is red earth, which is consistent with the landscape around Dubbo. That red earth would often penetrate our houses when massive rolling dust storms suddenly appeared, surrounding Dubbo and turning daylight into night in minutes. Dubbo was a solid country town, and I remember feeling safe there. We never locked our house even if we went away on holidays–just in case someone needed to come and borrow something, as Dad would say. The car keys were never taken out of the ignition, and the car was always unlocked, mainly with the windows left down. We were now living in a small three-bedroom fibro house that had neighbours on both sides and rear neighbours as well. Unlike the farm, this house had both running water and hot water. Across the very wide road was a caravan park with lots of people coming and going. The silence of the farm was long forgotten.

Kylie and I continued kindergarten at West Dubbo Public School, and we were placed in the same class. One day during the year, Mum was called up to the school to have a meeting with our class teacher. In class, Kylie and I were seated on opposite sides of the room, and our teacher had asked the class to draw something with a house, a tree, and a few other components. When we handed in our work, the teacher discovered that my twin and I had created identical drawings; apparently, they could have been photocopies. The teaching staff decided we should be separated and placed us in different classes, so we could learn from two different teachers with different teaching styles, and, learn in a more individualistic way. Mum didn't question the school; back then, you had complete trust in the education department, and the school principal was considered superior. Mum said that the school thought of it as a bit of an experiment. We were the only twins at the school. Kylie and I were not happy at all about being separated. This was the first time in our lives we were being treated as individuals and not as a set of twins. I remember that at lunchtime, we would gravitate back to each other like magnets, and the policy actually stopped us from socializing with other kids because we just wanted to be back with each other again. We would often walk around holding hands.

Dad was a 'bushy,' and never let the fact that we were all girls stop him from teaching us practical day-to-day skills, and he didn't care if the skill was usually reserved for males back then. We are very grateful for the skills our father taught us over the years, and all my sisters and I have the ability to think through a problem and work out a way to resolve most situations. We can change a car tyre, check the oil in a car, whistle like a pro, and shoot a gun. These skills helped Kylie and me get work later in life. I'm lucky I watched and learnt from my dad, as my husband didn't pick up many of these skills from his father, and we often call him 'Tim the tool man' as an inside joke. I am still the person who buys a drill and puts flat packs together in our house.

We moved houses and changed schools. In Year 4, the school didn't think one or both of us was progressing well enough. To this day we don't know if it was one of us, or both of us. Mum can't remember. Nonetheless, they decided to make both of us repeat the year. This involved doing a whole year of school again. I remember we felt embarrassed and sad at being repeated as all our friends were now in the year above us. They felt superior to us. Again, this caused us to draw together for a while, not knowing anyone else in the school year where firm friendships had already been established. We were each other's friends.

I have always loved sport, and we enrolled in a hockey team, the South Dubbo Wrens. I am a firm believer that sport is a great way to meet friends, and this was where I met my four life-long friends, including my best friend, Lisa. These friends still have a strong influence on my life today.

During this period, I met another girl named Talei. Apparently, she went home to her mother and said that she had joined the best group at school. She said all you had to do was to be friends with one of the Dickerson twins, and you were in the group. I didn't like the term 'the Dickerson twins' as I had started to understand that we were often thought of as a plural and not as individuals. When one of us did something, it was always referenced as something that the 'Dickerson twins' had done, even if it was only one of us. We understood that we were always thought of as a set. I don't recall having any particular influence in our group of friends, and I wonder if it was the self-assurance we had, as there were two of us, and that gave us some authority within our group. I guess it's not as easy to bully twins. Talei's family formed a lifelong friendship with our family. Her father was a local policeman, and we always treated him with the respect his uniform represented.

Over time, Kylie and I were starting to become more independent of each other, and we both found a best friend, but we still hung together in a big group at school. I was still protective of my twin, but at the same time, she would annoy me. We had also started to understand that we looked so similar that we could confuse people and began to play pranks on unsuspecting victims as they wouldn't know which twin was which. I don't remember who suggested it, but somehow, we decided that we would swap classes for the afternoon. We had a school uniform, and we both wore watches. My watchband was blue, and Kylie's was red. We knew that the teachers used the colour of our watch straps to tell us apart. So, we swapped watches with the intention of swapping classes. I remember I got cold feet and told Kylie that I wouldn't swap classes, so when the lunchtime bell went, I went back to my own class, but I forgot to swap my watch back with my twin.

As was probably expected from ten- or eleven-year-olds, someone told the teachers what we were going to do, and not long after lessons resumed, the teacher made me stand up in front of the other kids and told me to go back to my correct room. All the kids were giggling, and everyone was well and truly unsettled. Most of the students would have had no idea which twin I was, as most of them couldn't tell us apart either. I stood there pleading with my teacher that I was the right twin in the right class, but she wouldn't believe me. I started to tell her what we had been learning so she would understand that I was the correct twin. She still didn't believe me and made me go and get Kylie from her class. After some discussions and with our watches returned to their rightful owners, I was allowed back to my amused class with my sceptical teacher.

Being a friend of a twin is a difficult path for any friend. Can I be a friend to only one twin and not the other twin? Sometimes, it would hurt Kylie and me when one twin was invited somewhere special, and the other was left out. The reason could have been practical like their car wasn't big enough to accommodate more kids. I was much happier when I knew Kylie also had a best friend. Regrettably, this concern did not extend to our other sisters.

Our birthdays were also treated differently to our siblings. We did notice that, growing up, when it was time for our birthday presents, parents and relatives tended to reduce the amount of money spent on our presents because there were two of us. For example, if people usually spent fifty dollars on a gift, when it came to Kylie and me, we would get twenty-five dollars spent on each of us, or worse still, we would get a 'shared' present that was the dollar value of one gift. It was obviously a budgeting thing for most parents, but we definitely noticed, and we always thought it was unfair.

I also can't remember ever getting different gifts to my twin, even from our parents. If Kylie got a bike, I got a bike. If one of us got roller skates, the other got roller skates, and I don't think this changed until we had left home as adults. I rarely got to see her joy when she opened her presents as I wouldn't look at her; I didn't want my surprise ruined.

When I was in Year 6 in primary school, I was asked to do a school assignment on one particular type of working dog. I chose police dogs. Our father always had dependable working dogs, and I enjoyed watching him work his dogs in a farm setting. It's fascinating how a few whistles and signals can instruct intelligent working dogs to move stock from one place to another. Our Aunty Dale was a former police officer, and she would often tell my twin and me stories about her time in the police force. These stories were intriguing, and a little flame was lit inside me about becoming a policewoman.

Talei's father, Ian, always encouraged Kylie and me to join the police, and I can't remember anyone ever trying to change my mind. Another friend of ours was an Aboriginal boy called Matthew, and Ian encouraged him to join as well. I can't remember why Ian encouraged Matthew, but he had also obviously shown interest as well. He would have been well aware that I, Kylie and Matthew were not your obvious stock standard candidates for the New South Wales Police. In those days, most police officers were white males of Australian heritage who had a specific chest measurement and a minimum height requirement of 175cm. These requirements actually automatically excluded whole ethnic groups. This didn't deter me; the seed was planted. I was now twelve years of age and had decided I was going to be a police officer when I grew up and work with police dogs.

We spent our childhood mostly left to our own devices. A term we often heard was 'get outside and play'. We would wander the streets with all the local kids and go exploring. Our childhood was very much like the TV show Survivor. With no adults around, the country streets were survival of the fittest; the stronger groups of kids were the leaders. We would pack a bag with a sandwich and one piece of fruit and head off; if we wanted a drink, we drank out of someone's hose. We would explore for the day on our bikes, making up games and building cubby houses out of branches on the nearby abandoned railway line. Our imaginations were well developed. The only absolute rule we had to abide by was that we had to be home when the street lights came on.

Town life suited us well, and we enjoyed spending the weekends with our aunts, uncles and cousins. We would often meet up on weekends and play softball and cricket. I remember these days with great affection. Another favourite family activity was attending the many bush dances and picnic events scattered around the district. Every Sunday, we had a traditional roast for lunch, which we were expected to attend, no excuses. Most of our relatives were always available to help, and this was reciprocated by our family. Having these family traditions made for a predictable but stable upbringing, and we were having a happy childhood. This was about to change!

A Crisis

Beef

Turning thirteen meant starting high school, which I loved, particularly recess, lunch, and sports. Jacki and I were involved in many sports. Hockey and gymnastics were my favourites. I had a gymnasts build and no fear. Looking back, I felt like five-time Olympic gold medallist Nadia Comaneci, but the reality was I was only a regional-level gymnast. I had started the sport at an older age, and perhaps if I had started when I was young my gymnastic career may have been different. My twin and I played in various club and representative hockey teams. I always had a forward position, and she was a goalie. Most of our friendship group also played hockey, and within our loyal group of Dubbo friends, each girl had their individual best friend with whom she spent more one-on-one time; mine was Anne.

Jacki and I started working Thursday nights and Saturday mornings at Coles as check-out chicks. Our pay was around twenty-one dollars for eight hours of work. Our blue uniforms resembled the maid's outfits from the movie *The Help*, which were topped off with 'very attractive' black school shoes. As a check-out worker,

I had to pick up each grocery item, rotate it around searching for a price sticker, and then manually press the numbers into the keys on the cash register. Once completed, I would press the total button, and the cash drawer would open with a 'ting' sound. Each cash register had two staff, someone working the till and someone packing the groceries. Often, Jacki and I were put on cash registers next to each other, and we would catch some person, tired at the end of their working day and wrestling a wobbly wheeled trolley and a few kids, suddenly do a doubletake as they lined up to process their groceries. They would get confused if Jacki and I worked together in the same cash register aisle.

I once read a story about a McDonald's manager who employed identical twins. For fun, the manager often had one twin working at the cashier window and the other at the food collection window, just to mess with the customers' heads. Later we had second job, working as kitchen hands at a restaurant called Jules Crepes. We took turns working either Friday or Saturday nights, and full-time in the holidays.

My close friend Anne started to show a rebellious side, and I followed. I can remember as our group walked to school, Anne would get me to lag behind, produce a packet of cigarettes, and bully me into smoking with her. I started to understand that Anne was possibly not the best friend to have, but I mistakenly felt fearful that without Anne, I would be on my own, so I continued to hang out with her.

Jacki and I were at the age when we were stuck between childhood and adulthood. We were maturing and forging our own identities.

Now, this is hard for any teenager, but as a twin, that pressure is doubled, excuse the pun. A feeling of individual identity is important to all twins. I wanted to be noticed as me, an individual, not noticed because I was a twin. I would get outrageous haircuts or wear opposite-style clothing. Jacki often answered questions directed to me before I could respond, or she would use the word 'we' when talking about herself, which frustrated me.

Others often referred to 'the twins' when they were only talking about one of us. I felt that the people around us, intentionally or not, made our lives a constant competition, and I started to feel that I had to continually strive not only to be better but at least equal to my twin. I loved her dearly but would get annoyed when I was looked at as failing if I could not perform the same as her. I felt we were constantly being compared by friends, family, and teachers. I felt that I was judged on her successes or failures, as she was on mine. She was always more assertive than me; she still is. Because she was more outgoing, I was seen as sulky; if she lost weight, I was seen as the fat twin. At this point in our lives, she seemed to know exactly who she was. I didn't! I started to have a real identity crisis. Who was I, not twin me, but me, as an individual?

When our dad was not at work, he continued to want his girls close by. The problem was we were all growing up; we had school, more homework, part-time work, lots of sports and our friends, and we didn't want to go fishing on the river. Our father battled with this. He was always a drinker, loved his beer, and would jokingly tell friends that he would have to open two beers at the end of the day, because by the time he gave each of his daughters 'a sip' the first bottle would be empty. Over some time, our father started to drink more heavily, and gradually, he began overreacting to minor things.

When we were disciplined, he would send us to our room to be given corporal punishment, in our case, the strap, which meant several strikes of his leather belt. If we behaved unsuitably, we were sent to our room. Our father followed, the belt looped in his hands, and he would cruelly flick the ends together as he walked behind us. The sound of the leather clashing made us flinch before we received our first smack. If Dad had been drinking, the hits were more brutal. It got to the point that our friends started avoiding our home, and so did we.

Our family sat down at the kitchen table for dinner one day, and our younger sister accidentally spilled her cup of Milo. Our father exploded, stood up, started unbuckling his leather belt, and roared at her to go to her room. Defending her, we jumped up and protested. Dad violently turned his anger on all four of us, aggressively yelling at us to get out of the house and not come back. Fearful, we ran from the house in tears. Our younger sister climbed a tree in the front yard and hid, while we tearfully ran up the street, around the corner, and kept going. We ended up hiding in the dark for hours in a laneway a few kilometres from home until we felt it would be safe to return. Another night, our father held a knife at our elder sister's throat after he caught her taking a cigarette from his packet. This caused another tearful eruption of protests from us girls, resulting in us being kicked out again. This confused me, as on other days, he would give us cigarettes. Sadly, these sorts of incidents became more frequent, and our home life was now not a happy one.

Our father continued to spiral downwards and, as a result, lost his pool business. We found this very upsetting for many reasons; for one, it meant we were now moving to a different part of town. This was one of the most challenging periods of my life. Our father was unemployed, would regularly erupt into violent rages, and was a person I did not want to be around. We were now living in a new house that I hated, and our mum, the sole financial provider, was always working and was never home when we needed her. On top of all this, I loved my twin but didn't want to be a twin.

A new school year started, and my bucket load of troubles kept filling up. For some reason, I was put in the lowest English class, whereas Jacki was put in a higher-graded class. I never felt that I should have been in the top grade, but I knew I did not deserve to be in the bottom; my marks did not indicate that. Being in the bottom class meant I was surrounded by kids who didn't want to be there, and academically, the move took all my self-esteem away. I started to believe it would be impossible to fulfil my dream of becoming a policewoman.

Also, we were at an age where people often asked, "What do you want to do when you leave school?" Friends, family, and teachers just assumed my twin, and I both wanted to be policewomen because the other twin wanted the same profession. Between my class placement and the comments made, I begrudgingly felt that one of us would have to choose a different career, and I knew it would have to be me.

Our father became very controlling and possessive about us kids, but mainly about our mother; he was constantly checking her every move. Our mother was either working full-time, doing housework, or was with us, so her spare time was minimal. On rare occasions, she would visit one of her sisters or close friends for a coffee, and our father would continually phone to check she was where she said she would be. Of course, no one was checking on his whereabouts. Perhaps he should have been using his energy to try to find work.

One sad Friday night, Jacki and I were at home alone. Our mother finished work and ducked out to have a coffee with some family friends. Soon, our father arrived home and, as usual, suspiciously questioned us about where our mother was. Our mother returned soon after, and within minutes, our father's chest puffed out; he clenched his fists, and his voice raised as he started to ridiculously accuse her of having an affair. There was another violent argument, and our father ripped the telephone clean out of the wall, before chasing our mother through the house, trying to hit her. Jacki and I managed to grab our mother and protectively pushed her behind us down the small hallway as she ran.

Standing together shoulder to shoulder, shielding our mother, my twin and I blocked our dad's path. He angrily put his fists up and threatened us. I thought he would strike. I will truly never forget staring him in the eyes; all I could see was hate and anger, but we did not move. Our father backed down and temporarily walked away. Our mother begged us to leave the house for our own safety. We did. We walked in the dark streets quite a few kilometres to our aunties, knocked on the door, and embarrassingly asked for refuge. We were guilt-ridden for leaving our mother. It's hard to understand how a person can be so cruel to their own children, and we were at an age where we were both embarrassed by, and fearful of his violent actions. Gratefully, as a twin, I never had to spend the darkest of moments alone.

In the Amtambahoaka tribe in Madagascar, the elders believe raising twins brings misfortune, even death, to their families. In the past, if a woman gave birth to twins, the newborn siblings were taken into the bush and left there to die! Many elders still hold these beliefs, but now, a woman can choose to keep her twins, if she leaves the village. If she decides to give the twins away, refuge centres have been built where twin babies can be taken, often resulting in overseas adoption. Perhaps my twin and I had brought a curse to our family?

After several years of violence and unhappiness, our mother found the courage and fortitude to pack up us girls and leave. Our father accepted this; however, unlike the male emu, he had no desire to care for us and unlovingly said, 'You're better off living with your mother.'

I hated this new father we had been witnessing for several years and was happy to be free of the stress and emotion of being a child caught in a miserable marriage, but I also grieved for the father we had known and loved in our early lives. Our father needed professional help, but back then, men rarely went to a doctor or asked for help.

My confusion about being a twin continued. I felt I was seeing myself live two lives, hers and mine, I felt like we were two photos, double exposed. Sometimes I would sit and intensely observe my twin without her knowledge, watch her facial expressions and mannerisms. Did I smile like that? Was that how I sounded?

Often, when I take photographs of a group of people, an individual will say, 'Everyone looks great, but I look awful.' People are often more critical of themselves in photographs because they don't see themselves when they smile, or see how they look when they screw up their face a certain way. For me, I wasn't seeing myself in a photo but in real life. It was like talking to a mirror 'all the time'.

Jacki seemed to be the happier more confident version of myself. I believed that no matter how hard I tried, everything was easier for my twin, but at the same time, I wanted only the best for her. I felt like God had made a mistake; perhaps there weren't meant to be two of me. Around this time, I developed anorexia nervosa, an eating disorder. Food was one thing I could control. I perceived myself as fat, however, my weight was very low. My mother, concerned, did try to get me to seek professional help for the disorder, but I walked out of the specialist's office, and never went back. My struggles with food continued for several years. Despite the turmoils in my life, I continued to try my best at school, work, and sports.

Before long, we settled into a different but comfortable routine, and soon, the house our mother had rented started to feel like a home. I was maturing and began to grasp that whenever I was with my friend Anne, I seemed to end up in some sort of trouble, always minor, but trouble nevertheless, so I ended the friendship. I no longer had my one good friend, but that was okay, as I still had our whole friendship group, the wonderful Dubbo girls.

Our aunts, Joy and Dale, and our adopted Aunt Clelia were all involved in our lives; they always helped our mum or us whenever they could. Aunty Joy struggled to tell my twin and me apart for a long, long time. In her defence, often when I look at early photos of my sister and me, I can't identify myself. We were very fortunate to have these supportive women in our lives. Our father left town for some time and had limited contact with us girls. He did not provide any financial support, and our mother was left with the responsibility of supporting four girls single-handedly, so she worked two jobs, which meant we saw little of her.

We were all allocated chores; one job Jacki and I were given was mowing the lawns. I took a lot of pride in this job, but the second-hand lawnmower we somehow acquired made the job difficult. Often, it would not start, and I would pull and pull the cord until, if I was lucky, the motor would finally chug and spurt, the engine kicking in. One day, after one of my regular battles with the lawnmower, a kind elderly neighbour walked across the road and, with a gentle smile, handed me a cold glass of stout. He had witnessed my lawnmower battle and was jointly celebrating my success. I disliked stout but politely drank every drop.

At first, we couldn't afford to have a phone connected at the rented house, but we were lucky to have a public phone box about 100 meters from the home. Back then public phone boxes had one metal wall, two glass sidewalls, and a folding glass door that opened inwards. There was an open gap of about twenty centimetres at the bottom of the walls. One summer afternoon, I walked to the phone box to ring a friend. I was standing in the phone box with my back to the door, deep in conversation, when

I felt a snake-like feeling going up my leg and under my dress. I jumped, looked down and saw a man lying on the ground with his arm stretched up under the glass, his hand still going up my inner leg towards my underpants. I was trapped by the glass door but kicked at his arm, and he withdrew it. Terrified, I turned so my back was to the vile man, and I quickly tried to explain to my friend what was happening so she could get help. I turned again as he stood blocking the door, looking through the glass, grinning at me like a sly fox about to pounce on his prey. Suddenly he exposed his genitals before pressing his penis and testicles firmly onto the glass. I felt so vulnerable and frightened and was very concerned that worse was about to happen. I did what any smart girl would do in my situation; I loudly screamed! This startled him, and, fortunately, he began running up the street. I sprinted home, looking back over my shoulder on the way. Aunty Dale, the former policewoman, happened to be visiting. Distressed, I quickly told her what had happened, and she reacted immediately. 'Quickly, jump in my car.' Her old police instincts had set in, and she wanted to search for him. Unfortunately, we did not find him in the surrounding streets. We reported the incident to the police, but the man was never caught. Shortly afterwards, my mother had a phone connected at home, and we never had to use the phone box again.

It wasn't long before we were eligible to get our driver's licences. My twin and I both passed the Learner Driver's written test, and Aunty Dale took on the role of our driving instructor. She spent hours teaching my sister and me to drive. She had young children of her own but still found the time to be there for us. My twin and I went together to sit our Provisional Driving Test (Ps). She passed her Ps, and I failed. This was one of those times when being a twin can be cruel. She was excited to pass but upset for me; I was happy she passed, but upset for myself. I re-sat the driving test and passed. Jacki and I saved and pooling our money, we purchased our first car, a six-hundred-dollar, aging, faded blue Morris eleven hundred, five-speed automatic.

Recently, I was told a story about identical twins. One of the boys managed to save for a car. Soon after, the boys went to sit for their provisional driving test. The twin with the vehicle failed the test, and the twin without the vehicle passed. Simple: They both shared one car and one driver's license. This is where being a twin can be an advantage.

At the end of 1984, we had to pick our Higher School Certificate subjects. I wanted to do photography, but our family didn't own a camera. I was forced to do textiles, but this wasn't much help as we didn't own a sewing machine either. I had to do most of the sewing, very poorly, by hand. I was still upset about my English placement and found it challenging trying to learn in a class where most of the students were just filling in time. Our older sister finished school and left home, commencing her adult life. She is now married to a twin and did not need any training to understand their twin relationship.

Sport continued to be a big part of our lives, and both of us were selected as school sporting captains for different sporting houses. Jacki had quit gymnastics years earlier, but I had always continued with it. Gymnastics was one thing I enjoyed doing, separate from my twin. In 1985, I was part of a school team that went to Sydney to perform in the Sydney School Spectacular, hosted by Rolf Harris. Our group performed gymnastics to the song, *Where Are the Clowns*, and were involved in other performances within the show. It felt electric performing in front of a crowd of thousands. Weeks after the show, Rolf Harris sent signed posters to my home! I have no memory of how he got my private address. I still have the handwritten envelope and poster. In July 2014, Rolf Harris was convicted in the UK of twelve counts of indecent assault on five innocent victims. His court case and conviction brought back my memories of that time, which unsettled me.

My twin and I both played in the under-18 and 21 state hockey carnivals. We travelled to many towns and cities playing hockey, and although I was never selected for the state team from the large pool of field players, hockey was my refuge. Through the school years, eleven and twelve, Jacki was away in the winter school holidays for State hockey camps. Our mother sympathised with her and her conflicts with sports and study. However, I felt that she was fortunate to have some great adventures while I had to remain and work for both of us. So, she didn't lose her job; I exhaustingly worked both her and my shifts at the restaurant, which also meant little time to study. Although I did obtain a higher trial Higher School Certificate (HSC) mark than my twin, which I was pleased about, as for me, the mark justified my continual complaints about my English class placement. Our school graduation was held before we started Stuvac (study vacation), a period when HSC students could study or cram at home just before the final exams commenced. During Stuvac,

Jacki and I were home alone studying. We had not seen our father for many months, so we were surprised when we spotted him seated in his vehicle outside our home. Confused, we watched him for a considerable time from the window as he sat still in his car, staring straight ahead. Finally, he knocked on the door, and when we opened it, we were shocked to see our father standing motionless outside the door with his loaded .22 rifle tucked neatly under his arm. He quietly and calmly told us he was going to shoot himself. From his tone and demeanour, we believed every word and were petrified he was going to do it there and then in front of us. Another overriding concern was that he was going to harm us before harming himself. Together, we remained calm and reassured him. I don't remember who, but one of us managed to slip away and phone our adopted aunt for help; coincidently, she worked for a crisis support organisation. That day, our father was admitted to the hospital and received essential professional help. For Jacki and me, this incident was terrifying and upsetting and not ideal at any time, let alone when we were about to sit our final school exams. We did what we had always done and supported each other.

We completed our HSC exams and enjoyed our Year 12 formal. Despite the upsets in our private lives, my school memories are mostly happy ones. We had our wonderful friends and a great year group led by a supportive and compassionate year advisor, Miss Latta. After the exams I was still in limbo regarding my career choices. Miss Latta had been approached by a family looking for a governess for children living on an isolated property, in the far west of NSW. She asked if I would be interested and suggested I go to the property for a two-week trial. I couldn't see the harm, so soon, I was on a bus and headed west. I arrived at the property and met the family. I have never shied away from hard work, but I soon realised that the expected workload was immense. Then, alarmingly, the father privately made sexual comments to me. I asked to be put on the next bus.

During my outback adventure, it became clear to me, that I still really did want to be a policewoman; I always had since hearing our aunt's stories during primary school. I recognised that it was okay that my twin and I chose the same career. No one questions singleton siblings for selecting the same professions or fathers and sons, so why should I choose a different career path to the one I truly wanted? Many twins follow similar careers, but I feel it's because twins are so genetically alike, that the same things appeal to them; it's not just twins wanting to stay together. Now that that decision was settled, I felt more confident.

When our exam results were announced, Jacki and I received identical HSC marks. I am unsure how they found out, but several media outlets approached our school or our mother for an interview. 'Twins Score Identical Marks', 'Lookalike Sisters Score a Dead Heat', and 'Twins Score Same Marks in Exams' were headlines printed in several newspapers. I was very embarrassed by this unwanted media attention. Coincidentally and perfectly timed, the NSW Police and NSW Ambulance Services were holding recruitment drives in Dubbo. Jacki and I attended and filled out applications for both 'just in case'. It had been a rough few years, but I was looking forward to the adult world.

Reef

I remember going to high school with great excitement. I was ready for more responsibility, and I craved the freedom high school offered. Mum wouldn't allow us to shave our legs until high school, so with smooth legs, apart from a couple of razor nicks, I headed off to high school. I wore my first bra on that day as well. Why I bothered to wear one, I cannot say, as Kylie and I wore an A-cup bra until we hit our forties, but this added to the charade that I was now all grown up. Our group of friends, made up of boys and girls, subconsciously claimed an area we could call our own. It was here we spent our lunchtimes sitting in full sun, tanning our legs and, in doing so, achieving a distinctive ankle sock line stencilled by a tan that caused a few basal-cell carcinomas later in life.

Just before Kylie and I celebrated our thirteenth birthdays, Mum and Dad took the family for a holiday to Port Macquarie on the north coast of New South Wales. We stayed with friends of theirs. I was very excited to go to the beach. The family we were staying with had a surfer son, and as I loved any sport, I asked him to show me how to surf. He was probably not happy about having four girls arrive and cramp his style, so he was reluctant to show me how to surf. The first morning on the beach, he gave me a quick, unenthusiastic two-minute lesson and said there you go. I was a country girl who had rarely been in the surf, and I obviously had no idea what I was doing. On the very first wave, the surfboard flipped up, and as I was tumbling around in the surf, the surfboard propelled into my face. I struggled in the whitewash and managed to somehow get to the surface. The first thing I did was to check that my swimmers were in place and that my 'A' cup breasts were not revealed. Then I felt pain in my left eye. I put my hand to my eye, pulled it away and saw blood on my hand. I looked at my not-so-skilled surf coach, whose mouth was now wide open with shock. I stumbled out of the water and walked towards my oblivious parents, sitting under a beach umbrella further up the beach. As I walked blindly in their general direction, I noticed the looks on the faces of my fellow beachgoers. I couldn't see out of the damaged eye, and blood was streaming down my face and dripping off my chin. After my traumatised parents cleaned me up, it was discovered that, by some miracle, the board had hit the bottom of my eye and didn't actually get my eyeball. The only reason I couldn't see was because of all the blood. But I still had to walk around with a patch over my eye for the rest of the holiday to protect the wound.

The very next day, I awoke to my first period. This holiday already had far too much blood in it. I was upset and cried, as now I couldn't swim. I wasn't ready to try tampons just yet! It was a rare occasion for us to have a beach holiday. The worst thing was that my first menstrual cycle was now discussed by both families, much to my extreme embarrassment. Dad got the job of taking me fishing, but I didn't like fishing; it bored me. Two days later, Kylie had her first period. At least now I had my sister to go fishing with. Our personal predicament became a great comedy show for the adults who discussed it, laughing about how 'amazing' it was that 'the twins' got their first period days apart. This was possibly the worst holiday we ever had.

When the family pool business was thriving, Dad hired many off-duty police to work as labourers on their days off for cash to supplement their income. Dad enjoyed hanging with the police, as it made him feel important. If he was caught doing any minor traffic offence around town, the police would let him off and say things like, 'It's only Dicko.'

I became aware that our home life was changing. After an initial flourishing start, the business began to fail, which obviously caused tension in the house. Our father's personality worsened. Dad had always had a quick temper, but the atmosphere had altered, and he started drinking more. Arguments in the home were now common. With our parents' marriage and business failing, our home life was like one big pressure cooker about to explode. School and sports were my escape.

Our father had always been involved in our lives but more as an observer on the edge of the relationship. As we were all girls, he mostly left our upbringing to Mum. He never liked us to sleep in, believing the early mornings were the best part of the day. If we slept in, he would come into the bedroom in a rage and, pull the covers back and twist our toes to get us out of bed.

Ironically, he would often have an afternoon nap. Dad's temper surfaced quickly, and he could turn from Dr Jekyll to Mr Hyde in milliseconds. We learnt to look out for these triggers in an attempt to avoid this character flaw. We weren't always lucky. Dad had difficulty knowing how to parent us, especially when we reached high school, and he didn't like not having complete control over us. Looking back, I think he had quite an immature personality. Dad lost both his parents at a young age, and a relative once said that Dad knew how to be a son, but he had never been taught how to be a husband or a father.

The battles at home became more frequent, and my sisters and I were now living in a house filled with tension, domestic violence, and an alcoholic father. Dad had most of the police in town working for him, so going to the police was fruitless. It was also embarrassing because of the stigma surrounding domestic violence. Most families didn't discuss their 'private' life outside the home.

The business failed, and we had to sell our family home and move to rental accommodation. The street we lived on was the last before farming land commenced. This move isolated us from most of our friends who had previously lived in the same area as us. We continued to go to the same school, which was a blessing. We found out later that our form mistress had intervened and negotiated for us to stay at our high school, even though we were living out of the school zone.

During this tidal wave, Kylie and I became very close again, and we endured our hardship in solidarity. As the years passed, when our father became aggressive, we would stand up to him to protect our mother. We were like two little chihuahuas coming at him from both sides. As with most men in domestic violence, it was the power he craved. Once we had the guts to stand up to him, he would sometimes back down. There was one incident when we stood up to our father, and he kicked us out of the house in the middle of the night. We didn't know where to go. We ended up at our dependable form mistress's house, who happened to live in the same suburb. I don't know what happened at home, but we were at least safe for the night. Our little sister was three years younger than us, and we often had to leave her at the house with Mum if Dad kicked us out, which he often did. I remember feeling guilty about leaving both our mother and little sister at the house on their own and feeling powerless.

The house that we were renting had two telephones. One evening, I went into Mum and Dad's bedroom to use the second phone. I picked up the receiver and could hear voices. The male voice was my father's, and I couldn't recognise the female voice. My instinct was to hang up the phone, but my intuition told me to listen. I held my rapid breathing in, so I wouldn't be heard by either party and quietly covered up the mouthpiece just to make sure I wouldn't be heard. The conversation hadn't gone on long when it dawned on me that our father was having an affair. I was only young, but the contents of the conversation were so explicit that there was no doubt in my mind what was going on. I quietly put the receiver down, snuck off to the bedroom I shared with Kylie, and told her what I had heard. After an agonising debate with our older sister, we decided to tell our mother. There had already been so much tension in the house, we knew this piece of incriminating evidence would change the situation with their marriage. Mum decided to make plans to leave. School went on as normal, and apart from my best friend, I'm sure not many school friends knew what was going on in our house. Teachers still expected homework to be handed in. Our home life was a burden my sisters and I shared in secret.

Thankfully, this period of our life ended after a few years when Mum finally had the courage to walk away from the marriage, but now new struggles presented themselves. There were very few divorced families at our school, and this caused us embarrassment. Not that this meant everyone else's households were examples of domestic bliss. I remember the immense relief I felt the first night we slept in the new rented house without our father. However, my emotions were conflicted, and I felt incredibly sad for him because he was on his own.

Not long after we moved into the house, the Sheriff's Department arrived to recover anything of value to pay off creditors. I was at home at the time, and our mother did her best to remain composed and dignified during the experience.

We now had no car, and our mother would get groceries two bags at a time so she could carry them home from work, which was quite a distance. This also meant my sisters, and I now had to walk everywhere. I had to walk to hockey and training carrying a large, heavy bag that contained all my goalie equipment; although I was a lightweight, I was strong and carrying the bag helped me get stronger.

Since Kylie and I were tomboys, we became the male figureheads in the family. We mowed the lawns, but as we didn't have an edger, we had to do the edges by hand with a tomahawk. If there was any heavy lifting to do, we were called upon. Life was calmer; however, lack of money became our new struggle. I remember on one occasion watching our mother cry because she didn't have enough money to fill the car with petrol to drive us to the local pool for a swim on one of Dubbo's very hot summer days.

Despite receiving no child maintenance, Mum always had a meal on the table and did her very best to provide for us, but there were many nights when bread completed the meal to fill our stomachs. On one particular day, I was walking home from school, and my shoe fell apart. My shoulders slumped as I knew finding the money for new shoes would be challenging for our mother. I limped home with the weight of the world on my shoulders.

Somehow, Kylie and I managed to fit in a social life, and I had my first real romance with a boy called Trevor. I had known him most of my life as he sat with our group of friends. Our entire extended family loved Trevor. He had a great sense of humour, and he was the distraction I needed.

Hockey was becoming my standout sport and played a huge part in my life. I represented various hockey teams and was also part of the New South Wales Hockey Squad. I travelled away with the squad every second weekend to Sydney. These hockey trips gave me time away from Kylie and helped me develop my own personality, as most of the players in the teams didn't know I was a twin. I could enjoy the freedom of being an individual. Kylie and I played in different hockey teams for our regular Saturday afternoon comp. When we were about fifteen, we played against each other in the grand final. Our team led one nil my way until the last minute. Then, all of a sudden, Kylie, one of their forwards, made a break from the pack and headed in my direction. It was now one on one. The seconds on the clock were ticking down, and we only had minutes until the game was over. I remember saying out loud to myself, '"Come on. Kyl.' and moved towards her, stretching my arms and sticking out wide to protect the goal. As she came closer to me, I rushed forward and met her in the circle of the goal and at the last minute, I did a slide tackle. This meant lying down in a side position and using the momentum of my body to sweep my legs forward to block the ball and, at the same time, kick the ball out of harm's way. This type of manoeuvre usually resulted in the goalie cleaning up the player as well. Somehow, I timed my tackle perfectly and took out both the ball and my twin, also breaking her hockey stick. Kylie tumbled around on the ground, and the ball ricocheted off the field just as the final bell was sounded. We had won the grand final! This was one of those times my twin emotions were conflicted, enjoying my success but recognising my twin's despair. This has occurred many times in our lives. Parents of twins have to balance a precarious line between congratulating one twin and supporting the other. During this game our mum stood on the halfway line with streamers of both our teams in opposite hands.

Our father was still in our lives but was not a significant role model. Occasionally, he did make some effort to see us. Mum would have to go away for work training, and we would be left at the house on our own. Kylie and I used to panic when Mum went away, as our older sister enjoyed the lack of parental supervision and often held a party. I worried about getting into trouble. I also loved my sleep and knew that the party would go well into the night.

One weekend, Dad found out that Mum was away and turned up at our house, bringing with him a carton of beer for all the kids to drink. Dad stayed at the house well into the night, drinking with our sister and her friends. Kylie and I now had the responsibility of looking after our intoxicated father. Once our eldest sister left home, we made a pact that we never told any of our friends when our mother was away to avoid any of our friends or our father turning up to the house to party. We have responsible personalities and have always liked to follow the rules. I think I like rules and laws as they make things fair and equal.

Our year co-ordinator, Miss Latta, who was also our career adviser, held a meeting with everyone in our year and helped us develop a plan for our future. During this era, it was common for a person to have only one career, with the possibility of two, throughout their entire lives. The decision was one that would shape a person's life forever; it was significant. When I was called in, she asked me what I was going to do when I finished school. I told her I wanted to join the New South Wales Police. She said I had one big problem—two inches! I was aware that there was currently a height requirement for women in the police, with a minimum height requirement of 5'4 at the time. I was 5'2. I had heard media reports that the height requirement for both males and females was under review, and I firmly believed that I would get into the police, but to make my teacher happy, I did look at other options. I had completed work experience in Year 10 with the ambulance service, as the police wouldn't take work experience students. Towards the end of 1996, the New South Wales Police Force became the first police jurisdiction in Australia, and one of the first in the Western world, to abolish the minimum height requirements for both male and female police officers.

As the end of the year was fast approaching, and the higher school certificate exams were not far away, I started studying hard, looking beyond school and focusing on getting into the police. Our exams commenced, and although I had suffered from a recent bout of glandular fever, I felt moderately prepared to sit the exams that would secure my future. Waiting outside the school hall, students milled around nervously trying to memorise things like quotes and dates. While we were waiting outside the hall, our father turned up at the school grounds. He was threatening suicide again and was argumentative and crying. The .22 rifle in the car confirmed his intentions. He obviously caused a scene and was escorted from the school grounds. Kylie and I were used to being the adults in our relationship with Dad, but this disruption caused us embarrassment and a great deal of stress literally minutes before we sat one of our Higher School Certificate Exams. There was no such thing as an appeal process, and the mark we received for that exam was what we got regardless of the circumstances just prior to us sitting the exam.

The only way to receive your Higher School Certificate results was by post, and on the day the results came out, my twin and I waited anxiously for hours, sitting on bean bags next to the mailbox.

When the poor postie arrived, we almost knocked him off his bike. We both nervously opened up our results and quickly added up our marks. Once calculated, we discovered we had received the same final result—exactly!

We had received enough marks to apply for the police, and as a backup plan to please my teacher, we also applied to New South Wales Ambulance. Life had not been that easy over the last few years, and we could have been dealt an easier path. Our birth order might have helped us cope a bit better. We were the middle kids and twins. We believed we were in the best birth position in the family. We were mostly left to our own devices, and we had each other for constant support. My tumultuous childhood had shaped me, and I looked forward to the future.

―――― **Police Academy** ――――

Beef

Our mother and younger sister moved to Sydney to live, so Jacki and I were homeless and were forced to rent a basic small flat. At almost 19 years of age, this was the first time I had had my own bedroom. I was thankful to have my twin with me as I transitioned into the adult world and the responsibilities that came with it. We eagerly awaited a response regarding our police applications. Although my twin and I had filled out applications for the police force on the same day, I was not surprised when my twin received notification first; that's just how things were between her and me. Finally, I was told to attend Sydney for the necessary IQ, physical and medical tests. I passed all phases, although I had a little problem with my medical when the doctor questioned my low weight. Jacki and I were accepted for the same Police Academy class intake and would be attending together.

The New South Wales Police Academy was originally located in the inner Sydney suburb of Redfern at the old Police Depot. In 1907, the Police Depot was occupied by trainees of the Mounted Police section, and over the years, several other branches of the NSW Police occupied parts of the building. In 1954, the Police Depot changed its name to the Police Training Centre. The Redfern Academy was where all police training was held; our Aunty Dale also completed her initial training there. Our grandfather's first cousin, Peter Condon, was once the officer in charge of the Redfern Academy. In 1984, much of the training was moved to the new NSW Police Academy in Goulburn, 200 kilometres southwest of Sydney.

Our magnificent Morris 1100 had broken down while we were in Year 12, and we could not afford to fix it, but even if we could have, it certainly would not have made the 450-kilometre trip from Dubbo to Goulburn. Once again, our relatives came to the rescue when our Aunty Joy generously at her expense offered to drive us to the academy. We walked into the reception building with a mixture of anticipation and excitement and were met by an old sergeant sitting behind a counter. After a very 'welcoming' greeting and a brief introduction to the academy's rules, my twin and I were handed separate room keys. We were told our rooms were in tower one, the female tower, which was strictly off-limits to male recruits; similarly, the male towers were strictly off-limits to female recruits. Any breach was instant dismissal.

In 1987, initial police training lasted for twelve weeks, and if we successfully passed, we would graduate at the rank of probationary constable and start a twelve-month probationary period, before a further four weeks of secondary training. During the probationary period you were required to do assessments. Our first official day at the academy was on the 18th of May, 1987. Class 228, consisting of 190 recruits, 153 men and 37 women, was divided into six teaching classes. Our class had some of the first 'short' recruits, and my twin and I were the first set of female twins to join the NSW police. Class 228 also had the first married couple to enter together and the one-thousandth serving policewoman. The Police Academy was a mixture of an army camp and a university: lots of discipline, rules, study, training, and limited freedom.

The days consisted of classes on law, police powers, traffic law, common law, police and society, typing, court procedure, officer survival, firearms training, driver training, and the funniest, drill training. Well, most found it funny, but those with two left feet suffered greatly, which meant that the whole class suffered.

While walking around the academy, I would avoid senior officers because if I walked past them, I had to stop, stand to attention, salute and address them as 'Sir. I say, Sir, as from memory, there were no female commissioned officers at the academy. There were many rules, but I liked the routine and structure. A recruit packing their belongings was a constant reminder that it was a privilege to be there and that if we breached the rules or were found to be unsuitable, we were out. Recruits were continually told that we were about to start careers with a lot of responsibility and danger.

Apart from the freezing weather, I enjoyed the academy, and soon, we were in our final weeks, and our first police postings were announced. Jacki and I were both posted to Parramatta Police Station. I was disappointed not to be posted to a country posting, and that I had been posted to the same police station as my twin. I loved her deeply, but I wanted to step outside her shadow and be known as a singleton, just me, not 'one of the twins'. Without

Jacki's knowledge, I approached senior staff and requested to be posted to a different station. After I explained why, they agreed and soon notified me that I would be sent to 32 Division, which was right next door to Paramatta's, 18 Division. I would still be close to Jacki but at my own station. Perfect!

32 Division was about sixteen kilometres from the Sydney central business district. 32 Division covered roughly eight Sydney suburbs, and had a blend of residential, commercial, and industrial areas, with many low socioeconomic and ethnic communities. Flemington was home to the Flemington Markets, Silverwater Gaol and Mulawa Women's Prison. Our patrol was also home to Rookwood Cemetery, the largest cemetery in the southern hemisphere. The head police station for 32 Division was Flemington, where I was to be first stationed at, and there were two substations at Auburn and Lidcombe. At the time, Chief Inspector Allan Doyle was in charge of the ground floor, which comprised of general duties staff and patrol detectives. On the top floor was the Major Crime Squad Unit and the Tactical Response Group, specialist police whose primary role was to respond to and support the police in high-risk incidents such as sieges.

In our last week of training, we were issued our uniforms. A police uniform for women consisted of blue culottes, worn with specific Coltex Swede blue stockings. We were issued with ample shirts, a blue jumper, shoes, and an inner and outer belt. We were also issued with an Antron jacket and a female hat. The ladies' hats were hideous back then, similar to our grandmother's bowling hat. We prepared for our graduation, and the class formation was positioned according to height. Jacki and I were placed together in the front row, and the final week was filled with an enormous amount of parade practice.

On graduation day, we were issued our firearms and handcuffs. Firearms were first issued to policewomen only eight years previously, so I felt privileged to get a firearm and not a handbag. On that day, our entire family was present, including our adopted family, Ian and Clelia. Ian, at the time, was a serving chief inspector. Disappointingly, our Aunty Dale, the former policewoman, could not be there as she was living over 4000 kilometers away in the Northern Territory. During the passing out parade's formal inspection, the Commissioner of Police, Mr. Avery, and the Minister for Police, Mr. Paciullo, stopped and spoke with my twin and I, before we proudly marched off the parade ground as official police officers. The papers the following day read, 'Crims See Double', 'Double Trouble', 'Dubbo Twins Enter Police Force', 'Double Justice', 'Crooks Will Cop Two of a Kind'. We gratefully left the Antarctic Goulburn winter behind and drove to Sydney.

Reef

I started my application process for the New South Wales Police and could do nothing but wait to hear from recruiting. Kylie and I had to find somewhere to live, and we found ourselves a little flat. We still worked at the restaurant and they gave both of us as many shifts as they could. As we had been on the front page of the local newspaper, and on page three of the Sydney Daily Telegraph due to our identical marks, it was no secret that we had both applied to join the police force. We had trouble finding full-time jobs as everyone in our country town knew we were about to leave town or that we hoped that we would.

We tried to keep fit, knowing we had to pass a timed run, an obstacle course, and a medical to get accepted into the police. Part of the obstacle course was to climb over a sheer six-foot wall. We looked around town, and the only wall we could find to practice on was the wall between the Dubbo Court House and the Dubbo Police Station. Ian got us permission to climb the high concrete wall. It's not an easy feat, especially for us shorties. There was nothing more we could do but wait. I was still seeing my boyfriend, Trevor, who was now a mechanic, and he kept me occupied during this period.

I was thrilled to receive word that I had to go to Sydney and sit for my aptitude test at the police academy. We no longer owned a car, so I caught the train from Dubbo to Sydney to the recruiting section at the old Police Academy in Bourke Street, Sydney. I waited in the court yard with the other candidates, looking through a window and watching another group sitting their test. After the examination, I saw a few people get up and walk out of the room with disappointed faces, and it became apparent that they had failed the test. I became extremely uneasy. When it was my turn, I walked into a room with about thirty other people and nervously sat down. The time commenced, and I turned the paper over. Looking at the questions, I could have been reading a different language. I wasn't confident, and my writing hand was actually shaking. At the conclusion, the police officer at the front of the room collected our papers, and we had to sit and wait for the exams to be marked. The police officer from recruiting walked back in and said if our name was called out, it meant we had failed the test and had to leave immediately. We could reapply in six months. My name was called out, and I was devastated. I walked out of the room with the eyes of everyone in the room watching me. I caught a taxi to where I was staying, and my upbeat taxi driver asked how my day was going. I burst out crying, sensing that the taxi driver was now regretting that he had asked the question. He did attempt to cheer me up and proceeded to tell me that most 'cops' were arseholes anyway. I suspect this opinion resulted from traffic infringements he had received over the years.

I arrived back in Dubbo, shattered. Trevor tried to cheer me up, but I think he was secretly pleased as our romance could continue. I didn't know what to do as working in the police was all I had ever wanted. I was very lucky when a friend of the family made a 'little' call to 'someone' and somehow got me back in the recruiting pool earlier than the six months. I went to the newsagency and bought an IQ practice book and studied it for hours. I had never thought to do this before and didn't even know these books existed. Miss Latta, our dependable former form mistress, tutored me and helped me understand these unusual questions.

Three weeks later, like a ship setting course, my life changed. Kylie and I didn't have a telephone, and we had put our grandmother's name and phone number on our application forms as our contact for the police recruitment. Our grandmother received a phone call from recruiting asking for one of us to come to Sydney to sit the aptitude test. Our red-headed grandmother had a formidable personality and was not someone to argue with. She immediately said to the caller, 'What about her twin sister? There are two of them you know. It's very expensive for them to come down, and it would be much cheaper if they could go together.' She would have been very convincing. Whoever she spoke to told her to hold on a minute and went away for a while. The caller came back onto the phone and said they had retrieved the documents for the other twin and said, 'Alright, tell her to come as well.' This is how my twin sister and I ended up at the police academy together.

We both sat the aptitude test and passed. I was enormously relieved as I believed that passing this test was the most challenging part of the recruitment process for me. I was confident enough about the fitness and medical tests, the obstacle course and the interview. That same day, we had to do the obstacle course. Each person had to complete a specific course in a certain time frame. The course was designed much like those in Hollywood army movies, and skills such as balance, agility, and strength were required. I watched many people fail that morning, mostly women who couldn't get over the six-foot sheer wall. My twin and I completed the course well within the time limit. All those years trimming our lawn edges using the tomahawk weren't wasted and had helped us gain good upper body strength. Those that failed were now asked to leave. I still hadn't forgotten being sent away myself only a few short weeks earlier and felt really sorry for them. Our recruitment group was now taken over to Centennial Park to complete our run. We had to run 2.5 kilometres in under thirteen minutes. Start. Go! At first, I thought I was doing okay. As we completed the first lap, the recruitment officer would yell out the time. I soon understood that in my excitement, I had gone far too fast, too early, and was starting to feel exhausted. I honestly didn't think I was going to make it. The back of my throat burned as I gasped for air. My twin has always been a better runner than me, and she appeared to be doing it easier than me. She looked back at me and slowed down so we could run together. She started screaming at me with determination, 'Run.' I knew we were getting close to the time and something inside me literally lifted me and carried me across the finishing line. I felt like I had an out-of-body experience and can't remember my feet touching the ground over the last 100 metres. We crossed over the finishing line with the police recruitment officer and the completed candidates cheering us on. We finished dead on the thirteen minutes, and I wouldn't have made it within the time without Kylie's encouragement.

We went back home to wait for the next process. We were both cautiously optimistic that we would soon be going to the police academy. A few weeks later we got notice that we had to go back to Sydney for our interviews. The interview process was conducted on a Wednesday in front of a panel of three police officers, and I was asked random questions to assess my suitability to be a police officer. Kylie was interviewed in another room by a separate group of panellists at the same time. I have never been nervous sitting for an interview and felt it had gone well. After the interview, one of the panellists asked me if I had any questions. I inquired how long it would be before I would have my medical if I had passed the interview. I knew the medical would mean another trip to Sydney, and as we were still broke, I thought if it was soon, we could just stay in Sydney for a few days with friends to save on the train fares. They told me to go outside and wait. Outside, my twin was waiting for me. I told her what I had asked the panellists, and initially, she was annoyed with me as she thought it might affect my recruitment to be so forthcoming. Shortly afterwards, a male police officer came out and told us that we had both passed our interviews. Unusually, we were given permission to go directly to Police Headquarters for our medicals. We went around and had our medicals conducted by different doctors.

Afterward, we were told to wait because the senior police wanted to speak with us. They called us into a room and, with curiosity, had been looking at our separate files and had become aware that we had received the exact same HSC mark and told us that we had also achieved identical IQ results in our examinations. In a relaxed meeting, they discussed 'twin things' with us for some time and were fascinated. They said we would start at the Police Academy four days later. We would be the first female twins to join the New South Wales Police. We had four short days to get home to Dubbo, give notice on our apartment, quit our jobs, pack our meagre belongings, and somehow get to Goulburn, where the Police Academy was located. Family and friends rallied around us.

I decided to get a haircut before I left for the academy. I don't know if this was a subconscious decision to try not to look like my twin or whether I was being practical. I went into the salon with long blonde hair, and I walked out with possibly the worst hairstyle I have ever had in my life. I have experimented over the years with different hairstyles, but this was by far the worst. I walked out of the salon looking like a ninety-year-old with a tightly curled, permed short hairstyle with no fringe. The only thing I needed was a blue rinse. Nothing I could do about it; the damage was done.

We drove to Goulburn on Sunday, nervous and excited at the same time. Our aunty dropped us off with a quick kiss as she had to turn around and head straight back to Dubbo. We walked into the Police Academy with a suitcase and enthusiasm. There were two grumpy police officers on the front desk. The first thing that was said to us was, 'Names?' We said our names and one of the officers said, 'Sisters?'

We replied in unison, 'Yes, twins.'

He said, 'One's fat and one's ugly; here are your room keys.'

This didn't upset us for some reason, but we were simultaneously amused. Welcome to the Police Academy, I thought. I still haven't worked out which description I fitted more. I have always been the slightly heavier twin, but there was now my new horrendous hairstyle to consider. Once settled into our rooms we met the other trainees from class 228 and were placed into individual classes according to the alphabet. This meant my twin and I would be in the same class, 228B. At the academy, we had to wear smart casual clothes with police shoes, a gun belt without a gun, and a police hat without a badge. My new hairstyle was causing me further hardship as I now had to fit a mass of tight curls under the police hat. As our hair wasn't allowed to touch our collar, I had to wear my hair in two miniature ponytails like a small toddler in an attempt to give the illusion of longer hair. It looked ridiculous.

Soon after arrival at the academy, all cadets have their fingerprints taken to keep on record. This is so if police accidentally touch something at a crime scene, their fingerprints can quickly be identified. I suspect it was also to check that none of the new recruits had a criminal record. Police checks in the workplace were not conducted back then as they are today. We just ticked a box, and the name and paperwork we supplied were checked against the records. I learnt later in the job how easy it was to forge documents. Interestingly, identical twins do not have identical fingerprints, even though their identical genes give them very similar patterns. The foetus begins developing fingerprint patterns in the early weeks of pregnancy. Slight differences in the womb environment conspire to give each twin different but similar fingerprints.

During the first week, we were given nicknames. I don't know how these nicknames were decided, but I know my twin and I were given the nicknames 'Bib' and 'Bub', the gumnut twins from the book Snuggle Pot and Cuddle Pie by Australian author May Gibbs. During the first week at the academy, all 190 of us had a meeting in the big lecture theatre, and at the conclusion of the meeting, an officer called out trainees' names to hand out mail. During this process, he called out Constables Snuggle Pot and Cuddle Pie. Yep! Our mother had sent us a letter and addressed it thus on the front of the envelope. Everyone in the theatre started laughing, and we had to get up and walk down the front to collect our private mail. Our 'thoughtful' mother had sent us pocket money as she knew we wouldn't have any money for a week. The academy provided free food and board, and they also gave us a small amount of money as an allowance.

During the second week at the academy, Kylie and I received individual mail informing us that we had both been accepted into the New South Wales Ambulance Service. We wrote a letter and thanked them but told them we were currently at the Police Academy and would have to turn down the offer to join the Ambulance Service. They wrote back to us with a lovely letter wishing us the best and said if the police didn't work out for us, their offer stood. The letter went on to say how the two services work closely together in the community, and once we graduated, we found out how true this was.

Our day-to-day life settled into a routine, and I enjoyed most aspects of the academy. The instructors were hard on us, but this hardness created a bond within the class, which I'm sure was their intention. All of us would get picked on and yelled at for the most menial infringements, resulting in the entire class having to do push-ups on our knuckles on the concrete or having to run an extra lap of the oval. The instructors would line us up, standing us at attention like a typical scene in an army movie, and on one particular day, one of the instructors yelled in a female cadet's face and said, 'You stink. Have you got your period or something?'

She yelled back, 'No, Sergeant.' Then, the Sergeant moved along the line and yelled at someone else over something he thought would intimidate that cadet. This may seem hard or even sexist, but the criminals out in the big wide world have said a lot worse to us. The training helped us develop a thick skin and gave us the ability to have self-control when working on the streets. The insults also made us a stronger group.

The temperature of the Goulburn winters was unforgiving. It was as cold as an Antarctic Ocean, and the wind chill factor made it even colder. The medical staff gave us cadets up-to-date tetanus injections, and straight after this, we had a parade. Parade was where we practised marching and saluting and standing at attention for hours. Yet another form of discipline. So, with our freshly injected arms we headed to parade, and after some short instructions we were made to stand at attention for a very long time. Standing at attention required holding our arms straight along our sides, with our bodies straight and eyes looking forward. In the silence, the cold wind blew through us, and around us, and played and toyed with us as the minutes slowly ticked by. After what felt like forever, a drill sergeant appeared and hollered, with long drawn-out words, 'Parade, at ease.' We then went from the attention position to the at ease position, which required our legs to be separated and our arms to snap in one movement behind our backs and clasp our hands. After our arms had been in the fixed position for at least sixty minutes, the movement to the at-ease position caused all the cadets to moan at once with our stiffened, sore arms reminding us of the recent injections. Of course, we were reprimanded for complaining and then had to spend another thirty minutes standing in the cold wind. This did toughen up any weak personalities in the group.

Sitting at the desk studying in our university-styled rooms, on late nights or long weekends, the cold Goulburn wind whistled its way into my subconscious, squeezing through any small opening in the window frame. The wind toyed with my imagination and gave the impression that there was no one else in the world. It's strange how I felt so lonely surrounded by a lot of people, including my twin sister, only two floors above me. If I hear the wind whistle today, anywhere in the world, I think of the Goulburn Police Academy. The academy was a bustling place on weekdays, with cadets coming and going to different classes and police instructors delivering lectures. On the weekends, the academy would grind to a halt as most of the cadets, who came from Sydney, travelled back to their homes. The only cadets left were the country cadets who lived too far away to get home and back in one weekend. There were never more than about ten cadets at the academy on weekends. I remember feeling very lonely on the weekends, and I would not have survived the homesickness if it wasn't for my twin. Ironically, I didn't actually have a home in Dubbo to go back to.

To fill our weekends, Kylie and I would go for long runs around Goulburn, and as a result, our fitness improved significantly. To pass the fitness test at the Police Academy, the 2.5-kilometre run had a reduced time of twelve and a half minutes; my final run was 11.18 minutes. Kylie's time was comparable, and this improved time resulted in us getting paraded for good work. We were paraded for good work or bad work. When we were called into the office, we were never told what we were there for. The anticipation was all part of the charade, and the results were recorded on our academy records. Our run time hadn't only improved because of our own efforts, as we were made to do PT (Physical Training) most days and we would have to do long runs around the streets of Goulburn. While running in groups, we would do a cadence call. This is the traditional call-and-response song sung by the military. Singing a cadence while running helped us take deeper breaths and exhale more forcefully. This increased oxygen to our lungs and made us fitter. We must have looked quite the sight running around Goulburn, but the local residents would have been well and truly accustomed to it, as there were approximately 200 cadets arriving at the academy every six weeks.

Most cadets had difficulty with at least one aspect of the academy. There was one cadet who didn't have enough strength in her forefinger to pull the trigger on the gun. Another cadet had trouble passing the 100-metre sprint in the required time. The academic side of the course caused many cadets stress. My liability was the driver training. Part of the assessment was to drive a police vehicle in the city of Sydney. We left the academy with four cadets squashed in a car and the police driver instructor in the front passenger seat. Each cadet would take turns driving for short sections during the two-hour drive. When we got to Sydney, I was already really nervous. I was a country kid who had never driven in the bustling city. Dubbo's only road with two lanes was the highway that went through the centre of town. Needless to say, my driving in the city was a near-death experience for everyone in the car, and I subsequently failed. I was lucky that the pass or fail on my driving examination didn't affect my suitability for graduating; it just meant I had to redo the driving test when I was a probationary constable. But I wasn't allowed to drive a police car until I passed.

As we neared the end of our time at the police academy and closed in on our graduation date, Kylie and I were often called away from class to do media interviews to promote us as the first female twins to graduate from the academy. We did live radio shows, including one with a Northern Territory radio station, and newspapers interviewed us. It wasn't until years later that I understood the police used any opportunity to get some good publicity.

Towards the end of our academy training, recruits were taken into a room and questioned by a panel of three in regard to where we would like to be stationed. Being twins, they did our interview together. They said they would place us in police stations close enough that we could live together. I thought I had given a broad enough area, and I said I was happy to go anywhere in western New South Wales. They gave us a date when the appointments would be listed on a notice board outside one of the lecture rooms. On that day, I ran up and searched the list. The name Parramatta Police Station was written next to my name. I thought, did they think I said western Sydney or western New South Wales? There was nothing I could do about it. There was no appeals process; we just went where we were told. One cadet yelled out, 'I'm going to a place called Geurie,' and he pronounced it Guy-ree. He said, 'It's somewhere between Wellington and Dubbo.'

I giggled and said to him, 'You pronounce it Gear-ree.' He wouldn't have been too popular with the locals if he'd turned up and called it Guy-ree.

Our passing out parade was scheduled, and on the morning of the graduation, we were given our .38 Smith and Wesson firearms, with twelve hollow point bullets and a set of handcuffs. Each gun and pair of handcuffs was identified with a unique number. They didn't need to drop the height restrictions, as I felt two inches taller standing in that police uniform. The media took lots of photos of us with the Police Commissioner, and we had a half-page article in the Sydney Daily Telegraph. Anonymity about being a twin was now out of the question at my new station. I commenced work at Parramatta on the Monday after the passing out parade. As we only had two days between graduation and starting work, our mum found us somewhere to live. Kylie was stationed at Flemington, so Mum tried to find a central suburb where we could live together. We needed a home close to public transport because we didn't have a car. We ended up living in the densely populated suburb of Westmead, a bustling multi-cultural suburb. My adult life was about to begin.

Badge and Honour

Beef

On my first day, in my crisp new uniform, I felt like a child starting kindergarten, except I carried a gun and handcuffs instead of pencils and books. The gun belt was quite heavy, and for the first few weeks, it bruised my hip bones, however, I soon got accustomed to the extra weight. Over the years, this weight did nothing to help the condition of my spine. I had never caught city public transport on my own previously, but I successfully caught a train to Flemington and nervously walked into the Police station.

The first week was an induction week, where all new graduating Police in the area were taken to various locations. Our small group was quickly ushered to a minibus, and we were off. Other probationary constables, including my twin, were collected from different stations on the way. Our first stop was Westmead morgue! We were herded into a very cool room, and right in the middle, lying on a cold, stainless steel tray, was a dead body. The tray was positioned above a grill-like structure that ran parallel to the floor, which had a lip, and I presumed this was to catch any bodily fluids that may leak from the top tray. There were very bright medical lights hanging above, so there was no chance we couldn't see everything clearly. I had never seen a deceased person before, and I remember thinking, this person is dead! Are they hovering above, watching us? Is there truly heaven? We all witnessed our first post-mortem, from beginning to end, and some details are better left out. During the post-mortem, we were instructed to come closer and have a good look. As I stepped forward, I tripped on the grill at the base of the tray, lost my balance, and started to fall headfirst into the open chest cavity. A quick-moving cop grabbed my back, saving me from what could have been a very traumatic experience. Some police did not cope well with the confronting sight, some left the room and some almost fainted, but I found the inside of the human body fascinating. After several other stops, we were all dropped back at our respective stations and completed our first shift.

I walked to the train station, and as a naive country girl, I stepped onto the first train that stopped. I imagined that the train tracks were like those in Thomas the Tank Engine, one big circle. Unbeknown to me, the tracks veered off everywhere, and I soon passed train stops I had not seen that morning. It became obvious that I was on the wrong train. It was not stopping at any stations and was heading to who knows where. I later found out I had stepped onto an express train. Finally, after a long, nervous ride, the train stopped, and I anxiously jumped off. Where was I? I read a sign: Campbelltown. I had no idea where Campbelltown was in Sydney and did not know what to do. I needed help, and who did I spot but a policeman? Embarrassed, I explained it was my first day 'on the job', and that I was lost. He graciously helped me back on the correct train. The following day, I was cautious about which train I stepped on. My induction week flew by, and I was looking forward to the following week when I would start 'real' police work.

All probationary constables were allocated a buddy, who was our permanent partner for our first six weeks. My buddy was Constable First Class Mal, a tall, strong cop with sandy blond hair. Mal soon nicknamed me 'Sexy Legs'. My legs were not sexy, but I was happy to accept the nickname. Mal was a great guy, very kind, helpful, and fun. I could not have wished for a better buddy. My first official job was a car accident. At the scene, Mal guided me through the process as I pretended to know what I was doing. With Paramatta Road, Silverwater Road, and the M4 Freeway going through my patrol, this car accident would be one of hundreds, varying in severity, that I would attend over the next few years. Besides car accidents, general duties Police attended jobs such as break and enters, intoxicated persons, thefts, the death of a person, and domestic disputes, which I had firsthand training in. As there were many nursing homes in Strathfield, we also had many escaped dementia patients to track down and return. Occasionally, we attended fires, frauds, and armed robberies and searched for lost children. Any jobs we attended that were serious and required an in-depth investigation were passed on to the patrol detectives.

My first working day with Mal continued relatively smoothly, and several jobs later, we returned to the police station, where the endless paperwork was completed, all done on an old-style manual typewriter. The constant sound of click click click from typewriter keys echoed around the station. We were required to pass sixty words per minute in typing by the completion of our probation period, and my typing quickly improved, although I only typed with four fingers, and I still do. There was a police form to complete for everything: P40, P41, P69. I became familiar with a whole new Police language: alpha, bravo, Charlie… proceeded, apprehended, domestic dispute, in progress, suspect. Gradually, everything I was taught at the academy came together, and I soon learned what I hadn't been taught.

Our vehicles were F100 Ford Paddy Wagons. The truck's back had a metal cage for criminals, covered with a rubber tarp and a rear metal door. The vehicles had a plastic viewing section we could look through from the cabin to check on prisoners in the rear cage. Mal and I attended a break and enter in progress at a large factory yard that had piles of timber. He suggested we split up, and he quickly caught one offender. I made my first arrest when I caught another. He caught the third, and all three were handcuffed and placed in the cage of the paddy wagon. All three were simple old-time crooks who had been through this process before and did not resist. Mal unwittingly drove over a dirt mound as we drove out of the yard, causing the truck's rear to roughly bounce. One of the handcuffed offenders flew upwards, hit the roof of the cage, and landed heavily on the floor. When we arrived at the station, all three got out, one holding a sore arm and the other two laughing so much they couldn't contain themselves. Back then, very few complained.

I soon discovered that policewomen were rare. When a person was arrested, they were routinely searched for things such as weapons or drugs. Back in the eighties, female Police could search male offenders; however, male officers could not search female offenders. A call would go out over the police radio, referred to as VKG, for any available female officer to attend another district or division just to search a female suspect or prisoner. Flemington Police Station only had two other female officers in general duties. Many ladies left the Police when they had children, as it wasn't until 1988 that part-time maternity leave was first trialled for women police.

Within weeks, Mal and I sat in Lidcombe Court for my first court hearing. Constable Michelle from Auburn Police Station was called to give evidence for another case. The witness box was a small area with three steps leading up to it. When seated in the witness box, we were in full view of the magistrate and all those in the courtroom. The solicitor for the defence asked Michelle to stand up and demonstrate how an offender had resisted arrest. She stood up and re-enacted the incident, but in doing so, stepped back too far and fell backwards out of the witness box, landing heavily at the bottom of the stairs. The magistrate very calmly looked down over the top of his glasses, as the entire courtroom giggled. Later, I gave evidence for the first time, and I was very careful when stepping in and out of the witness box. Over the years, I attended numerous court hearings from local court, through to the Supreme Court.

I found the night shifts tiring and I struggled to sleep during the day. On the night shift, our first job was to drive into the city to collect the newspaper, fresh off the press, and then pick up milk from the dairy and bread from the bakery. There were usually two police officers working station duties, who looked after any prisoners in the police cells and attended any walk-in jobs at the counter. Four Police worked two cars on the night shift. A Regional Duty Officer was rostered on the night shift; they were usually of Inspector rank or above. Their job was to drive to each police station, ensure everything was above board, and sign some paperwork before moving to the next station. Some duty officers were very strict. If they arrived, and our uniforms were not up to standard, the police station was messy, or they spotted some other minor offence, we were in a lot of trouble. When the duty officer walked in, our number one job was to casually find out what police station he was visiting next. As soon as he left, we phoned that station and said the code, 'Whale in the Bay.' This gave the staff at that police station enough time to straighten things up, with the car crews disappearing, making sure they were out on the road. Some duty officers figured out what was going on and changed their route, catching some unsuspecting station staff out.

Nearing the end of one quiet night shift, I was exhausted, so I sat at a desk, too tired to concentrate on paperwork, and casually flicked through the freshly printed newspaper. Like a sleepy koala, my head slowly dropped onto the desk, and I fell sound asleep, only waking when the morning shift arrived. Everyone seemed extra happy that morning, and they were all smiling at me as I left. I drove home, and went to take a shower and caught my reflection in the mirror. Printed all over my face were the day's headlines, so clear, my colleagues could read the paper headlines. Jacki and I were often on opposite shifts, so we did not see much of each other. Occasionally, we would arrange to be on identical night shifts so after, we could have days off together. On those days off, we talked about the various jobs we had attended.

Sadly, after six comfortable weeks, my time working with Mal was over, and I was rostered to work with any of the other staff. They were a diverse bunch of different ranks, ages, backgrounds, and characters. On the whole, everyone got on very well at 32 Division, and each officer looked out for each other. However, there was one older sergeant that no one wanted to be rostered with. One night, he instructed me to drive to an isolated spot near a sign that read 'Danger - Polluted Water – Sharks' at Homebush Bay, where he unsuccessfully tried to make a pass at me. He was the only shark I was in danger of! I don't think there was one female officer who didn't experience this; however, the sergeant was never successful as every new female staff member was pre-warned by others.

One of the joys of being 'new in the job', was being made to do point duty. This job was regularly required at the main intersection of Silverwater and Paramatta Roads. I have many memories of standing in the middle of this large intersection, trying to keep the traffic flowing, and occasionally getting asked on a date by the driver of a passing car. Incidentally, there was no training for point duty; we were just told to stand in the middle of the intersection and direct traffic. This was daunting for a country girl who's home town only had a couple of traffic lights.

A few months later, a big intake of new probationary constables was posted to 32 Division. There were three policewomen in the group, including Constable Cath. She was an attractive blond and the same height as me. Coincidently, Cath was also allocated Mal as a buddy, and he instantly nicknamed Cath Sexy Legs. Mal was the envy of the other Police as he got another rare female buddy. Cath and I immediately became devoted and loyal friends and have remained so to this day. It wasn't long before Cath had finished her buddy period, and we would organise to be on the same shift. One day, we were rostered for the same shift and asked to work on the same vehicle together. All the boys were not sure what to do. Do we let two girls go out in the truck together or not? After some discussion, they reluctantly agreed, and we had an incident-free shift and proved our worth. From then on, Cath and I often worked out in the vehicle together. As we were both short, our blond heads were just visible over the dashboard, and I'm sure the F100 truck looked like it was driving independently. When we attended jobs, the public always looked shocked at the sight of two petite policewomen together, particularly two little blonds. At the time, some agreed with female police, and some did not, but I was lucky to be stationed at a progressive police station. Cath married a police officer and served as a police officer for thirty-two years, retiring at the rank of Sergeant. Today, it is very common to see two policewomen working together.

Jacki and I were now living within my patrol at Strathfield with our mother. Our home became a regular spot for Police from my station to drop in and have a meal, as our mother was always welcoming. The local residents must have thought that the house was full of criminals, as often there was one or more police cars parked outside. Although we shared the household chores, thanks to our mother, it was wonderful to come home after a late shift to a cooked meal.

Once I was rostered to work a shift with the tallest policeman at Flemington, Constable Trevor; he was around 196cm (6 foot 5 tall), and I was 157cm (5ft 2). Trevor and I were in the station when our Inspector walked past us and found our significant height difference amusing. He produced a camera and made us pose for a photo. A few weeks later, when I started my shift, I was mortified to see he had printed a large version of the photo, which was hanging in the police station's main foyer. It remained there for many years.

Every police officer gets to know repeat offenders and the homeless within their patrol. One repeat offender was an elderly drunk, Maria. Maria was continually arrested for relatively minor offences, usually involving alcohol, and all the staff and our local court magistrate knew Maria well. Maria had a piercing in her vagina, and often when drunk, she would drop her pants and show it to those arresting her, startling any new probationary constables.

Constable Michelle and I were now great friends, and one Christmas morning, after finishing the night shift, we decided to visit Maria. My twin joined us. We drove towards her home with thoughts that she might still be asleep, but as we turned the corner, we saw Maria in the middle of the road, drunk as a lord, her wispy uncombed hair poking out from under a bright-red Santa Hat. She was spinning in circles, her arms outstretched, repeatedly yelling loudly in all directions, 'Merry Fuckin Christmas.' Laughing, we got Maria off the street and into her home. We surprised her with a small Christmas gift that genuinely moved her. We told her to stay inside for the rest of the day and not upset the neighbours.

We had one more stop to make, a visit to Vergil. Vergil was a frail, elderly man with a foreign accent who lived in an underground tunnel along busy Paramatta Road. Again, we handed him a small gift and some food, and he was speechless. I am not sure if he even knew it was Christmas Day. I left feeling we had made both their Christmas days just that little bit better.

Suddenly, my first year as a probationary constable was up, and I had to attend secondary police training. Our graduating class was the last class to attend the old Redfern Police Academy for secondary training before it moved to the newer Goulburn Police Academy, where our initial training had been held. Secondary training was identical to initial training, with lots of lectures, exams, and fitness tests. On 8th August 1988, Jacki and I were attested as Constables. I thought of our Aunty Dale graduating from the same academy all those years before. Again, my twin and I were told we had to be interviewed by the media.

Each shift the jobs were varied and endless. One shift I was working out on the truck, and we got a call regarding a break and enter in progress. My partner and I arrived just as a large man leapt the back fence. I started to chase him while my partner sped off in the police vehicle to try to cut him off on the next street. The fences in this area were old and wooden, and each time the offender jumped a fence, he damaged it. As I jumped the fence behind him, the fence crumbled under me, hurting my knees. He leapt another fence, I followed, and down went the fence. I was calling my location on the handheld radio as we zigzagged through backyards. Despite the fences crumbling, I was catching up, and I started to wonder how I was going to tackle and handcuff this very large guy when I caught him. Finally, the crumbling fences were behind us, and he entered a street with me close behind, he threw himself under a parked vehicle. Trying to catch my breath, I lay on the road and used my police baton to try and get him out. Thankfully, the police car turned the corner, and more Police arrived to assist. We successfully dragged him out and cuffed him. My Coltex swede blue stockings looked like they had been attacked by an aggressive goanna. There was blood on my legs, and one of my knees was so badly hurt that after medical treatment, I was put on restricted duties for the next eighteen days. Being a cop was hard on the body, and over the years there were many injuries, scratches, and bumps. I know my body is paying for it today.

For some unknown reason, many people died on my shift, and I lost count of the deaths I attended. On arrival at a death, our first job was to ascertain if a death certificate was going to be issued by a doctor; if not, we were responsible for the death investigation. We would help the grieving family while obtaining all the necessary information for the report, and wait for the government contractor to attend and collect the body, which was transferred to either Westmead or Glebe Morgues. On most occasions, waiting for the government contractor could take many hours. After the body was collected, we would attend the city morgue and 'book in' the body. The following morning, regardless of what shift we were rostered on, we had to attend the morgue for an Identification Parade (ID parade). At an ID parade, any police involved in a deceased during the previous twenty-four hours attended and formally identified the body prior to a post-mortem.

Initially, most of my deceased people were taken to the Westmead morgue. The morgue staff had a reputation for being unfriendly, but they were always very friendly to me. I just put it down to the fact that I attended many deaths, and they felt sorry for me. As Jacki had the large Paramatta Hospital in her patrol, she also attended a good number of deceased. One day, I turned up at the morgue for an ID parade at the same time my twin did. The morgue staff finally recognised there were two of us. Combined, we had investigated a lot of deaths.

I found all deaths sad, but the death of a baby or child was so much harder. Police uniforms are just a bit of clothing; under the clothing is a real person, and as a human, it is impossible to attend a violent or traumatic incident and not think about it later. Some deceased, for different reasons, have remained fresh in my memory. One was the death of a frail elderly lady who had been married for a very long time. The lady was a smoker and had been diagnosed with cancer, but she still wanted to smoke. I suppose she thought smoking was not going to make any difference now. Due to her cancer treatment, the lady had lost her appetite and was desperately underweight. The husband devised a scheme where if his wife ate some food, he rewarded her with a cigarette. That morning, his wife woke and asked for a cigarette. He refused to give her one until she ate. Frustrated and angry, she struggled back to bed. Soon after, he lovingly went to check on her and discovered she had died. When we arrived, the husband was sitting beside her lifeless body, distraught, holding her hand. When I comforted him, he told me what had occurred and was so saddened that his last words to his lifelong partner and best friend were words of anger. As the government contractor carried this lady's body from the home, I watched as he walked slowly beside her, quietly sobbing, gently pulling her nightie down after it slipped and kissing her one last time before she was placed in the van. He remained in the street, a river of tears streaming down his face, silently waving goodbye until the vehicle was ultimately out of sight. When I think of this man, his love and his loss, tears still well in my eyes. Only a few months later, that beautiful man who had appeared relatively healthy for his age died. I am sure he died of grief.

A train track ran parallel through the Flemington markets' and a residential street ran parallel to it. One night, we were called to assist Police regarding a person who had been hit by a train and killed. When we arrived, we discovered that a man had parked his car on the street, and had been running across the train tracks, sneaking into the markets, and stealing watermelons, before returning for another handful. He made one trip too many and was hit by a fast-moving train. What made this incident more traumatic was that not only was he killed, but so was his very young son, who was with him at the time. Body parts were missing, so we had to walk along the stationary train, torches in hand, trying to find them. At one point, I stopped and flashed my torch near the train wheels, where I saw a mixture of brains and watermelon dripping. After thirty years, I have only just started eating watermelon again, although my thoughts still flash back to that night every time.

A job police hated to be rostered on, was prison escorts, where police had to escort detained prisoners to court. After arriving at a building at Zetland, we were allocated escort duties, sometimes requiring a plane flight. Normally, Police would be driven to one of the youth detention centres such as Minda, Cobham, or Revesby. On arrival, we collected our prisoner or prisoners, drove to the court they were appearing at, and sat there until their hearing was over, before returning them to goal. Whenever I did a juvenile escort, I would think of my Aunty Dale, who had performed the same duties many years earlier. One day, I was rostered for a two-person escort. When I arrived, I discovered the offenders were identical twin girls. It was clear from the start why the girls were in the detention centre as they were abusive and difficult, and the term 'Double Trouble' fitted them perfectly. They abused not only me but also the court staff, and the magistrate. The girls were sentenced, and I gladly loaded them back into a paddy wagon and headed back to the detention centre. While travelling, I looked back through the Perspex view hole and saw that they were trying to set the paddy wagon on fire. They had been searched, so I really didn't want to think about where the lighter had been hidden. In peak hour traffic on the freeway, we had to stop. I had to get the girls out onto the roadway, take the lighter, thoroughly search them again, and give them a lecture to behave, before finally, returning them to their centre. I couldn't wait to get rid of them.

One shift, my partner and I arrested a girl. We took her back to the police station and sat her in the interview room, where she provided her name and date of birth. My partner left the room to run a criminal check on her. While he was gone, I was writing notes when the offender suddenly looked at me, sighed, and said, 'That's not my real name; it's….'

I looked up and asked, 'Why did you decide to tell the truth?'

She said, 'You arrested me in Paramatta a few weeks ago. It will be only a matter of time before you remember.'

I thanked her and told her the arresting officer at Paramatta was certainly my identical twin. Jacki had a similar incident happen to her when a female was arrested for a fraud offence. She gave her name but had no identification on her. Jacki noticed she was far too familiar and comfortable in a charge room setting and suspected the name given was false, so she threatened to take her fingerprints and take them straight to the fingerprint section for immediate analysis, as the fingerprint section was only a few blocks away. Defeated, she sighed and said, 'Can't you remember, you arrested me at Flemington last week.' Smiling, Jacki phoned me and soon had her correct details.

Late one evening I was driving home after a night out drinking with off duty work colleagues, and although I was sure I was under the legal alcohol limit, my heart still raced when I saw police lights in front of me. A stationary Roadside Breath Testing Unit (RBT) was set up, and my car was waved in. I nervously waited as a police officer came up to the window. 'Oh, hi Jacki, are you on your way home.'

'Yes.' He thought I was my twin!

'Have a good night.' He just waved me through, and I drove off. I have never been more grateful to be a twin in my life.

I was selected to join a Task Force named Anzac, a joint operation involving the Drug Unit, the Surveillance Unit, and the Drug Enforcement Agency (DEA). As a result of Anzac, forty-four offenders were arrested for numerous serious offences, including attempted murder and armed robbery. I felt privileged to be a junior uniformed officer working with experienced detectives. I liked the look of plain clothes work and started to consider this career path.

Occasionally, the Drug Unit and Major Crime Squad would conduct operations at Silverwater and Mulawa prisons. There were no female police attached to the Drug Squad, and several times, I was rostered to work with them. The Major Crime Squad detectives were experienced detectives who had all previously worked in a patrol detectives' office. I thought they were like the Gods of the Detective world! The esteemed positions at the Major Crime Squads were sought after and competitive. They asked if I would consider applying for the Undercover Course (UC). I was young and keen to impress, so I thought, why not. I don't think I even considered how dangerous UC work could be. In February 1991, I commenced the second Special Forces Undercover Course. I was very aware that I was one of the few uniformed Police selected for the course. Most attendees were designated detectives, so I was inspired to start the process of becoming a detective. I started the investigator's course, a stepping stone to becoming a designated detective.

On the 17th of August 1991, I arrived at work to discover that there had been a mass shooting at our local shopping centre in Strathfield, which was only about 100 meters from the home I had once shared with our mother a few years earlier. That afternoon, Wade Frankum was seated in a café when he suddenly pulled out a machete-style knife and horrifically stabbed a teenage girl who was sitting close by before producing an SKK semi-automatic rifle from a bag. In a craze, he started randomly shooting innocent people as he weaved through the shopping centre before heading to the rooftop carpark. From there, Frankum shot down at the first responding Police before attempting a carjacking. He then shot himself. That day, seven innocent people were killed, and several people were injured. Thankfully, unlike other countries, shootings like these were uncommon in Australia.

I started my shift and was given the job of delivering the death message for the first victim, a fifteen-year-old girl. Death messages were always very tough. I was acutely aware that when knocking on a person's door, I was about to sadly change their life forever. Attending that home has stayed forever in my mind. I had a new Probationary Constable with me at the time, and I am certain he has never forgotten that day. The distraught family followed us to the Glebe morgue so they could formally identify their innocent, beautiful and much-loved daughter. Witnessing the intensity of their harrowing pain was just awful. I slipped off into the back area as all the victims were arriving in white vans. The young girl had had no injuries to her face, just a smear of fresh blood. She was so young, not much younger than I was at the time. In my weak attempt to lessen the family's grief, I pleaded with morgue staff to wipe her face clean, which, of course, they refused to do. The bodies of deceased people were not touched until the official post-mortem. Over the years, I have often thought of that family.

Recently, a crime program aired on TV about the Strathfield Massacre. In the young victim's honour, the family provided a scholarship to her former school. As I watched the program, memories flooded back.

Our mother was now remarried and had moved to a country town and we saw very little of her. Jacki and I were now living together in Wentworthville. Over the years, I was asked out on several dates, but although they were all very nice men, none of them ignited any spark. One policeman was happy to date either of us, so he asked me out for dinner. That didn't go anywhere, so he asked Jacki out. Again, he was unsuccessful. Recently, I was at a doctor's appointment, and the discussion turned to twins. My doctor said his son was married to a twin and said, 'He didn't care which twin he married as long as he married one of them.' For twelve months, I did date a policeman, Tom, who was a police prosecutor, basically a lawyer for the Police, but when this relationship ended due to infidelity, I was comfortable being single.

We turned twenty-one, and apart from each other, we had no immediate family to help us celebrate, but thankfully, my police family was there. Constable Michelle and her parents organised a big birthday party not only for me but also for my sister. This resulted in their family's backyard being full of both 32 Division and 18 Division police. Police from neighbouring patrols all knew each other well. I have never forgotten that kindness.

Jacki and I rarely had time together due to our conflicting shifts and individual friendship groups. Jacki had started dating a policeman, and she obviously spent a lot of time with him, which meant I was doing all the domestic chores. I was not Cinderella, so one day, after a heated argument about this, she abruptly told me she was moving out. I wasn't expecting this, but I thought it was time! Throughout our lives, we had been entwined. Now untangled, we could entirely and independently be our own person. One of my work friends, Constable Leanne, offered me a room to rent at her house. I was very grateful, and this gave me time to find something permanent.

As a uniformed officer, I had learned and seen a lot, maybe much more than I needed to. I had made wonderful friends. I loved 32 Division, and it remained my favourite police division throughout my police career, but I felt it was time I tried something new.

Reef

I had never actually been inside a police station until my first day on the job. I was allocated a buddy for six weeks and placed with a competent senior constable. He was a top bloke. Over the next few weeks, I worked whatever shifts he did, and his job was to teach me the ropes. We worked a rotational twenty-four-hour roster. Usually, the senior person on the car crew would be the observer or passenger. The junior officer would drive. As I still hadn't passed my driving test, my buddy had to do all the driving. There was still a lot of scepticism amongst the ranks about the new breed of short Police, and I was aware that I had to prove my ability early on to get any respect. At the time at Parramatta Police Station, we had about 200 male police and approximately ten females.

My very first job was an incident when someone's pregnant pet rabbit was killed, and all the dead baby rabbits scattered over the backyard. The family, including the children, were standing in the backyard amongst all these dead rabbits, crying. I thought, Toto we are not in Kansas City anymore. By the way, this type of job was not covered in the police academy manuals and was one of the thousands of weird and unusual jobs I encountered while in the Police. When my buddy found out I didn't own a car, he would often pick me up on his way to work and drop me home when we finished. If he wasn't able to, the car crew would drop me home, especially if it was the night shift, so I didn't have to catch a train at 11 o'clock at night on my own. Not that I had any fears about doing this because I still had country naivety and trusted everyone. This changed very quickly.

I was nineteen years old and had been in the police force for three weeks when I had to attend my first cot death. At the time, a vast study was taking place to try to work out why sudden deaths in infants occurred. The infants' bodies were all taken to the city morgue as part of the study, and all the post-mortems were conducted at the same facility. There was finally some support being offered to the parents, and counsellors would attend the scene with the Police. Part of the new guidelines was to allow the grieving parents to hold their dead baby for as long as they wanted, and when they, and only they, were ready to hand the baby over to be taken away, that would take place. I remember standing watching this heart-wrenching scene play out in front of me. I didn't know how to react and tried to hold it together. I felt a tide full of emotions, I wanted to burst out crying but had to hold the grief in, and it sat hard at the back of my throat. A few silent tears escaped, and rolled down my cheek. Whatever I did or said would have been inadequate. I can still describe that small room and visualise where everyone was standing. I see the mother reach out to pass her child across, only to pull her back for one last cuddle. This scene was played out many times over some hours. When I smell the scent of a newborn baby, my thoughts go back to that day, and on occasions, I still feel the grief that encompassed that small child's bedroom.

I was growing up quickly, whether I wanted to or not, and learning to have my own life without Kylie. We would debrief together when we had shifts off at the same time, but often, we were like ships in the night, passing from one shift to the next. Soon after we had moved into our little flat in Westmead, we noticed a man who lived in the flat directly above us. He often wore army camouflage clothing, but he wasn't in the army. As naïve as we were, we sensed that he didn't like us and knew he was aware that we were Police. Our uniforms hung on the shared clothesline, and my colleagues regularly dropped me home from work in marked police vehicles. One night, when Kylie was at work, and I was in bed asleep, a noise woke me. I realised there was a domestic violence incident taking place with the army camouflage guy and his female partner in the unit above ours. I lay there to arouse my senses and felt the incident was escalating. When fully awake, I was about to get out of bed and phone the incident into the Police, but then I recognised the noise had changed and could hear our neighbour trying to break his way into our flat. He was ramming the front door with his body. I ran to the hallway and saw that with each crash, the doorframe was giving way. At the same time, he was yelling out, 'Let me in, you copper cunts!' Panicking, I ran into my bedroom, looking for something to protect myself with. As a uniformed police officer, I kept my gun and handcuffs at work. I grabbed my trusty hockey stick and then ran into the kitchen to get to the phone, which in those days was fixed to the wall. I dialled 000. As an afterthought, I grabbed some fly spray to spray it in his eyes if he managed to get in.

The phones back then had a dial on the front in the form of a circle. The circle was numbered one through to zero. To dial the number, we put our finger in the required hole, manoeuvred it around to a fixed position on the phone, and then released our finger. The dial spring would take the dial back to the start.

'000' felt like forever as I waited for the circle to retract back into position so I could dial the '0' for a second and third time. When I spoke to the operator, I told them I was an off-duty police officer, and someone was trying to break into my apartment.

Triple zero calls to the Police are graded by their gravity. Two beeps announced before a message meant the call was a really serious job, such as armed robberies or jobs that could place members of the public in imminent danger of serious injury. If New South Wales Police heard three beeps over the police radio before a message, they knew the job about to be broadcast was what we call a 'signal one', that is, an announcement to the force that a police officer was in immediate danger of serious bodily harm or death. These calls are not announced lightly.

Unbeknown to me, the operator that night put the call out as a two-beep signal, and this got everyone's attention, including Kylie's, who was working approximately ten kilometres away. She heard the two beeps and then our address. The caller announced that there was an attempted break in with an off-duty police officer in 'immediate duress'.

My heart was beating, and I was trying to think clearly and make smart decisions quickly. I was standing in my pyjamas with my back against the wall in the hall where I could still watch the door. I had already decided that if he managed to get inside our flat, I would run as quickly as I could through my bedroom, climb onto the balcony and jump from the single story down to the ground. I had unlocked the external balcony door and opened the blinds in readiness. I would have about a six-meter head start, and I would have to be quick. Within a very short time, about twenty police vehicles turned up at our house, and I saw the comforting blue lights flashing through the windows. I then heard my twin sister at the door, and when I opened it, I saw her giving the male intruder a verbal assault as he was 'carried' downstairs by other Police. I collapsed on the lounge with relief; two women were now safe that night, my neighbour and myself.

Our neighbour was charged, and he pleaded guilty and received a fine. This incident shook both my sister and I, and soon after we decided to move into a house with our mother who was still living in Sydney. We both took out car loans, and this made us much more independent, and it was safer for us travelling to work and home after dark.

Soon after this, my relationship with Trevor fizzled. I was meeting all these new friends and enjoying my policing. Trevor had hoped that I would be able to transfer back to Dubbo, but as a junior officer, it was out of the question, and I was enjoying the excitement of the city. We both went our separate ways. As a side note, he ended up becoming a police officer himself many years later.

After being at the station for a few months, I was called up to redo my driving test. I had to go to the Mona Vale driving facility. I passed the city drive this time, having gained a few months of driving experience around the city in my own car. All I had to do was pass the highspeed component of the course. I got into the driver's seat and felt confident enough. The instructor got into the passenger seat and had me drive around the police driving course just like I would on a Sunday drive to get familiar with the track. Once we were back at the starting line, he said, 'Go.' Off I went with him, screaming in my ear, 'Faster, go faster.'

My immaturity revealed itself, and I did as I was told. I went faster and faster and faster. I was driving down a long, straight section of the track and came to a wide, gradual bend that had a slight camber on the surface of the road. As I started to negotiate the bend, I could feel I was losing control of the car and knew I was going way too fast. The car slid off the roadway and cleaned up some small pine trees that were once firmly rooted at the end of the roadway. The car came to a sudden stop. I looked at the ashen-faced instructor and said, 'Failed.' He confirmed this just prior to radioing for a tow truck.

I was annoyed at myself for being so reckless, and the officer told me that they didn't care about the actual speed at which I completed the course; it was all about driving to our own ability. He was yelling in my ear as he knew this is what happened when we were working on the road. It is up to the driver to drive to their own capability, not the demands of the passenger. I arrived back at Parramatta Police Station, slightly embarrassed. I had a message on our telephone log to phone a male person unknown to me. I dialled the number, and the person at the end of the line said, 'Parramatta Speedway.' It was a stitch-up by all my work colleagues, and they were all in on it, having got word about the 'incident' before I arrived back at the station. We all had a good laugh, and although I was disappointed, it wasn't such a big deal. I did finally pass the driving test the third time.

Once we finished working with our buddy, we worked with Police of all different ranks and length of service. On one shift, I was rostered with a chubby male senior constable on a car crew. This rank meant he had been in the Police for at least ten years. At the start of the shift, I got into the F100 Ford Police truck and slid the bench seat forward to reach the pedals with my feet. This created a problem for the senior constable; due to his long legs, he now had his knees up around his face. This was a dilemma that other new 'short' police recruits had already experienced. I heard a big groan coming from the senior constable, and he told me to, 'Get out.' He was driving, and he wasn't happy about it.

One of the first jobs we were called to was what we referred to as a concern for welfare. Someone had rung the Police, concerned for the safety of a person. When we arrived at the job, the distressed family were standing outside a dark, locked house. We found one 'very small' window closed, but it was unlocked. The window was positioned high up near the facia of the roof. With a slight smirk, I thought the recent drop in height restrictions might now come in handy. After removing the screen, the senior constable gave me a leg up. I went head-first through the window, and I had to negotiate the sill with my thick gun belt catching on the rim. Somehow, I manoeuvred my way in with my head now hanging halfway down the wall. The Senior Constable let go of my legs, and all I could do was drop down, my arms outstretched in front of me and roll my head so I didn't hurt my neck. Somehow, I fell into the house and didn't injure myself. The house lights would not turn on, so with torchlight, I tried to open the front door, but it was deadlocked. I discovered that the windows were also deadlocked. I walked around the house and was aware I was in the kitchen. My foot touched something, and I flashed the torch down to discover the dead body of the elderly lady on the floor.

This was now a delicate situation as I had to let my senior officer know what I had discovered while her family stood alongside him. I thought for a second and yelled out through the window that I had just come through. 'I'm sorry, I have found her, and unfortunately, she is deceased.'

I heard the familiar gasp of a shocked family hearing of a death and then heard the senior constable yell, 'Are you sure?'

I said, 'Yes.'

He said, 'How do you know?'

He was aware I was new to 'the job', and he was probably worried I might not have been certain. I yelled out, "I'm certain," and he yelled back, "How?"

I was thinking now, oh God, the family are just outside. After some time, with everyone losing their patience, I yelled out, 'I know because I accidentally kicked the kitchen bin. The old dear's arm was resting on it and is now standing up in the air.' Rigor mortis had set in. I was no doctor, but this was a given.

This satisfied the senior constable, and he decided he better come into the house and investigate if there were any suspicious circumstances. Up he went, trying to get into the house through the same small window. Picture a boiled, shelled egg trying to squeeze into the top of a milk bottle. I was pulling his arms, and the distraught family was pushing him from behind, and eventually, he 'flopped' into the house. After about an hour of searching and discovering that the old lady had turned her power off at the electrical box, probably to save money, we found the house keys, hidden in the most random place. This type of work was common, and although the death of the old lady was very sad, the comical side of the whole scene got me through to the next job.

We were probationary constables for twelve months, and during this year, part of the training was to work in a few different police sections so we could observe what they did and be shown different aspects of policing. We went to sections like highway patrol and detectives. I worked with the Parramatta Detectives during this period, and I didn't know it at the time, but these two weeks changed the trajectory of my life, both professionally and personally.

Before any shift, the rostered car crew would check the police vehicle, testing the lights and sirens and filling the car with petrol. I had only been observing the detectives for a day or two and was given the task of driving down to a building we referred to as the Ferguson Centre three blocks away. This building housed several specialist sections and was the head office for our region. I drove down to the building in the unmarked police vehicle. I did my errand and was on the way back to the station when the vehicle lost power. I glided the car to the side of the road and quickly discovered that it had run out of petrol. I hadn't thought to check the fuel gauge as I was only driving three blocks, and the car 'should' have had a full tank of fuel. I had no way of filling the car up and had to call for assistance via a back channel on the police radio.

A junior detective was sent down to me with a jerry can of petrol. The detective was well-mannered and good-looking. I chatted to him, and he drove the car back with me. Over the next two weeks, I knew I liked the work that detectives did, and I became conscious that I liked the young detective who had helped me. I went home after work three weeks later and said to my Mum, 'I met a really nice police detective, and I think I'm going to marry him.'

I was getting into the routine of work life and feeling more comfortable, but I never knew what I would encounter from day to day. We had a job where an armed holdup alarm was activated at a local brothel. We arrived and spoke to the madam of the establishment, but it was a false alarm. She had quite revealing clothing on, and the male officer I was with was staring at her really huge bust. The madam was enjoying the attention and, with a grin, said to the senior constable, 'What are you staring at?'

He comfortably replied, 'Your tits.'

The madam laughed and turned to me, saying, 'Do they stare at your tits as well?'

I nervously said, 'Not really, I don't have much there.'

Very quickly, she reached forward and grabbed both my breasts. Then this gruff old prostitute said, 'Don't worry luv, more than a mouthful is a waste.' I stood there, shocked, and everyone laughed at me. I nervously laughed back.

This was an era well before the 'Me Too' movement, and policewomen had to negotiate some difficult situations. When we were working with a police partner, we often saw more of them, than our own families. We drove around in a car for the entire shift, dealing with emotional issues and often need support from one another to cope. Sometimes 'support' was read incorrectly by a partner.

I was working on a car crew with a male police sergeant when we were called to investigate an alarm that had gone off in someone's house during the day. We arrived at the house and walked around to see if anything was out of the ordinary, and we found an open window at the rear of the house. This window was small and high. Climbing through small windows was beginning to become a habit of mine. Up I went through the window into the house with a leg up from the police sergeant. When I was inside the house, I unlocked the external door from inside and let him in. We checked the house, but nothing appeared out of place, and it looked like no offence had been committed. It was more than likely a mouse or something that had activated the alarm. While checking all the rooms in the house for any offenders, we ended up in a bedroom, and the sergeant grabbed me and pulled me close to him. I was only nineteen or twenty; he was much older. He tried to kiss me.

I had my police hat on, as it had to be worn at all times as part of our uniform. It had a small rim at the front and was made from a fabric that had a bit of flex in it. I used to pull the hat down firmly on my head so it wouldn't fall off while I was working. I put my arms up in front of me and attempted to push him off, but he was far too determined and much stronger than me. I could feel against my body that he was aroused. I continued to keep my head down, so my hat acted as a barrier to his face, as he was much taller than me. He released one hand, grabbed my hat off my head and threw it like a frisbee across the bedroom. He managed to get his lips on mine, and he was kissing me hard and determined. I wished I had a piece of driftwood to hit him with.

One advantage I had was that our uniforms included a heavy, thick leather belt. It held our gun, spare bullets, handcuffs and any other equipment we needed. They were difficult to remove. We also wore culottes, which are a mixture of a skirt and shorts. They looked like a skirt but had a centre seam that created wide-legged shorts underneath the skirt. It was also compulsory to wear Coltex swede blue stockings that had control tops on them, so they were firm-fitting and high-waisted. In a frantic and desperate manner, the sergeant grabbed underneath my culottes, clawing around, trying to get access, rubbing around my genital area. I was grateful for both the gun belt and the stockings. I continued to struggle with him and pushed as hard as I could to get away from him.

While he had one hand under my culottes and only one hand holding me, I managed to break his hold by rolling my body away from him. When I did defensive training at the police academy, I didn't think I would have to use it against a colleague. I escaped from the home and waited out on the street alongside the police car. The sergeant had the keys. After some time, he came out of the house, and we both got in the vehicle. He handed me my hat, and I said to him, 'That will never happen again.' He didn't reply, and without any discussion, we went to the next job. I never had the courage at the time to tell anyone what had occurred, as his rank intimidated me, and I was well aware it would not have been advantageous for me to say anything.

Some years later, at a police women's night out, something came up about this particular sergeant and after a bit of alcohol, we relaxed, this gave us some courage, and it became apparent that this sergeant had assaulted and sexually harassed quite a few young female Police with varying degrees. Like me, they had all kept it to themselves.

I was quickly grasping the failings of humankind, and some months later, I saw the worst of it. I was working on a car crew when we heard the distressing sound of a three-beep call. One of our officers was in immediate peril. When Police hear this, they stop what they are doing and get to the scene as quickly as possible to do whatever they can to help. My partner and I were some distance away, and by the time we arrived at the scene, the ambulance was already in attendance. Two male officers had attempted to arrest a male offender after a domestic dispute. The offender had run outside to his truck, locking himself in the cabin. He started the vehicle and attempted to flee the scene. The two Police had jumped up onto the step of the truck and smashed the window, trying to arrest the offender. The offender started to drive off while the Police clung to each side of the truck. As the vehicle sped forward, one of the officers managed to jump off, and he fell heavily on to the road. The second officer was partially inside the cabin when the vehicle collided with a tree, crushing the male officer between the truck and the tree and severely injuring him.

Watching one of our workmates fight for his life was not something any police officer wanted to see. The ambulance officers worked frantically on our colleague for some time at the scene, performing CPR. I was a junior officer, so I was asked to do crowd duty, to keep the prying public back, attempting to give the injured police officer some dignity and also preserve the crime scene. I remember telling a mother with young children to move back as she stood there watching my colleague fight for his life. I said to her, 'Do you really want your children to see this?'

She still had to be pushed back with the rest of the onlookers. We spent a long time at the incident, and while we were there, other police jobs piled up. Later, the policeman was taken to hospital, where he died from his injuries. Once there was nothing more we could do, we radioed in and were given a list of the many outstanding jobs, some of which had been called in hours earlier. My partner and I looked at the list, prioritised which was the most important job to do first and worked our way back. The most pressing job we had was to convey a death message to some grandparents and tell them their grandchild had passed away. The baton of grief was being passed around that night.

There was little help in the way of counselling offered to Police, and if we said we wanted counselling, we were regarded as weak by our colleagues. I was a short female police officer and had a lot to prove. If I had a particularly bad day, I either had a drink at the station or went to the pub and talked it out there. My home was my sanctuary, and I was lucky to have my supportive twin sister living with me, a sister who knew precisely what I was going through. When we did manage to get our rosters aligned and actually spent some time together, we would often exchange our shared experiences.

Our police divisions boarded each other, so when backup was required, Kylie and I sometimes came across each other at work. I was rostered to perform crowd control at a soccer match held on the border of Granville and Lidcombe. Mostly, we just walked around, keeping an eye on things. I didn't mind watching the soccer games, as the rules and plays are very similar to hockey. I hadn't played hockey since I joined the Police as it was challenging to commit to a team when my rostering was so erratic. I quickly learned that some soccer fans are fanatical and very passionate. There were often flares let off in the crowd, and this always caused a disturbance, especially if the flares went onto the field and disrupted play. When this occurred, we would have two groups of inflamed supporters from opposite teams screaming and yelling at each other, and a riot would almost certainly ensue.

We did our best to keep the two packs separated. The only way we successfully achieved this was by forming one line, wielding our aluminium batons in figure eight and chanting the words, 'Back, back, back.' This did not always keep the supporters apart, and often, we had to call for backup. On one particular day, all hell broke loose, and the inevitable call went out for backup. In these situations, I was always aware of my colleagues around me, but not necessarily precisely who was next to me. I was thrashing away with my baton when I heard, 'Oh hi, Jack!' It was Kylie. Side by side, we swung away. 'Back, back, back.' I'm sure some of the supporters were slightly confused when they saw twins.

Because Kylie and I often had conflicting shifts, there was usually at least one person at our home, but during a narrow opportunity, someone broke into our house when we were both out. All our meagre jewellery was taken, along with our mother's jewellery, and she had much more valuable and sentimental possessions stolen. We were so annoyed at this 'person' for destroying the only sanctuary we had to find peace away from all the depravity at work. We lost the tranquillity that the home offered. Kylie and I wrote notes and put them in our jewellery boxes that read, 'There's nothing left. You took everything the last time you broke in.'

Our Mum remarried and moved away, and we were now living on our own again. It wasn't long before we were broken into a second time. This time, the offender didn't take anything as there was nothing of value left. Instead, he sat on our beds going through our underwear drawers, probably masturbating at the same time, a practice that had been revealed to us through our police work. We knew this as we always kept our doona covers very smooth and could see the shape of a bottom pressed into the doona where a person had sat. He would have known we were Police as our uniforms were hanging in our wardrobes. On this occasion, the front door was kicked entirely off the hinges and found halfway up the hall. What frightened us most was the thought that if one of us had been on night shift, we could have been sleeping when the intruder broke in. If they had found someone at home, the situation might have had a very different outcome. This second break-in rattled us, and we decided it was time for a move.

After a few years, I transferred to a new section of the department called Beats. We would work with a permanent partner in a specific geographic area. This distinct area would become our own. Within our 'beat', we had schools, businesses, homes and community centres. It was a different method of foot patrolling than had been done in the past when Police randomly walked around aimlessly from one location to the next.

My first problem working in this section was that I weighed only forty-eight kilograms, and my waist was the size of my present-day leg. I needed to fit my gun, handcuffs, spare bullets, a baton, torch, pocket knife and a large bulky radio to my waist belt. As women didn't have a top pocket in our police shirts, I had to find somewhere to store my official notebook and pen as well. I didn't have enough room around my waist, and I remember talking to my boss and trying to decide what the most important equipment to have with me was. We carried an extraordinary amount of extra weight on the belts that rested on our hips. Some policewomen wore men's shirts if they could get away with it, as some bosses were really strict about our uniforms. I was short and had no bust; the smallest men's shirt had pockets level with my waistline, so this option was out of the question for me. Police now wear vests over their shirts to carry all the equipment. This provides a great spot to store vital equipment and helps distribute the weight more evenly on the body. The new unisex cargo trousers also have lots of pockets for storage.

Being a country girl, this type of policing suited me. We were placed with a permanent partner and were allocated any police jobs within our Beat, so we got to know the community really well. We developed trust and provided support to those in the area. Parramatta had such a diverse community, and conversing with business people and the homeless fifteen minutes apart was common practice. The cultural diversity was wide, as was the age of the individuals within the Beat. The community got to know us well. We walked around school grounds, went to community meetings and were invited to office functions. It really was a great initiative in city areas, but nothing new for country policing.

Our boss decided we would do an operation, which is a term police use when they focus on one specific type of offence or crime. This operation was to combat an increase in crime at Parramatta Mall during the early hours of the morning. Our team wore plain clothes or civilian clothes, and we were positioned around the central business district on our own or one out. I was put near the post office. We used police radios as our only means of communicating, on a back channel, and we kept the radio off unless we were checking in. The sound of a police radio squawking in the dead of night is not very discreet. I sat on the cold concrete for hours, with my arms wrapped around my bent legs to try to keep warm. I watched and waited in the dark. A young couple walked past me and looked in my direction. I stayed as still as possible, but there was some lighting. After some time, they walked back and approached; they had seen me. They thought I was a homeless kid and offered me somewhere to sleep at their house for the night. These encounters gave me continued hope in mankind; there were still good people out there. I showed my shocked saviours my police badge, thanked them and sent them on their way. Obviously, even though I felt grown up at twenty-one, I still looked like a twelve-year-old. This type of operation fuelled my desire to become a detective, and I started inquiring about the process.

My hope to work in the Police Dog Section had been dashed years ago when I discovered they had never had a female in their section, and the talk around the station was that women's menstrual cycles interfered with the scent-driven police dogs. Of course, this was ridiculous. There were a lot of departments within the Police that still struggled with the idea of having policewomen in their sections. The first female was not accepted into the dog section until five years later, in 1994, and she came first in her course.

However, I was still learning and going to such a varied number of jobs, and my enthusiasm for police work was not diminished. In Beats, we were lucky enough to go to a lot of sporting events to bolster police numbers when required. We were rostered to work at first-grade rugby league matches, standing alongside the ground, and got a bird's eye view of the games. We worked amongst the colourful 'hill' crowds at the one-day cricket matches. I did not particularly enjoy the races, but I loved fashion and could look at the stunning outfits. We were even given one dollar each to have a bet. The pleasant atmosphere at the Royal Easter Show would turn even the most cantankerous police officer into a ball of mush. Beat Police didn't have much of a social life as we worked almost every Friday and Saturday night and most Sundays. I got on well with my partner, and we had a great time anyway. I never felt like it was work, as we had so much fun.

Out of nowhere, I received an invitation to go out to dinner from the good-looking detective who had brought me the petrol. This was soon followed by another date, then another and another.

During one of my shifts, my partner and I were walking up the Parramatta Mall and had to arrest a man who was wanted on warrants. He wasn't too impressed about it, and it resulted in a struggle when we tried to handcuff him. We had him pinned down on a bench seat in the middle of a busy lunch hour and were providing entertainment for the lunchtime crowd. There are usually two types of onlookers; the first are those who wonder if they should step in and help but are hesitant. The others cheer on the baddie, hoping he escapes or at least lands a few punches on the cops. We called up on our radio requesting assistance. We managed to get one handcuff on one wrist, and I was firmly attached to the second arm, being waved around like a ragdoll. I didn't let go. The second call went out on the radio for help. The struggle continued for some time, and although we couldn't actually complete his arrest, he wasn't going anywhere. My partner and I were now on top of him, using our body weight to hold him down, and were still waiting for backup. We sent out a third call: 'Parramatta 42, we require urgent assistance.'

I heard the sound of police sirens and was relieved. I looked up and saw an unmarked police car driving up the pedestrian mall to get to us. There were four detectives in the vehicle, and one was my knight in shining armour, my new boyfriend. He recognised my call sign and came to my assistance. If I wasn't in love before, I definitely was now. The offender was quickly bundled into the police car.

I didn't see Kylie as much at work anymore, as I was confined mostly to my Beat, but occasionally, we would run into each other at the morgue. It was not the sort of place I normally would catch up with my sister, but we would have a quick chat and a laugh with the morgue staff, who were always surprisingly friendly; everyone had their own coping mechanisms. Going to the morgue regularly, I saw how a post-mortem was conducted. The process fascinated me; I was shown things like what a heart bypass looked like on the inside of a body and the effects of pleurisy on the inside of the lungs. I also discovered that blood was scooped out with a tool that looked similar to a soup ladle so the amount of blood in the body could be measured. Often, a deceased's major organs were still at toxicology after the funeral had taken place, particularly if there were suspicious circumstances surrounding the death. After the post-mortem is complete, the cavity was filled with cotton wool to fill in any gaps. My relationship with the morgue staff became so friendly that I told them if my body turned up there, would they mind stuffing extra cotton wool in my bust area. At least my small bust could then look big in the afterlife; it was cheaper than breast augmentation. I also asked them to reduce the amount of cotton wool in my bum area, as my larger bum was not yet in fashion!

One Christmas, Kylie and I were both rostered on the day shift at our respective stations, and somehow, we were invited to have Christmas lunch with the morgue staff and their little white mascot dog that hung around the place. Christmas day was always a busy shift, particularly around lunchtime when many child custody court orders outlined that the kids were to have half a day with each parent. We often had one parent who refused to hand the child over to the other parent. This defiance never worked out for anyone, especially the distressed children who were emotionally torn. By some good luck, we were both free at lunchtime, and we managed a quick half-hour Christmas lunch with the morgue staff in their meal room. Death doesn't frighten me, only the way I'm going to go. Kylie and I have different views on the way in which we would like our bodies to be disposed of when we die. I would like to be cremated, and she would like to be buried. I don't know if the different opinions of her Christian husband and my agnostic husband have influenced either of our decisions. But I don't want to take up any space on our increasingly crowded earth, whereas Kylie, living on a vast cattle station, probably feels there is enough land to give her a small burial plot. She is happy turning herself into compost to feed the soil.

Sometimes I just click with a person, and my partner Sam and I had great chemistry. He had a great sense of humour, which was needed with the types of jobs we were doing. We would talk about almost everything just to fill in the time walking the streets at all hours, and Sam heard everything about my twin sister. I hope he picked up a few hints about twin relationships because he fathered twins many years later. One evening, Sam and I were walking around the streets of Parramatta in driving rain on a freezing, very wet night. We had to work rain, hail or shine, and the only protection we had were vinyl raincoats that reached our mid calves and a cover for our police hats that looked like the clear freebie shower caps given away in motels.

We were patrolling around the back of the Town Hall, an area that was dark and wet. We were walking side-by-side in water that was almost ankle-deep. As we were walking, I unexpectedly dropped and was standing waist-deep in water. After the initial shock, we realised that a construction site had not been cordoned off. I had fallen in a trench. My partner and I burst out laughing, and after a struggle, he pulled me out of the wet muddy hole. We had to walk back to the station as my gun was utterly drenched, and guns don't tend to work too well when they are wet, so it needed to be cleaned. I was also able to change my uniform as I kept a full set in my locker for emergencies; they happened every now and then. I was with a team of Police that arrested a paedophile once, and his house was riddled with fleas; they swarmed around him. We could actually see a haze of the insects as he walked to the police car. Our uniforms were infested by the biting insects. We were often covered in vomit and faeces when arresting or helping people, so having a spare uniform was handy.

Kylie and I were now very busy at our own stations and making lots of friends on our own. We were not spending as much time together, although we still lived together, and when our shifts aligned, we would spend some time together. One day, after we had been out shopping together, we pulled back into our driveway. We were giggling about something random as we opened the front door and saw that the hallway cupboard was open. Kylie and I gave each other a glare. The house was silent. Walking towards our living room, the noise returned. We heard the blinds flapping against the wall and the heavy sound of someone's feet scurrying (not either of ours). As we turned the corner, we saw him. He was desperately trying to get out of the backdoor before we reached him, and he was successful. He scaled the back fence quickly, his tall frame out of sight in seconds and headed in the direction of the mowed reserve that sat parallel to our townhouse.

Out of instinct or twin telepathy, as neither of us spoke, Kylie chased him on foot, clambering over the back fence while I ran in the opposite direction, out the front door and got in my car. I took off in my red Mitsubishi Colt, revving the engine as I mounted the footpath, turning my little car into a four-wheel drive. Kylie was starting to get breathless after a long sprint and had dropped back a bit. I had a faster engine on my side and quickly caught up with the guy, to his shock, as I don't think he expected four wheels to be after him. I drove my car right up behind him and could see he was scurrying around like a wild animal being chased by a much larger prey. He was darting in every direction, trying to find the best means of survival. I was impersonating a driver from a Fast and the Furious movie. As I got close to him, I opened my driver's door in an attempt to take him out with it. He was right in my sight, and just as I got close enough to knock him off his feet, he darted to the right and ran back up the hill towards the rear of other townhouses. I jumped out of the car reaching, my fingertips almost touched him. At the same time, I noticed movement behind me, quickly turned and watched as my car looked like an autonomous vehicle driving down the hill. In my haste, I forgot to put the handbrake on my manual car. To catch the baddie or save my car? I opted to save my car as I could see my twin had now caught up and was hot on his heels. She did her best, but as I manoeuvred the car around, I saw the tall male, who had more to lose than we did, scaling a back fence. In seconds, he was gone. We really didn't have anything of value to steal (it had all been stolen in the first two robberies). He was on foot, so he was probably only looking for money and jewellery. The only thing he got that day was a huge fright, and I bet he shit his pants when he knew we were after him and got so close. We didn't think he would be back in a hurry.

I was spending a lot of my free time with my new boyfriend, and after a delightful day out, I came home to find Kylie upset and angry because I hadn't been home earlier to help her clean our townhouse. As with most arguments, the disagreement was over something trivial, and the bigger issue was probably that I was always out with Scott and not paying her any attention. I was lovestruck and was only thinking about myself. After a heated argument. I turned to her and said, 'I'm moving out.' And I did. We forgave each other quickly, as we always do, but moving out from each other was like going through a terrible divorce. We had to separate our joint possessions. You can have the jug, and I'll have the toaster. Do you want the frying pan or the slow cooker?

A dilemma many twins face is how to negotiate a relationship with a partner – someone who may not understand the strong bond twins have and why each of them would want to continue to have such a close relationship with their twin. I have known of relationships that have ended because the partner cannot accept the relationship twins have. From a twin's perspective, we are constantly cheating on our romantic relationship to be with our twin, and vice versa. When I told Scott about my argument with Kylie later, I knew straight away he didn't understand how she was feeling. This was going to be a delicate situation. I felt like I was being pushed and pulled by both of them. However, I recognised that our twin relationship was beginning to feel like a tropical storm slowly developing offshore, and it had reached peak atmospheric pressure. We needed some time apart to calm the seas.

Detectives

Beef

After three years in uniform, I transferred to the Georges River District Special Operations Group (SOGS), based at Bankstown. The SOGS was a small section that supported uniform police with crimes such as break and enters, stealing and car thefts. However, SOGS staff were not detectives. We did not work out of a police station or wear a police uniform; our uniform was jeans and T-shirts, a bit like the movie 21 Jump Street. If there was an escalation of break-and-enters in a particular suburb or an increase in cars stolen in a specific shopping centre, we would patrol that area in unmarked police cars or on foot. I enjoyed the SOGS. It was different, and I worked with a good group of police.

The New South Wales Police wanted to try a new approach to identify and arrest offenders and recover stolen goods. They decided to run an original sting-style operation where police would lease a shop front and open an imitation but genuine-looking pawnshop, which would be run by three Undercover operators (UC). The operation was named Honeypot. The

SOGS job was to conduct surveillance on the shop, and follow and identify offenders after they had sold suspected stolen goods to the UCs at the shop. When we weren't involved in surveillance, we attempted to track and trace the owners of the stolen goods. We were rostered in pairs and worked set surveillance shifts. This all seemed simple enough; however, standing near a busy road, trying to blend in at a small city shopping centre for many hours was not always easy, and following an offender from the location without being seen was even more challenging. Some days, there was no action at the pawnshop, and the hours would drag by. On other days, there were so many offenders in and out of the pawnshop that we couldn't follow them all.

One day, a suspect left the shop. However, I was having trouble following him without being seen. On the noisy, busy road, I crouched behind a parked car but still had a clear view of him. I was so occupied watching the bad guy that I didn't notice an occupant get in the car and start to reverse it out of its parking spot. I was knocked hard by the car and dived onto the path. As I lay there, I watched the oblivious driver drive off. Another day, I hid close to a bushy garden bed but was bitten by a few bees. Soon, watching the same shop for weeks on end became a little tedious; however, I found Ben, one of the UC police running the shop, very attractive, and I thoroughly enjoyed watching him.

Despite Jacki and I divorcing, I enjoyed forging my individual life path. We occasionally caught up with each other or our lovely Dubbo friends, who had also migrated to Sydney, and I became Jacki's backup when her boyfriend was absent. I continued to socialise with the old Flemo crew and was soon called back to attend an award and dinner night held by the Lidcombe Rotary Club. Somehow, I was awarded a Rotary Club yearly 'Pride in Workmanship' award. I was not sure why I was singled out to receive this award, but it encouraged me to keep trying my best. I did love my job.

I searched for my own rental and found a little granny flat, a garage actually, in the backyard of a home at Blacktown; it was optimal downsizing. The layout was straightforward. As I walked in the door, I instantly stepped into the kitchen, consisting of a sink with a gap for the fridge on the left and a small two-door cupboard on the right. If I walked two metres forward, I stepped into the combined shower and bath. If the shower curtain wasn't closed, the water would spray and wet my food; however, if I was cooking while showering, I could turn the food and shampoo my hair all at once. To the right, off the door entrance was a second, slightly larger room, which I turned into a combined lounge and dining room, and following that was my bedroom. The toilet was outside. It was very basic but clean and cheap. It was the first time I had lived entirely on my own, and I found that I was happy with my own company. At the time, Blacktown had a reputation for being an unsafe suburb, mainly due to the 1986 abduction, horrific rape, and murder of Anita Cobby from the Blacktown railway station. Fortunately, I felt pretty safe in the backyard.

My SOGS job continued for five months before a large operation was held, which resulted in the recovery of 1.1 million dollars' worth of stolen goods, 500,000 dollars' worth of drugs seized, and sixty-five people arrested with a total of 400 charges. Due to the successful operation, each member of Operation Honeypot was awarded a Commissioners Commendation. These are not given out lightly, so receiving it was a great honour. To celebrate our success, the team decided to let our hair down and have an informal debrief, so we travelled to the south coast for a weekend of fun. The undercover operatives joined us, and I got to know Ben, the good-looking UC, a little better. Within the following months we were dating.

After only seven months at the SOGS, I was asked if I would like to become a full-time member of the Drug Unit at the South West Major Crime Squad. I seized the opportunity. I had only been a police officer for four years, and it was very rare for someone who was not a designated detective to get a full-time position with a Major Crime Squad. At the time, Ben was working at another regional drug unit. With a mixture of excitement and nerves, I started my first day at the drug unit, which was led by Inspector Geoff Steer. It was quickly arranged for me to go before a regional assessment to be placed on A-List, commonly known as the Bull Ring. This was necessary to become a qualified detective. The next problem was my firearm. Like most police, I had a six-shot, which was quite big and difficult to hide under civilian clothes on my petite body. It was replaced with a much smaller five-shot, which meant one less bullet if needed. I had to get a shoulder and ankle holster; however, like our Aunty Dale, on most occasions, a handbag did the job. The South West Major Crime Squad encompassed a quarter of the state of New South Wales, and we often travelled away on drug jobs. At the Drug Unit, our job was to arrest the drug suppliers, those who sold drugs to the street dealers. It would often take many months of surveillance and other police tactics to get enough evidence to enable an arrest and successful conviction in court. Another role at the Drug Unit was to assist the other Major Crime Squad Units with surveillance of their suspects, including armed robbers and murderers. I was twenty-four years old, not designated as a detective, and the only female in an office of men, few of whom would fit the 'normal-looking' police mould. Not long after starting at the drug unit, I was promoted to Constable First Class.

The staff at the drug unit were great and looked out for me. Often during surveillance, I was teamed up with one of the guys, and we just looked like a couple dating, or in some cases, like a father and daughter. In unmarked vehicles, we would follow suspects all over Sydney, and when the pressure was on, we were forced to slip through red traffic lights, drive over medium strips, or up one-way streets the wrong way, all witnessed by many shocked civilian drivers who were not aware we were police. At times, our cars would surround offenders' vehicles when they stopped at traffic lights, and when we were directed to do so, we would suddenly jump from an assortment of unmarked police cars and, with guns drawn, arrest the offenders. Sometimes, our jobs were in country towns where remaining covert was harder to achieve. I loved these trips; and missed the country lifestyle.

When conducting searches of offenders' homes, we had to enter quickly so the offenders did not have a chance to dispose of any drugs or get an opportunity to reach for a weapon. We often wore bulletproof vests. Early on, one of the boys handed me a heavy bulletproof vest to wear, which was obviously made to fit a standard sized male body. I lifted it on, but it was so big on my petite frame that it hung down to my knees. I couldn't even walk in it, let alone run! I was sure if I fell over, I would be stuck on my back like a little turtle. I decided I would be better off risking a bullet and went without. The suspects were often armed, and their homes had security measures in place. With my gorgeous mullet hairstyle and build, I did not look like a police officer, so the boys would hide near the front door and get me to knock. The offender would peer out, see a 'young girl' and open the door, and the guys would suddenly thunder in behind me like a mob of wild brumbies, trampling me as they went. On one of these occasions, I dusted myself off and came in behind them, but I turned right into the first room while they charged down a hallway. I came face-to-face with five stunned, seated men. Shit, five to one, where was everyone? I pulled my gun and held it on them until I had backup. That was a little scary.

After we had raided a house, it was thoroughly searched. Due to my size and junior rank, I was always given the job to search the roof. I lost count of the number of manholes I was lifted into. Sometimes, I had success up in the dark, spider-filled rafters. I was also given the job to search any females or children. Yes, searching children is very sad, but these people would often hide drugs in children's nappies, clothes, cots, or toys. When doing so, I did try to make the children comfortable and turn it into a game.

I was now doing the occasional undercover job. I looked at undercover work as just acting, playing a role, just like my Mary role in kindergarten. While doing UC jobs, I prayed that Mary, Mother of God, would protect me. I chose the undercover name,

Lisa. Specialist police would wire me up with a listening device, and I would meet with a drug dealer, often numerous times over several weeks and months. Each time, I would purchase drugs before their eventual arrest. Being recognised as a police officer was a constant worry, and when I was doing undercover work near my twin's police division, my anxiety was heightened. I knew who I had arrested previously, but I didn't know who she had. I don't think my boss ever considered this added danger. When I met with the drug dealers, it was frightening. These were bad crooks, and there were times my heart pounded so hard that I was sure they could actually see it pulsating through my clothing. I greatly admire and respect the police who do very dangerous, full-time undercover work. It is not like the movies!

At one job, I was in a private home with an ex-bikie and was in the process of buying several ounces of amphetamines from him. We were standing in his kitchen weighing the drugs when the police team started to enter the house. However, he spotted them sneaking down the side of the house. He grabbed the drugs and ran towards a bathroom in an attempt to flush the drugs down the toilet. I tried to act just as shocked at the sight of the police as he was, but at the same time inconspicuously block him. He was a fit, solid-looking guy, and he aggressively grabbed me and literally threw me out of the way. I felt like Kermit the Frog being thrown by Miss Piggy, as I flew through the kitchen, hitting the fridge mid-air, before landing heavily on the kitchen floor. The guys entered the house and tackled him at the toilet.

Occasionally, we travelled to country towns for UC work. Once, we drove a few hundred kilometres to Orange. I was grateful for my large family tree; I had relatives in many towns, so I went to my aunt and uncle's home to prepare. Later, the four offenders were charged and appeared in court. My aunt later sent me the Orange local paper. The headline read, 'Secret Tapes in Drug Case'. Not long after that, I did another undercover job at Bathurst with offenders arrested. Afterwards, I stood in court swearing on oath that I was a police officer before giving evidence. The offender was still not convinced I was a police officer. He wholeheartedly believed I was a prostitute working for the police.

I commenced the Detectives Education Program, which is the final phase of becoming a designated detective. I had a close friendship with two policewomen, Despina and Julie, whom I had met in my earlier Investigators Course. They were both married to policemen, and both worked in the eastern suburbs. All three of us were selected to complete the same detective course, so we decided to travel to Goulburn together, having many laughs along the way. After thirty-three years, Despina is still a serving policewoman. She currently holds the rank of superintendent and remains a treasured friend.

When the parents of murdered Anita Cobby and young Ebony Simpson were introduced to each other, they established The Victims of Homicide Support Group. As part of our detective training, the newly established group was brought in to talk to our class. Listening to the detailed, honest feelings and experiences of this group of immediate family members, all of whom had lost a loved one to some of the most horrific murders in our state, was informative, helpful, and deeply deeply emotional.

My boyfriend Ben and I were very happy in our relationship, so we decided to move in together. I left my cosy, little western suburbs garage and moved into his flat in the eastern suburbs of Sydney. Although our shifts often conflicted, we did manage to spend a lot of time together. The Maroubra flat had brilliant ocean views, and I loved the early mornings when I could watch the rolling waves while I sipped my cup of tea. Ben loved the ocean and any activity associated with it. Even though I was a country girl, I have always loved being near water. However, I was very inexperienced in the ocean, I still am! Ben spent hours holding my hand, trying to assure me I was not shark bait as we floated off the shore. Sometimes, he would take me for little spearfishing trips, but I soon found I was more comfortable lying on the beach with a good book while I watched him surf, or waited for him to surface from a scuba dive. We spent many hours fishing at one beach or another, and thanks to my father, this was one thing I was okay at. Ben enjoyed photography, and my inner creativity started to resurface, igniting the photography passion that I had felt when in high school.

Over the years, my sisters and I tried to maintain a relationship with our father, which was at times turbulent. I have sadly seen a person kick a dog, but the loyal dog will still return to its owner and obediently sit at its owner's feet. I sort of felt like this was the relationship I had with my father. He would kick me in the guts, metaphorically, and I would obediently keep going back. Once, Ben and I met my father in the country, and we headed off on an enjoyable fishing and hunting trip on the Bogan River. My father's happy place was seated in the tinny on a river, and Ben enjoyed fishing in my father's company. Around our work commitments, Ben and I went on many adventures together, and as we cruised along the roads in his van listening to Neil Diamond, I felt life just couldn't get any better.

As I had sort of skipped the 'normal' patrol detective phase, I started to wonder what other forms of detective work were like, and I felt inexperienced amongst the group of seasoned detectives. I loved working in the drug squad, but after two years of full-time drug work, I decided to transfer to Mascot Detectives within the Botany Patrol. Here I enjoyed the variety of work, and felt that I was gaining more needed skills to help me become a more competent Detective. The drug squad still contacted me on occasions to do undercover work for them, so I didn't completely abandon ship.

One shift, a man burst into the police station, fearing for his safety due to a domestic situation with his adult son, who could be heard erratically yelling loudly up the street. My partner and I were close by, so we walked out of the station, followed by two uniformed officers and the father. Suddenly, the son appeared and, like a raging bull, ran at me and my partner, violently swinging two large knives, one in each hand. He pointed the blades at us, swinging them and threatening us both as we jumped back to avoid being stabbed. The very agitated man ran between us and towards the two uniformed officers who were standing with the offender's father near the station door. The two uniformed police pulled their firearms and yelled several times at the offender, 'Drop the knives, drop the knives'. The father, although fearful, did not want his son shot, so he jumped in front of the police, yelling, 'Don't shoot. Don't shoot!' and grabbed at his son, just as my quick-thinking partner grabbed an arm, and they both fell to the ground. I dived and grabbed the other arm, holding it firmly at the wrist. My partner freed one knife, and a uniformed officer removed the knife from the hand that I was struggling to hold. As this was happening, the second uniformed officer dived on top of the son's legs. The man had injuries, and as we all struggled to hold this raging bull down, he spat at us, and soon we were covered in blood. Several other police came running from the station, and with difficulty, the man was finally handcuffed. Every second of every day was different, and circumstances could change in an instant. The risk to my colleagues' safety and my own was always at the back of my mind.

Detectives were called to attend the sand dunes at Kurnell, where a man walking his dog had a surprise find, skeletal remains. We attended, and soon the area was swarming with homicide detectives, as there was the possibility the remains were connected to an underworld murder. I was fascinated watching the forensic police work, removing the remains with little disturbance to any evidence. The following day, I attended the post-mortem and watched as staff painstakingly used little paintbrushes to brush away every bit of sand meticulously. The homicide squad took control of the investigation. Years later, while sitting out in the bush, I was watching TV with my family when a crime investigation program aired. The program was about a group of well-known underworld figures and the number of skeletal remains linked to them that had been found in the Botany Bay area. Some old news footage flashed up on the TV, and there I was, looking much younger, standing watching the removal of the skeleton by forensic police.

I had wanted to learn more as a patrol detective, and I did. Each day was new and different. I could be investigating a million-dollar theft, attending a violent home invasion, or investigating a large industrial fire. I could be responding to an armed robbery or being seated on a plane travelling interstate to interview an offender or witness. Once, I worked undercover at a Sydney airport protest, and like a mob of sheep, I marched, chanting, 'Third Runways got to go, oh ho, hey hey, third Runways gotta go….' I was promoted to senior constable and completed the Advanced Criminal Investigation Course.

One afternoon, Ben walked into our flat and quite suddenly ended our relationship. I was completely devastated and felt like I had literally been bucked off a wild bull and trampled in the dirt. I was still very much in love with him. As I was in 'his' flat, I had to find somewhere to live quickly! I found a cheap, dark, dingy flat at La Perouse, and despite being a self-confessed clean freak, it was infested with large cockroaches that I could not control. I had some very dark days in that flat and spent many hours desperately trying to mend my broken heart. Although I felt like my world had ended, crime continued, and I had bills to pay, so for many months, my life was simply to get up, go to work, and at the end of my shift, crawl home to my shitty flat and kill cockroaches.

I was working when a man walked into the police station and asked to speak to a detective. This man was a criminal and was involved in vehicle theft, but he wanted to change sides. I started to interview him, obtaining as many details as possible. It was apparent his information involved a very large-scale car theft racket, and he became a registered police informant. I passed this information on to the South Region Major Crime Squad, which soon formed Task Force Hedgehog. Police from various areas were seconded to work full-time on the investigation. I was seconded to Hedgehog and spent many hours collecting and collating information from the informant. I found stolen cars and converted motor engines, one of the most tedious jobs I had been involved in.

I had had enough of the cockroaches, so I moved to a granny flat only a few blocks from my work. The house had initially been a two-story home. The family lived upstairs, and they had recently converted the ground floor into a flat. The husband, a Greek man, and the wife, an Italian lady, often had heated arguments in both languages at once, and I learned many foreign swear words in Greek and Italian. After getting permission from these landlords, my beautiful friend Despina surprised me with a gorgeous fluffy ginger kitten, and he became a welcome part of my family.

While I was attached to the task force, I was selected to be interviewed for the 'Eighty Years of Women in Policing' celebrations. I had to attend a media training course, and later, various media outlets interviewed me. The headline of one paper read, 'Beauty on the Beat.' I have never considered myself beautiful, I'm quite plain looking really, but this paper was worth keeping. Hundreds of policewomen from all over the state gathered in Sydney for several days of celebrations. The first female police officer was Lillian Armfield, who was sworn in in 1915. In our initial graduating class in 1987, the 1000th serving policewoman was sworn in, and in just eight years, there were 1719 policewomen in the state, with seven ranked as commissioned officers. Jacki and I marched together in a policewomen parade through the centre of Sydney. Some people hate the police, and some people like them. Despite how people felt, I knew that day I was very proud to be a serving female police officer.

Reef

After a few years of policing, I applied to be in the detectives. Becoming a Detective in NSW is a long and involved process. After a minimum of two years working in general duties, I could put my name down as an expression of interest to work in that section. The next process was sitting for the 'Bull Ring'. The bull ring is an interview we had to undertake to gain acceptance into the detectives' office. A panel of three senior detectives fired random questions at us in relation to law and the practices and procedures of the police force. This process was very intimidating. When I went into the interview, I recognised the most junior detective on the panel, as he was a sergeant working with my boyfriend. He knew who I was. There was also a superintendent and an inspector on the panel. I passed the bull ring and was accepted into the Parramatta Detectives as a plainclothes constable, which meant I was not a qualified detective…yet.

Although I couldn't play hockey, some policewomen organised an indoor cricket team. We registered a bigger team, so if some of us were working, we would still have enough players to fill a team. Kylie and some of her work colleagues also joined the team. When the competition started, we realised there was a team from Mullewa, the female section of Silverwater Gaol, and a team of prison officers. The prisoners' team wore their prison uniforms. It was very interesting when we played against the inmates. Most of the inmates had their friends and relatives come and watch, as it was as close to a visit as they were going to get. While the game was underway, we were always heckled by the crowd, and it was worse for any of our subs who had to sit outside the nets close to the intimidating spectators. Many of the female inmates were built like 'brick shithouses' and could hit the balls with as much force as most men, and they also used any opportunity they could to carefully aim their strike straight at us. There were correctional staff supervising the inmates, and sometimes, the tension between our two teams was very evident. I think it is fair to say they were the better team or that they used intimidation to elevate themselves to that position.

I loved working with the dedicated detectives, who are the people assigned to investigate some of the most horrendous and confronting crimes in the community. I read once that a detective has to have a special set of skills that includes an analytical mind, emotional resilience and a persistent personality. Being a detective requires working long hours, often on call, investigating a broad range of serious crimes. The evidence surrounding crimes is like building a big jigsaw puzzle. The evidence has to be put together piece by piece to enable us to see the bigger picture, working within the frame of the law. Experience and education do make putting these puzzles together a lot easier, though sometimes we also needed a bit of luck. It was surprising how some serious crimes were solved because the offender had dropped their wallet or some sort of identification at a crime scene. There was a lot more freedom given to detectives, and it was up to us to work independently and get our work done. As I was a junior plainclothes officer, I was partnered with a fully designated or qualified detective to learn whilst I studied for the role.

I was working long hours but still managed to catch up with my four girlfriends from school whenever I could, as we were all now living in Sydney. Kylie would often try to come with me. The six of us had all commenced interesting lives. My twin and I were in the police. Two became WAGS married to first-grade footballers. One became a nanny for the rich and famous and worked for some very well-known identities, and one was a makeup artist and hair stylist for Channel 9. She went on to work freelance for different Australian movies and TV shows. We were all working irregular hours, and the WAGS were travelling all over the place to keep up with their football husbands, but we still managed occasionally to catch up together. With all our different lives, there was always something interesting to talk about. The girls heard about our police lives, and my twin and I heard stories about the inside of the rugby league world and the lifestyles of the rich and famous.

Driving home from one of these catchups, Kylie and I noticed a large fire in an industrial area near Ryde. We did a drive-by out of curiosity, and, arriving on the abandoned street, we noticed we were the first people on the scene. Our training told us that the first thing to do was to check that no one was in immediate danger. We ran along the perimeter of the building, yelling out to see if anyone was inside and, at the same time, checking for any forced entry into the building. This information would be vital for the inquiry by the coroner who investigates fires and explosions which have caused damage to property. We were running under a large carport that ran the length of the building when we heard a loud cracking sound; the noise was coming from the light pole, as the power transformer was now also well-lit. A powerline fell down, and the heat of the fire was very intense. The sparks from the transformer were cascading down onto the ground and would have made a spectacular light show on New Year's Eve. We knew we had to get out of there really quickly as the fire was now engulfing the entire building, and the roof was about to cave in. I could feel the radiating heat on my face. Kylie took off back towards our car, and for some reason, my feet just would not move. I was scared. The fire had started trailing under the awning that I was standing beneath, and sparks were flicking in all directions from the electricity. I was in real danger. The sound of the fire was deafening, but over the noise of the fire, I heard my twin yell, 'Run, Jack, run!' This shocked me back into reality, and I ran like hell out of there. Kylie has always been braver than me, and I couldn't believe that fear could paralyse a person's body like that.

There have been many cases where twins have died together or close apart. I believe one of the reasons for this comes down to, proximity. Twins play together, drive together, holiday together, work together, live together. The 'unnatural' death of twins has occurred because of an accident or natural disaster, and they were close to each other when this occurred.

Twin deaths are common when one twin attempts to rescue the other twin. In Dubbo, we had a family that lived in our neighbourhood, and they had young twin girls who died together. One had somehow gotten onto the roof and was electrocuted; the other twin went to rescue her sister, and she also was electrocuted. In Nagoya, Japan, twin boys fell to their deaths from a seventh-floor apartment minutes apart due to misadventure. In Barrington, USA, ninety-seven-year-old twins died after one fell over in their driveway during a snowstorm; her twin sister fell as she went to get help. Both were found deceased, lying in the elements.

Kylie and I were decreasing our proximity and spending more time apart. I went on my first overseas holiday with Scott, and we went to Fiji. On the first day, we booked a group cruise on a big old wooden sailboat out to a beautiful island. The sunny day started with Jamaican-style music and a few cocktails, and the atmosphere gave the impression that it was going to be a great day. I mentioned the dark, menacing clouds on the horizon to the staff on the boat, and they assured me that all was fine. Our boat literally sailed into the eye of a storm, and the waves were getting huge just as we arrived at the island. There were small tender boats to take us onto shore. I didn't know much about the ocean, but the huge swell creating massive waves didn't look like the boat landings were going to go too smoothly, so I opted to leave my camera on the sailboat. The optimistic Fijians said we could swim on the island if we wanted. I took the boat option and waited to go on one of the last boats. As I watched from the rocky sailboat, I saw two tourists who had decided to swim get pulled away really quickly from the boat in the big swell. They were floating away from the island. They needed to be rescued, so Scott, being a strong swimmer, dived in and helped them get to shore. Our tender boat was behind two other tender boats, and as we approached the island, I could see the landings of the other boats hadn't gone well. Tourists were being flung out as the waves turned the boats over in the swell. The Fijians were grabbing beach bags and tourists from the water and dragging them to shore. One courteous Japanese tourist kept smiling as his wet camera dangled from around his neck. I braced myself as we approached but was lucky; my boat landing went a lot more smoothly. The storm arrived with impeccable timing, and the rain came with tremendous force, heavy and hard. As I sat under my beach towel in the rain on the beautiful beach island surrounded by tourists from all over the world, I smiled at the chaos around me. I was still enjoying travel.

Back on shore, we caught dodgy private transport back to our resort, one hour away. The rain continued to pelt down, and as soon as we left, we discovered that the windscreen wipers on the vehicle weren't working. The driver was leaning forward like the cartoon character Mr Magoo, the eccentric millionaire who had terrible eyesight but refused to wear glasses. We couldn't see five meters in front of us. Foolishly, we continued our journey, with Scott leaning out the passenger window and using his straight arm as a windscreen wiper. The rain streamed into the car. I had a towel up to try to protect myself, and also to shield me from seeing what was sure to be an accident. After about fifteen minutes, the rain eased, and Scott collapsed back into the car.

After a week on the tropical island, our holiday ended. When we arrived at the airport, we discovered that a plane had run entirely off the end of the runway on landing. The plane had to be moved and examined by an engineer, so all flights were cancelled. We had another unscheduled night in Fiji, which was so romantic that we had to share the hotel room with another couple as there was no accommodation left. We took it in turns to rest on the one bed. Needless to say, we didn't get much sleep. Getting on a plane the next day was scary, but we had to get home and back to work. We landed in Sydney safely, and despite the few holiday incidents, I now had the travel bug.

I continued working in the detectives and was involved in the investigations of some really interesting crimes. Some matters were investigated solely by my partner and me, but sometimes, when there was a serious crime like murder, a team of us would work together using our individual skills and knowledge as a unit to try to solve the case. In our office, we had a staff of twenty, including four women. My office was very progressive, and the women detectives were treated as individuals and not by their sex. It was not uncommon for two female detectives to be rostered on together to cover the entire H District during the night shift, which encompassed an area that took us all the way to Richmond. When I was in general duties, there was one shift I worked where the three-car crews were manned solely by women police, although this was rare due to the limited number of female police at the time.

Detectives worked a ten-day on, four days off roster. Obviously if we had a serious crime to solve, our four days off were cancelled and taken at a later time. During one particular ten-day period I worked, I was required to investigate a new sexual assault every day for ten days. The workload piled up very quickly, and so did the emotional load.

Scott and I did whatever we could to get the four days off together, and our relationship continued. My office was investigating a double murder in Parramatta, and I had to travel to Melbourne to follow up some leads with a senior detective. While I was packing at home, my boyfriend unexpectedly turned up at the house. He had just been told he was heading off to Queensland to follow up on some armed robberies with the Armed Hold-Up Squad. This was the type of life we were living, but it was all we knew. A quick kiss, and we were off in different directions, to different states. On my way back from Melbourne my colleague and I shared a motel room to save our travel allowance money. This was a common thing to do amongst detectives as we could keep any money we hadn't spent. While in our motel I went and had a shower and took all my clean clothes in with me, careful not to 'encourage' any unwanted male attention. When I came out of the bathroom, the senior detective was lying on the bed in his underwear, attempting to look like Burt Reynolds in his Cosmopolitan centrefold pose. He indicated by patting the bed with his hand that he wanted me to join him. I grabbed my handbag and left the room. I was now in a very difficult position, alone and a long way from home. I went and found a seat, where I waited a few long hours, hoping my long absence had given the detective the tip-off that I wasn't interested in him. When I got back to the room much later, the lights were out, and I quietly slid into my own bed in my clothes, but I didn't sleep very well at all that night.

A week after this incident, my boyfriend, who had found out what had happened, confronted the detective at a well-known cop pub and a few choice words were exchanged in front of a big police crowd. On the Monday I was called into the senior detective's office, who I had travelled to Melbourne with and he said, 'If you don't learn to shut your mouth, it might adversely affect your position in detectives.' I knew better than to make a complaint; it would only result in me getting a quick transfer with a reputation to follow. The rest of the staff were good people, and I loved working in the office.

Soon after this, a detective was needed at Mount Druitt Detectives to work a six-month secondment as they were having trouble filling the position. I was 'coincidently' selected by that same detective. I was the first female to work at Mount Druitt Detectives, and I found out later that the male detectives had a meeting about who was going to be my partner. No one wanted a female partner. Policewomen were still having to break down barriers. One of the detectives finally gave in and agreed to partner me. He was a great bloke; we got on well, and we still catch up and share stories today. It was a great experience working in another area, but I was happy to go back to the familiarity of Parramatta station at the end of the six months. It was also great to have the other female detectives for friendship and support.

I had been dating my boyfriend for a few years and thought it was time to introduce him to my father. Kylie and I had continued to maintain a sporadic relationship with him. We were adults, and police, so he was generally well-behaved. However, occasionally, his unstable mood swings surfaced. My boyfriend and I planned a shooting and fishing trip out in the bush and took some friends with us. We met up with my father and his latest partner. We had decided to go to a property that Dad knew inland from Warren. Scott always thinks he is a country bloke due to the fact that he grew up on the outskirts of Sydney where there were a few cows in the odd paddock and a prison farm nearby, the term 'farm' being referenced loosely. It was time to test his capabilities. We took our police guns with us to use for a bit of practice. Being detectives, we kept our firearms with us all the time, as we were often called out in the middle of the night. We technically weren't allowed to take them away with us, but this was not policed, and our bosses generally turned a blind eye to this. We took some paper targets with us to hone our skills. Gun laws in Australia were just beginning to be tightened, and there had been gun amnesties that involved federally funded gun buybacks. These occurred before and after the 1996 Port Arthur Massacre. More than one million firearms were surrendered. Police now have much tighter regulations in regard to their firearms, and they are secured at the station when officers are off duty.

After a long drive out west, we set up our camp. Dad had a well-organised camp system with camping kits made up for powered locations and a camping kit for no power. Dad was at home in the bush, and this is where I would see the best come out of him. Soon after our arrival, Scott needed to go to the toilet. Being a bit precious where this area was concerned, he cautiously headed into the bush to do his business. Off he went with some toilet paper, with the rest of us laughing at his hesitation. After a while, we started to worry about the length of time he was taking. Dad said, 'You better go and check on him Jack,' so I went looking for him. I found him deep in the thick scrub, standing naked from the waist down. He had his underwear in his hands and was wiping them with the toilet paper. When I asked him what he was doing, this 'skilled' countryman replied, 'It got a swing up and landed back in my undies.' Laughing about the 'incident' around the fire that night, my father very quickly recognised that my new boyfriend was indeed a city lad who needed supervision in the bush.

The following day, we all went hunting for feral pigs. We always hunted responsibly and walked spaced out in a line so we wouldn't accidentally shoot each other. Scott was particularly careful as he had an uncle who had accidentally shot and killed one of his relatives years earlier on a shooting trip. I always stayed close to Dad, as he was the only person I trusted to keep me safe from the feral pigs. These wild animals are very dangerous. I was tasked with carrying the spare bullets, and the only gun I had was my .38 Smith and Wesson police gun. All the men had different types of shotguns. Walking through the bush, we were all quiet, waiting and listening for any sound. In the middle of our silence, there was a sudden squeal by a pig and a yell from my dad. Dad let off two rounds but missed both times. The pig was ducking and weaving through the scrub, with us running in our line behind it. Dad yelled for more bullets, but I wanted a shot. I knelt on one knee, and when the pig ran into a clearing, I fired off one round. The bullet hit the dirt straight in front of the pig. All of a sudden, everything went quiet, and all I could hear was my controlled breathing. I breathed out and shot again. The pig hit the deck. Suddenly, everyone was yelling and jumping. I had managed to shoot the moving pig straight behind his ear and killed it instantly, not an easy feat, in that distance, and with a pistol. Dad was impressed with my shooting. I walked over to the dead pig and felt sorry for it instantly. I have never liked killing animals, even if they are feral and cause enormous damage to the environment. However, I was pleased that the repetitive police training had fallen into place. The rain started, and the red dirt turned to mud. I was well and truly ready to head back to the comforts of the city and a shower.

We hadn't been home long, and Scott asked me to marry him. It wasn't a complete surprise as he had asked Kylie what sort of ring I would like and filled her in on his proposal plans. He was going to take me to dinner in the city and tell me we were going to stay over for the night. As a surprise, the next day, he was going to fly me to the Gold Coast for the weekend. Kylie knew this plan wasn't perfect. I would be packing a bag for one night in the city of Sydney and would then have no resort-style clothing for a Queensland weekend getaway. Of course, she told me!

I knew the proposal would happen, just not when. We got busy organising a wedding while I was still undertaking my educational requirements to become a detective. We managed a social life, and had a great group of police friends and went out regularly. Most of the men worked at the North West Crime Squad, and a couple of the wives were also police. The tight-knit group had a special bond, and I likened it to being in a big 'mafia' family, except we were on the other side of the law. The men watched out for us and made sure we were safe and looked after. I trust these men with my life. They were very experienced detectives and had a special set of skills that got the job done. We formed lifelong friendships with some of these people, and some of the men went on to have very distinguished careers in the police. I finished my detective training and placed third in the course. Kylie was also working in the detectives by this stage, and we were having trouble finding time to catch up in person, Detectives work erratic shifts, and an eight-hour shift can quickly turn into a fourteen-hour day if a serious crime occurs. It's odd, but I can't remember many occasions we were together during this time, as we were living on opposite sides of the city and busy.

In early 1993, Scott and I were married, with my twin sister as my maid of honour. My two other sisters were bridesmaids and walked down the aisle first, followed by Kylie. One of the police wives told me after the ceremony that when Kylie walked down the aisle, and there was a short pause before I entered the church, her husband said it was weird I wasn't wearing a wedding dress and had the same outfit as the bridesmaids. She had to tell him that was my twin. They all knew I was a twin but some of the guests had never met her and didn't know how alike we actually were. We had a big wedding, and we had just as many police at the wedding as we did family. My old school friends from Dubbo all made it as well, and the policemen thought it was pretty cool having a couple of first grade footy players at the wedding. When it came time to throw my bouquet, I made a pact with Kylie that I would let her catch it, hoping the tradition that the person who catches the bouquet is the next person to get married would come true; Kylie caught the bouquet. We headed off for a two-week honeymoon, spending a week at Port Macquarie and a week at

Coffs Harbour, not knowing at the time that we would be living there very shortly. We had decided that we would start trying for a family straight away and would just let nature take its course.

Soon after my wedding, my friend Lisa and I went to visit our friend Jo from school at the Channel 9 studios. She gave us a tour, and we sat in the studio audience for the Midday Show with Ray Martin. After the show, Ray spoke with the audience and asked a few questions. He then looked in our direction and asked us if either of us was pregnant. We both laughed and said no. He told us that we were sitting in their pregnant seats, and most women that sat there were pregnant. We told him that we both were trying, and he wished us luck. A few weeks later we both found out we were pregnant, and were, in fact, pregnant when Ray had asked us. Those special seats had worked their magic. I was as fertile as a sea horse and fell pregnant before our wedding photos were delivered.

I decided not to tell my boss I was pregnant straight away as I didn't want to go on restricted duties. I was only pregnant for a few weeks when I had an incident with an offender in an interview room where he pushed me up against a wall. This frightened me, not for my safety, but for the safety of my unborn child. I told my boss that day. The detectives were really great about my pregnancy, and my day-to-day work life didn't change as much as I thought it would. I was even rostered on call right up until I finished work. Being on-call meant being called out in the middle of the night if a serious job occurred. At thirty-eight weeks pregnant, I was called out in the middle of the night for a murder. I waddled up to the scene, showed my identification badge to the police officer guarding the crime scene, and asked what was going on. He told me that they were waiting for the detectives. I said to him, 'That would be me.' He was shocked and showed me to the crime scene. I finished work a week later before the murder was solved.

A week later, our little girl was born at a private hospital on Jamison Road, Penrith. This was the same road my husband was born on, but having an impatient personality, he was born on the back seat of a car. Incidentally, this was also the same road his father eagerly joined the world, born in a horse and sulky.

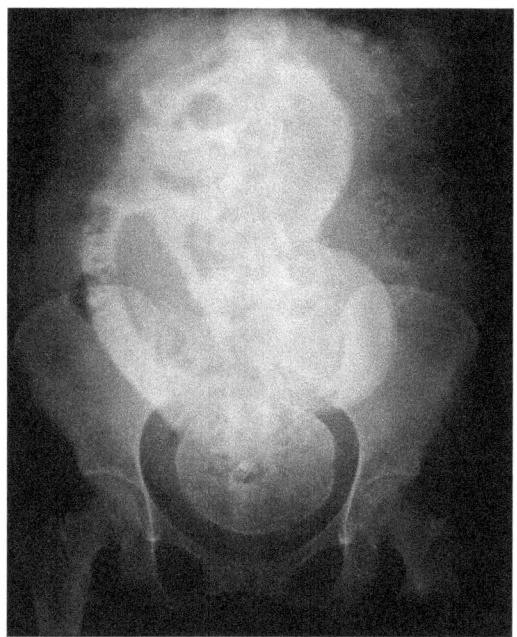
Our mother's pregnancy X-Ray, with our fetal outlines visible.

The rocks we left at the Cruz de Ferro, during our Camino pilgrimage.

Our mother Narelle, standing outside Orange Base Hospital with two Nurses holding us, on the day we were discharged from Hospital.

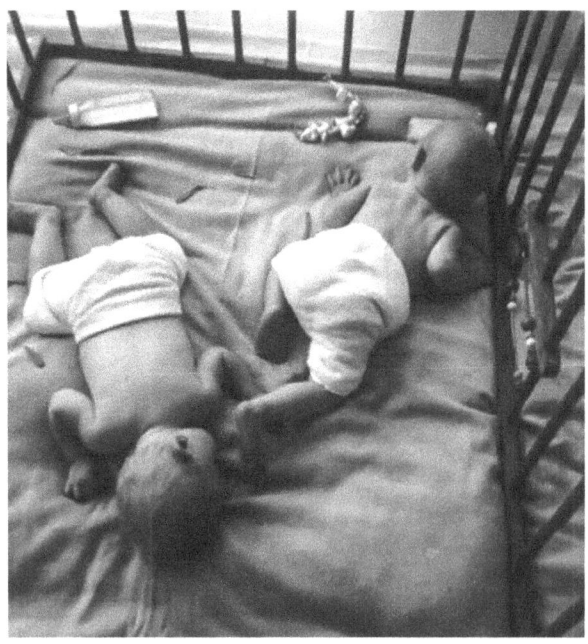

Having some play time. Taken at Allambie, Stuart Town 1968.

Our father, Graeme Dickerson, with Kylie on the left and Jacki on the right.

Jacki and Kylie in their twin pram, taken at 'Allambie' Stuart Town.

Our first day of School in Dubbo NSW. Taken 1972.

Kylie and Jacki standing at the Dubbo Hockey Fields in the 1980's.

Jacki and Kylie on Graduation Day, at the NSW Police Academy Goulburn, 7th August, 1987

Double justice!

• Twins Kylie and Jaqueline Dickerson of Dubbo were among the graduates to pass out of Class 228 from the Goulburn Police Academy today. They were two of the 190 graduates to

One of the many Newspaper Stories after our Police Graduation.

Jacki, a.k.a Reefs husband Scott James.

Kylie, a.k.a Beefs husband David Fisher.

Jacki and Kylie walking the Camino de Santiago, in Spain in 2018.

Jacki and Kylie in Dubai in 2018.

Scott and Jacki James, and Kylie and David Fisher, taken in 2021.

Separated by over 1000 kilometres, Reef's home on the NSW coast and Beef's home in far north western NSW.

1000 Kilometres

Beef

I was still mourning my breakup with Ben; I was losing the buzz of city life, and I started to feel like I was trapped in a set of stockyards. I craved space, fresh air and gum leaves. I decided to apply for a transfer to the bush. I didn't care where I went, as long as it was west of the Blue Mountains. Detective positions were hard to come by; however, a position was advertised for Bourke Detectives, so I applied and was successful. Bourke was classed as both a regional and remote posting. Most isolated rural towns had a working tenure of three years, and at the end, we were basically offered a free pass to the station of our choice. My plan was to do my tenure while gaining some bush policing experience and possibly apply for a promotion before heading to a dream coastal location. In remote communities, police housing was available to rent at a reduced rate, so I also had a financial advantage.

At the time, the rural town of Bourke had a bad reputation, with low employment, a high drug and alcohol-related crime rate, and it was generally believed to be an unsafe town. A little concerned for my safety, I contacted the Police Dog Squad and asked if they had any dogs that were looking for a home. They offered me a police dog called Harley, who, although very well trained, he had failed one final phase of the police dog training course. I was expecting Harley to be a German shepherd but discovered he was a Rottweiler. I arranged to collect Harley from The Rocks Police Station at a pre-arranged time. Harley was massive; his head was bigger than mine, and after I was handed the lead, Harley enthusiastically led me out of the police station.

I was grateful to have had eight years of city life experience and I had learned a lot as a city policewoman. I was sad about leaving the Dubbo girls and my wonderful city friends, but I knew that distance would not diminish our strong bond. Jacki and I would now be over 1000 kilometres away from each other, but I knew this would not hinder our special connection. I was looking forward to moving back to my natural habitat.

Soon, I left the city smog behind me, and with my fur family in toe, I headed west to inland Australia. I foolishly sedated Otis, my cat, and Harley, my new dog, thinking this would help with the long car trip. After a stopover in my hometown of Dubbo, I continued the drive towards the western sun. I sat the cat cage containing Otis on the front seat; he was not happy about being locked up like a criminal. He let out a continuous drugged-up, drawn-out meeeooow for the entire car trip. As I drove, I pushed my finger into the cage to caress him, but his protests turned physical, and he embedded a claw deep into my finger. The small but painful hole bled considerably. Harley, seated on the back seat, decided to lean forward, and position his massive head next to mine. He drooled so much I wished I was wearing a raincoat.

I stopped at one point to give Harley a rest stop. The sedation had worked a bit too well, and resembling a meth addict, he stumbled out of the car and unsteadily went to relieve himself. Somehow, he urinated all over his legs. After I cleaned him, I found he was too drugged to walk back to my car, so I had to drag his 55-kilogram body over to it, lift his front paws onto the seat, wrap my arms around his wet legs and waist, and use all my body weight to lift his back half into the car. His face slid across the seat as I pushed and shoved his dead weight. I drove on, bleeding and smelling of urine, soon the traffic lessened, the road got straighter, and the handful of vehicles that passed gave me a country wave.

I was relieved when, finally, after a nine-and-a-half-hour drive, I read the sign, Welcome to Bourke. I quickly found the police station, was handed the keys to my police house, and in two minutes located the small, three-bedroom fibro home. I unlocked the door and wearily walked inside, navigating my way around a mountain of boxes and furniture that had been delivered by the furniture removalist the previous day.

The fur babies were excited to be out of the car, and although I was tired, I immediately started some essential unpacking. My double bed mattress was just inside the front door. I tipped the mattress onto its side and slid it, inch by inch, up the hallway. Finally, I got it to the bedroom, the furthest room away, where, exhausted, I collapsed on the bare mattress and heavily fell asleep. I woke up early the following morning, suffering from severe vomiting and diarrhea. After six hours, I knew I was very ill, so I attended the hospital, where it was recommended that I be admitted. Tired, sick, and upset, I explained that this was not possible. I was new in town, only had a few days to unpack, and had animals that needed care. I was given a needle and strict instructions to return in an hour if I wasn't any better. They never saw me again. I returned to the police house, collapsed back onto the mattress, and prayed for the needle to take effect.

Days later, I heard a knock at the door, and looking somewhat dishevelled, I opened the door where a friendly uniformed police officer was standing in the bright sunlight. 'Hi, I'm just here to check on you; your sister has been trying to ring you for days.' Back then, there were no mobiles or cordless phones, and the only phone in the house was in the lounge room. Unbeknown to me, while the house was vacant, the phone ring volume had been turned down. Lying weak and sick at the opposite end of the house, I had not heard the continual phone calls from my worried sister. My twin had phoned the police station, stating she was concerned for my welfare. I phoned her and reassured her I was 'just alive.' Days later, I emerged from sickbay several kilograms lighter to a house full of unpacked boxes. It wasn't a great start.

In 1995, I started my first shift as a bush detective. The police station was a historical, single-storey building with an internal courtyard, and after entering the station, I was directed to the detectives' office. I walked past the old, bar-style prisoner cells towards the office and was heckled by nine male prisoners. The Patrol Commander, Inspector Cross, informed me that I had to do an interview with the local paper. I discovered I was the first female detective to be stationed at Bourke, and this novelty was newsworthy, not just to the prisoners but to the entire small country town. I soon got the name Detective Lady. Some locals would say, 'You're like Maggie, aye?' They were referring to the hugely popular Australian television show Blue Healers that debuted the previous year. One of the main characters in the show was a small blonde woman, Maggie Doyle, played by actress Lisa McCune. In the first episode, Maggie arrives at an all-male country police station. Thankfully for me, there were three uniformed policewomen stationed at Bourke, so I wasn't entirely like Maggie.

In keeping with the 80's style of fashion, I was wearing my best detective outfit, a long-pencilled skirt with a matching blazer. I entered the office and was met by the Detective Sergeant, Bob and the second Detective, Greg, both of whom were very welcoming. Bobby offered to take me on a tour. In the city, all the detectives' vehicles were sedans, but here, all police cars, including the detective's car, were high off the ground four-wheel drives. As I am short, I went to climb in, however, my straight skirt prevented this. I hitched up my skirt and jumped up, making a mental note never to wear a skirt in Bourke again. Bobby filled me in on patrol issues as we drove. Bob told me that both he and Greg were heading to Sydney for a court hearing and would be away for a week. This meant I would be on my own, which also meant being 'on call', after hours if detectives were needed. I was thrown the car keys and wished good luck.

Our patrol was roughly 110,000 square kilometres covering Brewarrina, Louth, Tilpa, Fords Bridge, Enngonia, Wanaaring and Nyngan, and everywhere in between. Bob, Greg, and I were responsible for all serious crimes and any rural crime, including stock theft, within the entire patrol. At the time, Bourke had only twenty-four uniformed police, all of whom were married or living with a partner. Enngonia had two uniformed officers, Wanaaring had one officer, and Brewarrina had a small number of uniformed police. Uniformed police were extremely busy, grossly understaffed, and often had to work singularly. Understandably, I soon found out that police morale was not very good. There were some areas in the town where police were not allowed to attend alone, and often, police had to escort the ambulances or fire trucks to certain areas or homes.

One of my first jobs was a fire; a shearing shed had burnt down on a property near the village of Fords Bridge. I jumped in the car and, following instructions from a uniform staff, headed west seventy kilometres on a bush road until I got to the Fords Bridge Pub. I turned right and travelled north until I reached the property. I was met by a man who said, 'I knew you weren't far away.'

Bewildered, I said, 'How did you know?'

He replied, 'The publican rang. He told me the police car had gone around the corner and it's a Sheila.'

The shearing shed had certainly burnt down; there was nothing left except hot, twisted sheets of iron. In the city, detectives in the same situation would call the scientific police, who would arrive and assist within an hour or so. The nearest scientific police were stationed 500 kilometres away from my location and attended five days later. After doing what I could, I had a nice cup of tea and left. Driving back, I couldn't help but laugh; policing was undoubtedly going to be different in the bush, and as I bounced along creating a dust trail, while avoiding kangaroos, I felt peaceful. I think my heart is connected to the country earth.

There was no specific stock squad, so my next job was the theft of eighty-five feral goats. My knowledge of goats and the goat industry was zero. I attended a set of stockyards and spotted the man I was to speak to, standing in the centre of a pen overflowing with sharp-horned, multi-coloured, noisy goats. For his entertainment, I am sure, he waited for me to walk to him, so unperturbed, in my immaculate suit, I climbed into the yard and pushed my way through the smelly goats towards him, conscious of the smirk on his face. I took the report, cautiously avoiding goat horns in the process.

I had a murder-suicide involving a firearm at one of the small villages. The victim and offender were Aboriginal Australians. Although I had grown up in a town with a high Indigenous population, I had no understanding of their beliefs about spirits and the smoking ceremony. When I entered the home, the deceased people were both in a bedroom. Things did not add up, as there was a large pool of blood on the kitchen floor. I eventually discovered the blood in the kitchen was animal blood. A freshly killed sheep or 'killer' had been recently hung in the kitchen. I had to arrange for the two deceased people to be transported to Sydney, 860 kilometres away, and organise a destitute burial for one. Policing in the country came with many different challenges.

I had wanted some country policing experience and was getting it thick and fast. With every job came a mountain of paperwork, reports, victim and witness statements, and briefs of evidence to be prepared for court. I was very grateful that technology had evolved and we no longer had manual typewriters. The continual callouts at night meant little sleep, and I was soon exhausted. On many of my rostered days off, I was still 'on call', so I couldn't leave the town for a brief break. It was sixteen months before I was granted my first period of holiday leave.

I believe police work is police work wherever you are, but there are two major pitfalls to country policing. Firstly, in the city, if a patrol is overwhelmed with work or needs backup, a neighbouring patrol assists; in the bush, the distances are just too great for this. Secondly, in the city, when a police officer is off duty, they have anonymity and blend in with the community. As a country cop in a small town, all the bad guys know where you live, which took me some time to get used to. One day I arrested a man who had severe mental issues and threatened to come to my home and rape me. I would often see him staring at my house as he slowly walked past, and I was grateful to have my police dog Harley, who I knew without a doubt would protect me if needed.

Not only did the bad guys know where I lived, but the entire town did. Early one evening, I was enjoying a rare night at home and had just sat down to eat my steak and veg for dinner when there was a knock at my door. I opened the door to see a very upset lady, a victim of a domestic dispute. The offender, who had followed her, suddenly appeared out the front of my house. He yelled abuse at both his partner and me, so I ushered her inside my home, locked the door, and called the police station. Unfortunately, the car crew were busy out of town, and there was no one available to attend. I tried to calm the victim, hoping the agitated guy would leave. A short while later, our two Aboriginal Community Liaison Officers (ACLOs) Willie and Trev arrived. The ACLOs were Aboriginal people trained and employed by the NSW Police to assist police, and I felt they were invaluable. Trev was also an identical twin, and we often talked about our siblings and twin life. The ACLOs removed the male offender from the street and then came and helped the lady. Finally, I could eat my dinner. Relieved and hungry, I went back inside and went to pick up my plate; my steak was gone! I turned and Harley was licking his lips. I knew he would not need to be fed that night.

Willie had a female Rottweiler, so we arranged for Harley to have a date night, and Harley soon became a father. I kept a female pup and named her, Narla. One night at home, Harley and Narla were inside the house and started to bark aggressively at the back door. I opened the door and caught sight of someone jumping over my side fence. Another day, I came home, and the lock on my house gate was broken. Harley and Narla had been let out; however, well trained, neither had left the front yard. I was woken another night to sounds at my front door. I snuck to the window and saw four men, so I quickly brought Harley and Narla inside; Harley's protective barks scared them away. From that point on, Harley and Narla slept next to my bed. Unfortunately, most police in town at one time or another experienced these sorts of incidents at their homes.

Witnesses and victims of crime were reluctant to assist the police or provide statements as they were understandably fearful of reprisals. The bad guys also knew where 'they' lived. This made things difficult and frustrating for police. We often knew who committed a crime but could not get the necessary legal proof through victim and witness statements to enable an arrest, and a successful conviction in court. Or, we arrested the offenders and they were bail refused by police, before being given bail by the magistrate. As soon as they were released, they would commit another crime, whilst on bail of the previous offence. The disgruntled public, unaware of the legal process, mistakenly felt that the local police were not doing their job to stop the crime.

Work continued! Many jobs involved very serious assaults and sexual assaults and we had at least one murder a year. One case I had been investigating was the horrific child abuse of a young baby. I contacted the suspect, and asked him to attend the station for an interview. About half an hour before he was due to arrive, I received an anonymous phone call, informing me the suspect intended to stab me. I alerted the station staff, who stood hidden on either side of the door. As the suspect walked through the doorway towards me, police grabbed him. I searched him, and sure enough, he had a knife secreted down his shorts. I was thankful to the informant who potentially saved my life.

I was reluctant to go out socially, as inevitably a crime would occur while I was out and the community would expect action, off duty or not. It was easier to stay at home. I was asked out on several dates, but my break-up with Ben was still raw, I felt that dates in a small community could lead to a conflict of interest, and I was too busy at work for dates, so I declined. This started country town rumours that I might be a lesbian. I phoned my twin regularly and filled her in on my experiences, and she did the same. We were living so far apart and were so busy with our individual lives that it occurred to me that we had not seen each other for almost twelve months.

Morale at the police station continued to be very low, and crime and unrest in the town was on the rise. The community were frustrated with the police, our staff numbers were low, and police assaults were common. Once I was walking down the main street and passed three males. One of them, for no reason punched me hard in the back. I was at home one evening when I got a phone call from the station. The police were expecting a riot, and all officers in the town were put on standby. Thankfully, things quietened down, but for days, the atmosphere was tense. The Police Association attended Bourke several times, attempting to support police and boost morale. Only a few weeks later, I arrested a man who later drove past my home and smashed my car window. He was later charged and had to pay me compensation, ten dollars a week. My twin worried about my safety regularly, and at times, I was also a little concerned.

Because of the tenure, some police left, and fresh staff arrived. Bourke now had six policewomen in uniform, with a staff of twenty-five. Three policewomen were pregnant, and a male policeman was on restricted duties, so only twenty-one police were operational. Two policewomen were single, so finally, I wasn't the only single policewoman in town. A new sergeant was chatting with me one day, and it came up that I was a twin. He told me how he and his wife were told they could not have children. Years later, his wife became unwell. The doctor suspected gallstones and sent her for an ultrasound. He accompanied her, but due to delays, he decided to slip down to the barber. When he returned, he found out it wasn't gallstones, but astoundingly, they were expecting twins. They had twin boys who were fraternal or dizygotic twins.

Two years later, his wife fell pregnant again. He stayed with his wife for the ultrasound this time and said to the technician, 'I hope it's not twins?'

She replied, 'I'm sorry, but there are two babies.'

They had another set of fraternal twins. His wife told me after the birth of the second set of twins she knew what was ahead of her, and was reluctant to leave the hospital. The nurses politely asked her to leave the hospital on day ten.

I started attending the Catholic Church with a few of the police, and I found that I thoroughly enjoyed my spiritual time. Soon, I decided to become a Catholic. Once a week, when possible, I would attend church class led by a nun, Sister Marietta. Sister Marietta was a beautiful lady, and I loved her basic approach to Catholicism. She would often say, 'You don't have to attend church to pray,' or 'Oh, I don't think God would care.' Interestingly, our grandmother was baptised as a Catholic and later converted, becoming a Presbyterian. At this stage in my life, I respect the values of all faiths and sit comfortably in any church. I also started playing hockey in the small-town competition. I hadn't played Hockey since my Dubbo days. Our team had several members who were police or nurses, and due to shift work commitments, we had to have extra team numbers. There were only four teams in the competition, and we won the grand final!

A new detective arrived, and Greg left. It was hard to establish firm friendships as the rotation of police was continuous. I was interested in becoming a police negotiator. These positions were not full-time, but a negotiator could be contacted at an instant to attend any location in the state, if needed. To my knowledge, there were no qualified negotiators west of Dubbo. I decided to apply and after a rigorous and selective process, which even requiring psychological testing, I was accepted. I was excited to start the three-year course which required several training blocks at the Goulburn Police Academy.

In 1996, uniform staff numbers were still low, so to boost police numbers, the detectives were asked to work at the Enngonia Races. I reluctantly left town with Bobby, driving one-hour north. Throughout the day, we mingled with the well-behaved crowd. I spotted Gavin, one of the Enngonia policemen, standing with his partner, Trish, a local lady, talking to a good-looking guy. I thought, who's he? I haven't seen him before. Later, I spoke with Gavin and Trish and casually asked who the handsome guy was.

'That's Dave. He lives west of here on a property. He's single. Do you want to meet him?'

'No!' Laughing, I walked off, but soon after, they approached in company with a 6'4" tall, fit, olive-skinned, dark-haired, blue-eyed cowboy with a gorgeous smile. Gossip travelled fast, and Bobby, who had been concerned for some time about my lengthy single status, encouraged me to make a move.

Later that night, we had officially knocked off and were having drinks with other off-duty police and locals. Who was at the bar, cowboy Dave! We started talking and his group of friends joined us. Dave asked me back to his camp, and while sitting by a campfire, we chatted quietly, getting to know each other a little better.

Sometime later, the detective's vehicle came bouncing across the paddock, the headlights annoying other campers, as the car swerved around their campsites. I could hear Bobby yelling loudly, 'Kylieee, it's Bobby, where are you? We have to go.' I was mortified. Bobby located us and had a quick chat to Dave, before we headed back to Bourke. Unbeknown to me, before driving off, Bobby slipped Dave my phone number.

Later, Dave and I made contact, and he asked me out on a date. Now, I knew this potentially broke my rule about dating local men; however, as he lived out of town, I thought the rules could be bent. Dave arrived in his unregistered Ute, and after an enjoyable evening, he dropped me off at home, where he politely asked if he could kiss me goodnight. I was not accustomed to this type of gentlemanly country charm and replied, 'Yes.' He leaned down and kissed me softly on the cheek. This seared my face like a brand on a heifer, he won me there and then.

Dave later said he fell for me at the bar at the Enngonia races when he discovered I had a Smith and Weston .38 pistol in my handbag. We officially started dating, and Dave got his Ute registered. Dave was a true bushman with a quick-witted sense of humour, and we thoroughly enjoyed each other's company. He was the perfect distraction from the stress of work.

Dave's parents lived on one of the three properties his family owned, and Dave invited me for a visit. While there, Dave told me we had a job to do. A steer had wire caught around its leg, and we had to remove it. Dave's dad chased down the steer with his vehicle, while Dave stood in the back. As we got close, Dave roped it, jumped off the ute, and pulled it down. I thought to myself, 'Gosh, he's a real cowboy!' Dave and his dad dealt with the wire, and I was handed the rope that was still attached to the steer's neck. As I held the rope and watched, I took some photos with my little film camera. As Dave dug in to cut the wire wrapped tightly around the steer's swollen leg, it violently flung its head back, hitting my leg and knocking me backwards into a patch of burs. Embarrassed, I jumped up and assured Dave and his dad that I was okay. Afterwards, in the privacy of Dave's bedroom, I burst into tears. The pain in my leg was intense. I asked Dave for some ice, and he returned with a frozen leg of lamb. I was thinking frozen peas would have been better. The pain was so bad I had to leave, so I drove myself hours back to town, feeling every bump and jerk along the way, and went straight to the hospital. I had a fracture, and I spent the following weeks juggling work while on crutches. Despite my unpleasant first experience, I continued to visit when it was possible.

Dave's family owned a 172 Cessna plane, and Dave had his pilot's licence, which he qualified for before he could legally drive a car. He took me for a flight, giving me God's view of the expansive and beautiful landscape. On the ground, I followed Dave around the properties like a sheepdog, and with my limited skills, helped where I could. At night, we would sit on the roof of his farm ute under the canvas of stars and shoot feral pigs as they approached stock troughs. Not a typical courtship, but parts of it were romantic. When I was often 'on call', and couldn't leave town, Dave would drive into town and spend the weekend with me. Through the week, Dave would shoot feral pigs, putting them in a cool room, and then on Fridays, he would arrive at Bourke and sell the carcasses to the chiller before staying the night. The next day, he would get his food supplies and head back to the property to work.

One Friday afternoon, Dave arrived at the police station as my shift was due to finish. Uniformed police called for urgent assistance, so I left Dave standing in the foyer as I jumped into a police car and rushed to assist officers dealing with a large group of aggressive males throwing bottles and fighting. While standing amongst this angry group, I happened to glance to my right to see Dave, who had apparently decided to 'back me up'. He drove past in his ute, very slowly, before turning and driving back again. It reminded me of a scene from the 2008 film, *Grand Torino*. One Christmas day, I was on call and could not leave town, so Dave and I had a quiet Christmas day together in Bourke. That evening, I received a phone call, all police were recalled to duty due to a large brawl. A concerned Dave sat on the front porch as I left the house wearing my Merry Christmas t-shirt. When I returned hours later, he was still sitting in the same spot, he wrapped his strong arms around me. Being an old-fashioned country guy, he found it difficult watching his girlfriend leave him to attend violent incidences.

I read once that for countrymen, a weekend at a rural agricultural show can be compared to a romantic getaway. I agree! At the yearly Bourke Agricultural Show, David introduced me to one of his closest friends, Jamie. We all enjoyed the evening around the bar. Only a few weeks later, I arrived at work and was told there had been a car fatality on the Mitchell Highway between Bourke and Nyngan. It was Jamie. I phoned Dave and had great difficulty breaking this devastating news to him. I supported Dave at the funeral, which was unbelievably sad, as this was the third young son the family had lost in dreadful circumstances.

I was involved in the investigation of the tragic drowning of an eight-year-old girl. This young girl had often visited me at the police station, and I would buy her chips and gravy. As she ate, we talked, and I encouraged her to become a policewoman when she got older. It was a difficult investigation as most of the witnesses were young children. Later I received a file to note; the Deputy State Coroner had commended the police investigation, along with the support I gave to the young, traumatised witnesses at the coroner's court. Many police jobs are mentally difficult to deal with, which was amplified when I knew the people involved. I was fortunate that I could phone my twin and receive therapy. She understood.

My boss Bobby sadly finished his tenure at Bourke, but he was replaced by Craig, a detective I had worked with in the drug squad in Sydney. Soon after, Dave and I decided to drive to Dubbo to celebrate my birthday out of town. That weekend, over a candlelit dinner, Dave nervously proposed. Dave was my best friend. I loved him as equally as I loved my twin, and although our lives were like peas and carrots, I knew we could somehow make it work. Later, Dave told me he had used the feral pig money to pay for the engagement ring. I laughed, as my father had broken in horses to pay for my mother's ring. Dave and I happily started to plan our wedding for the following April.

I headed to Goulburn for the final phase of the negotiator's course. Soon after returning to Bourke, I received my first call out as a negotiator; a man in Dubbo had barricaded himself inside a house with two female hostages. Negotiators work as a team and come together from all over the state when needed. We worked alongside the State Protection Group, the policemen who wear black. The siege continued for two days, with both hostages eventually released safely and the offender arrested. Later, all police who attended that incident were awarded a NSW Police Deputy Commissioners Commendation. It was an honour to receive it.

Another detective position opened at Bourke, and was filled by plainclothes constable Frank. With our large workload, having four staff in the detectives' office helped immensely. In 2025, the Bourke Detectives Office staff consisted of two detective sergeants, five detectives, two rural crime Detectives and a separately staffed Child Abuse Investigation Unit. These staff numbers would have made a huge difference.

We received a job; a man had been shot near Fords Bridge. We headed to the property to find nine men, one with a close-range shotgun wound to the abdomen. We assisted the ambulance staff, and the critically ill victim was rushed to Bourke Hospital, but he died shortly afterwards. We were left to interview eight distraught men who spoke very poor English. It appeared the group was visiting from interstate and had been hunting. The victim had shot a goat but had not killed it. To save using an extra bullet, he turned the firearm around and used the butt of the shotgun to hit the goat over the head, and in doing so, the firearm discharged, shooting him at very close range. An autopsy was conducted, and the results baffled us. There were enough pellets in the man's abdomen for two cartridges, not one. We became suspicious that we had not been told all the facts. After several days of investigating, the full details were finally discovered by scientific police. Apparently, when the accident occurred, the man was wearing a belt holding extra shotgun shells. As the firearm discharged, it hit one of the cartridges on the belt, which also exploded. We were not aware of the belt as it had been removed before police and ambulance initially arrived.

The town of Bourke received a large flood thanks to the mighty Darling River. There were fears the town was going to be entirely isolated on one big island, so emergency plans were prepared. Eventually, the water peaked lower than expected. However, a large volume of water surrounded the town, bringing a plague of massive mosquitoes. I became quite ill and soon discovered I had caught Ross River Fever. Between sickness, the wedding plans, and the abundance of work, I felt physically run down and had a brief stint in hospital to recover. The doctor suggested I take some stress leave.

Unfortunately, we had a death in custody at Brewarrina, and a fatal police shooting at Bourke. In the country, if the police were directly involved in a police shooting, they were transferred out of town overnight. As a result of the shooting, racial tension in the town was high, and all police and their families were threatened. These threats were real and intense and included threats to burn police homes to the ground. Many police officers chose to send their families out of town for several weeks.

As I lived alone, Dave was anxious about my safety and bought a handheld UHF radio to town that I could carry with me when I was off duty. The police station had its own UHF radio base, which was separate from the official police radio equipment. Rather than use a telephone, locals would often call the police for help over the UHF radio. Eventually, countless police were brought to Bourke to support us, some from the city. They were accommodated in motels, and for weeks we could not turn a corner in Bourke without seeing several police officers, on foot, bikes, cars or horses. We appreciated this much-needed assistance and support.

Not only was there tension in the town of Bourke, but only a few months out from our wedding day there was also family tension regarding aspects of our wedding plans. This was not what getting married was about! Dave and I decided to postpone the wedding. Dave left the property and moved into my police home in Bourke. He secured a full-time job as a grader driver for the Bourke Shire Council, and at night and weekends, he studied a Meat Inspector's course.

Late in 1998, Dave and I booked a holiday to Hamilton Island on the Whitsundays in far north Queensland. While we were there, we got married. We had been planning our covert elopement since our initial wedding plans were postponed. Dave and I had driven to Sydney and booked into a motel before heading to the casino. We thought we might win some money and start our marriage in a good financial position. Well, this didn't work out, so we returned to the motel to discover a main water pipe had burst, and there was no water for showers or the loo. Early in the morning, we arrived at the airport, and when we checked in, we were told that someone with the same name had already checked in. Our first thoughts were that our cover had been blown, but we soon discovered it was just another random person who coincidently had the same surname. On the flight, our headsets were faulty, and the hostess forgot our meal.

On our wedding day, we woke to pouring rain. I went to a hair salon, and as my hair was being styled, Dave phoned me. I had a poignant moment. This was the first significant life event that I had not shared with my twin, and I felt sad that she was not with me. A few minutes later Dave came walking backwards into the salon holding a bottle of champagne, which he passed to the hairdresser. He slipped back out without looking at me, much to the amusement of a lady sitting with rollers in her hair. I explained we were about to elope, and she excitedly shared the bottle of champagne with me; actually, she had one glass, and I drank the rest. She kindly asked would I mind if she popped by the church to have a look.

I was collected in a bridal car and driven to the All Saints Chapel, a tiny white church high on a hill overlooking the ocean. As I started to walk down the aisle towards Dave, who was nervously standing at the altar, I spotted my new friend from the hairdresser dressed in her finest, complete with pearls, sitting in the front row with her husband. So, to the sound of the Randy Travis song, I'll Love You for Ever and Ever Amen, with the rain falling heavily on the chapel roof, Dave and I finally and officially became husband and wife in front of two complete smiling strangers.

We arrived back in Bourke; however, we did not disclose our elopement to anyone as Jacki was away holidaying at the time. We wished to tell all immediate family members on the same day. Our marriage felt quite surreal! Several weeks later, we decided that we would finally phone our immediate family and tell them our happy news. My first call was to Jacki. She answered, but before I could say anything further, she abruptly replied, 'I'm too busy to talk,' and hung up. She did have small children, so I mentally excused her. Next, Dave phoned his parents, but they genuinely thought he was joking and moved on to more serious cattle talk. Our announcements weren't going well. We continued the phone calls to other family members with a little more success. After hours of the phone being engaged, my twin got through to me. Through the family grapevine, she had received an excited telephone call and realised perhaps, busy or not, she should have asked what I wanted before hanging up. Soon, our elopement was big news around town and made the local newspaper. That Christmas our family held a surprise wedding celebration for us. Dave was almost finished his course when he successfully applied for a job at Taree Abattoirs. He moved to Taree, and I applied for a transfer and waited. After several months, I was offered a transfer to Forster Detectives, which would take effect several months later. Soon, we would be back together, living near the beach, and I would only be a few hours' drive from my twin.

While waiting for my transfer date, work continued, and tensions in Bourke exploded again. There was another large riot, and many business properties were damaged. Over nine days, we arrested thirty-four people for numerous offences. Due to official crime statistics and the recent unrest, Bourke was labelled in the media as 'The Most Dangerous Town in The World'. I think this was somewhat exaggerated; however, from a police point of view, things were pretty tough. Over several months, we tried new approaches, and finally, it felt like we were getting a handle on the crime wave. The Bourke community had some great people, and most residents just wanted to live their lives safely.

There is a country song, A Bushman Can't Survive in City Lights, and after several months, it was obvious Dave wasn't surviving living over in Taree. I did not want Dave to be unhappy, and although this would impact my transfer, I suggested he move back. I cancelled my dream transfer and wasn't quite sure how we would make things work to create a happy result for us both. David's parents had recently bought a fourth property, and they wanted him to return, and move there to live.

Due to my initial transfer application, my position at the detectives' office had already been advertised and filled, which meant I had lost my position. At first, I was disappointed, but I was offered a new role as a Community Safety Officer. When I thought about it, this job was appealing; the hours were only Monday to Friday, 8 am to 4.30 pm, no on-call obligations and very little overtime. I had been at Bourke for four and a half years and had had more than my fair share of country detective experience. I was burnt out!

I accepted the job. This was a uniform position, and I hadn't worn a police uniform in nine years. I was excited to be issued with a new style police leather jacket to replace my old mothball-smelling Antron jacket, and received comfortable female police trousers, no more culottes or Coltex swede blue stockings. The police school shoes had been replaced with practical boots. Dave and I returned to our weekend visits.

I enjoyed my new role and the change of pace and considered applying for a promotion. Some months later, we were very excited when I discovered I was pregnant. Dave was like a proud emu, saying he wanted at least four kids. My time back in a police uniform was brief. As my abdomen expanded, I was soon back in plain clothes, but this time, they were maternity clothes. Dave wanted me to live with him on one of his family's properties, but for many reasons, this was a major decision for me. The property was too far from town to allow me to continue working, and I did not want to give up my financial independence, but I also wanted to live full-time with my husband and be a family. He had given it a go, living my town life, but I hadn't tried living his. Could a town person survive with no city lights? I wasn't sure. We agreed I would move out to the property when our baby was born, and after all my eligible leave was exhausted, re-evaluate things.

Dave's parents brought a new home to be erected on the recently purchased property. A kit-style home that resembled a Meccano set arrived, and construction commenced. I continued working and concentrated on looking after myself and our unborn baby, who was due early in the new millennium.

Reef

Scott was feeling restless, and he told me that he might apply for an advertised position at the North Region Drug Squad based in Coffs Harbour. I amused him and told him I didn't mind. Hundreds of police would apply as being on the north coast was a sought-after position. I didn't think he had a hope in hell of getting the position and didn't think too much more about it; after all, I was coping with the birth of our first child. Six weeks after her birth, Scott came home from work and told me he had won the transfer. This put me in a difficult position as I was still attached to the Parramatta Detectives. I had been approved to work at the detectives' office on a part-time basis after the completion of my maternity leave. All I could do was hope I would get transferred to Coffs Harbour on compassionate grounds.

I was sad to leave my work colleagues as I had really enjoyed working in the office, but I looked at it as an adventure. I was hesitant to leave our friends and family who lived not far from us. They would all have been invaluable support with our new baby. I was a nervous first-time mother and had the support of my friend from school, who was the nanny. She gave great non-judgemental support, and at the time, I didn't understand how much I would miss this support and was quite naïve about the whole move. Within weeks, with a now ten-week-old baby, we packed up our house and two dogs and moved to Coffs Harbour.

Scott had travelled to Coffs earlier and found us somewhere to live. The house was on two acres in the rural suburb of Bonville. When we arrived at the house, we discovered there hadn't been a telephone connected and this isolated me from the only support I had. It took quite a few months for us to get one connected. Scott travelled up and down the coast with the drug squad and would be away for days, working out in the bush looking for drug crops. I remember many days when I would drive the few kilometres to a phone booth with my tiny baby and ring anyone who was up for a chat. Having just left full-time work and becoming a mother for the first time was already a huge adjustment. I was very lonely in the early days, and the person I missed most was my twin sister.

I strongly felt that I wanted our daughter baptised, and Scott didn't care less either way as he has always been agnostic. I wanted our daughter raised with Christian values and was adamant that she would attend a Christian school one day. Scott and I both were baptised Anglican, and I was aware that with our jobs, we could be transferred anywhere in the state, and I wanted consistency for my child. I knew the Catholic Education System had far more schools scattered in most towns and cities in New South Wales than the Anglican Church. After communicating with a few priests, I found a deacon who was also a police chaplain who was prepared to baptise our daughter with my promise that I would also convert to Catholicism. I had always had a strong faith, as has Kylie, and we were raised with Christian values even though we hadn't attended church regularly for many years. It is widely agreed that religion has biological foundations and that faith is influenced by genetics. Interestingly, our sisters do not have the same conviction in faith as Kylie and me, even though we were raised in the same environment.

When we moved to Coffs Harbour, I made good on my promise and commenced my Rite of Christian Initiation for adults to learn about the Catholic faith. The course was conducted over twelve months in a group, so I would have a social framework for assimilating the experience. Our participants met at my house each week as I was the only person with a young baby. The group were a delightful assembly of people of all age ranges, and a few had just recently moved to Australia from countries all over the world. We each had a support person allocated by the church, and as luck would have it, I was given the local magistrate's wife. For years, I was involved in the local Catholic community, teaching children about their sacraments and assisting with church functions like altar servers' picnics.

I would attend church weekly on a Saturday night, and Scott would attend his own 'church', the local pub. We would meet up with him afterwards and have dinner at a pre-arranged venue in Sawtell. One evening, I was sitting towards the rear of the church when, during the priest's homily, Scott walked into the church through the side door. Most of the families attending mass from our small school recognised Scott and turned to give me pleasant smiles and nods of approval, shocked at the sight of my husband attending mass. They all knew his opinion on religion. As he walked into the church, the priest kept speaking but looked up at my husband, and my devoted husband gave the priest a two-finger wave; this was not normal church etiquette. Everyone seated in the rear of the church watched and reacted with stifled laughter. I ignored this, straightened myself, sat up tall, and was as proud as punch as my husband sat next to me in the pew. My fellow parishioners shuffled along to fit the new Christian in. Scott then whispered to me, 'The pubs too busy. We will meet at the bowling club.' And just like that, he stood up and walked back out of the church through the same side door while giving the priest another wave goodbye. I shrank with embarrassment as my neighbours continued to silently laugh, and even the priest gave a little smirk.

Over the years, I have started to feel I don't need to belong to any particular organised religion, and I believe there are aspects of quite a few religions that support my faith. I believe in God and sit comfortably in a Catholic church, but I sit equally as comfortably inside 'any' church and even feel God when I am amongst nature. I have always tried to move through life with the values of kindness and compassion. There are a lot of people who never step foot inside a church that live with Christian values without even knowing it, my husband being one of them.

After what felt like a lifetime, Kylie managed a visit, and we played tricks on my baby. Our daughter was going through a clingy stage where she only wanted me. My mum was also visiting, and my daughter would cry if my mum held her. I would send Kylie into my baby's room without me, and my daughter would give her the biggest smile and hold her arms out to be held, obviously thinking it was me. I would walk in afterwards and she would keep looking at my twin, and then me, trying to work out what was going on. It was free entertainment that my daughter may require therapy for in the future.

After living at Coffs Harbour for some time, I was eventually transferred to Coffs Harbour on compassionate grounds, but could only secure a position in general duties and was the first female working part-time in general duties out on the road. There was one other police woman, who had given birth just prior to me, and had also started working part-time, but she had been working in an office position prior to her child's birth and would be returning to the same position. I hoped that after some time, I could apply for a detective's job when there was a vacancy. I found a wonderful babysitter, but on my first day of work, I cried the entire drive to the police station, guilt-ridden at leaving my four-month-old baby. I knew I would be a better mother working, and was keen to remain independent and not reliant on my husband. We also needed the extra income. On arrival at the station, I was called into the boss's office. After a few pleasantries, he said to me, 'I think it is in everyone's best interest if you remain in station duty.' I was stunned at his suggestion and suddenly felt my breasts have a 'let down' from the shock. I could feel my breast milk starting to leak. There was nothing I could do. I thought with time, he would come around, and I would just have to be patient. At that moment, I just wanted to get out of his office as I felt two wet patches on my freshly ironed Police shirt.

I had been the go-to girl at Parramatta Detectives if someone had an issue with computers and could work my way around one pretty easily. In the short time I was on maternity leave, a new computer program had been introduced. I walked into the station and looked like an incompetent fool as I couldn't even enter a simple job like a lost wallet. No training was offered to me at all, and I had to fumble my way through. There was some animosity among the ranks with my quick transfer to Coffs Harbour, and they had no idea how to deal with a part-time police officer. It didn't help things when a few days later, one of the police officers, who used to work for my father in his pool business, walked into the station and recognised me. He came straight over to say hi. I hadn't seen him for about fifteen years, and he happened to be the area commander. He was a superintendent, which is quite a high rank. Most of the lower ranks in the police have a love-hate relationship with the commissioned officers, inspectors and above. It didn't help that he promptly landed a kiss on my cheek and told everyone in the station that he knew me when I used to run around in my underwear. He left out the fact that I was about eight at the time. I knew I was being watched with suspicion.

After some months just watching and keeping my mouth shut, I understood very quickly why, during this period, the Coffs Harbour Detectives had a reputation for being a 'boys club'. The office had never had a female detective work there, which was so unusual for me after working in Sydney. I discovered there were other policewomen who also were fully qualified Detectives still working in uniform. Some of the women had applied for the detectives when there was a vacancy and had not been successful. The position was given to a male who required full training, which would take many months and at a cost to the station. At this stage,

I wasn't too concerned about getting into detectives. I would have been happy just being allowed to go out on the road and work on a police truck. In the two years I worked at Coffs Harbour, I worked on a car crew twice and was kept in the station the rest of the time. Officers on general duties usually do both jobs unless they have a specific reason not to, like an injury. I considered my confinement a complete waste of resources.

We had been at Coffs Harbour for twelve months, and my husband transferred from the North Drug Squad to the detective's office at Coffs Harbour. I knew they now would use this as a reason not to let me transfer there, as the conservative staff wouldn't want a husband and wife working together in the same small office.

On one particular shift, I came into the police station, and the duty sergeant told me that I was working on the car crew. I tried to contain my excitement that I would now be able to show some of my policing ability and walked out to the police truck, where I found I was working with a female officer. I was stunned, as I had never seen two females work together at 'this' station. We had only driven one block when we received a call over the radio to return to the station. We walked back in, and the sergeant was in a panic as he had just realised two females were working together. I was pulled off the truck and had to work station duty. Again! I couldn't believe it, and tears welled up in my eyes. I had come from Sydney, where we were always treated as a unit and not by our sex. I was getting very disillusioned with the station.

We were making friends in the town, and Scott signed up to play football with the Sawtell Rugby League Club. I went along to the games and met the wives, and we all had young children about the same age. The wives then formed an indoor netball team. I had never played netball, and the girls worked out quickly that it was better to put me in the position of centre, as I went all over the court anyway. The women then decided we would all take our babies to playgroup. I was concerned I was going to meet a boring bunch of women who just wanted to talk about their children, but I was surprised to find a diverse group of ladies who had all sorts of careers. They gave me the stimulation and support I needed. I also met an ex-policewoman who had resigned after being equally disillusioned with the Coffs Harbour Police Station. I finally felt I had an ally.

Fifteen months after the birth of our first daughter, I fell pregnant with our second daughter. I wasn't making friends with management at the station. Being pregnant in general duties automatically confined me to station duties. I accepted this.

My netball team and playgroup friends decided we would form a babysitting club. Basically, we earned one point for every fifteen minutes we babysat, with double points earned after midnight and during 'happy hour', meals and bath times. No money was exchanged, and we were able to go out regularly knowing that our children were safe, and it didn't cost us a cent in childcare. The babysitting club ended up having weekends away together, regularly booking cabins at idyllic locations up and down the north coast. We had ten families and about twenty-eight kids. We bred well. Not one of us had family living close by, so we became each other's family. The children are all grown up now, but the parents still get together regularly. If we are lucky, our now adult children and their children join us as well. The support and friendship I received from the babysitters club was invaluable.

My maternity leave was running out, and I made the heart-wrenching decision to resign from the police. We loved living at Coffs Harbour, and we didn't want to move again. But I was very unhappy at the station and couldn't see anything changing on my return from my second daughter's maternity leave. I was sick in the stomach with the thought of having to return to work only to remain on station duties again for another two years while working part-time. I was dreadfully disappointed that I wouldn't get more opportunity to learn from the senior police, particularly the detectives, and felt that I had a lot of experience I could have offered to the station.

I made an appointment to see the patrol commander, the boss of the station, and told him I was resigning. I can't remember what he said, but I can remember what he didn't say. He didn't ask why I wanted to resign. He made no attempt to try to persuade me to stay or care that the police department had invested thousands of dollars in training me. He didn't ask if I wanted more time to think it over or check on my mental health or postpartum health. He didn't suggest any ways we could make the job work. The entire process took less than five minutes. They had worn me down. They won!

— **Multitasking** —

Beef

On a hot January day, two weeks early, my contractions started, and Dave unnecessarily sped to town. Twenty-six hours later, after a slight mishap where my amniotic waters broke all over Dave, we became proud parents to a little girl who we named Isabella. I was extremely grateful to have had only a single birth, and no twins! With genuine country hospitality, the small Bourke hospital staff provided Dave with meals and put me in a room with two beds, one for each of us. Five days later, all 'three' of us were discharged from the hospital, and we returned to my police house.

Finishing the house build at the property was now a priority, as not only did we wish to live as a family, but there had been heavy rains up north, falling in the Warrego catchment, and a large flood was expected in the following weeks. After twenty-four hours bonding with tiny Bella, Dave reluctantly returned to the property, while I started some packing. After a week alone, my mother arrived, and I was thankful for her help and company. Together, we drove out to the property so Dave could see his daughter, and I could see the new build, for only the second time. The new home sat adjacent to the original historic homestead; a pise home constructed in 1893. Walking through its ghostly rooms, I thought, if the walls could talk, what would they tell me?

My mother left and I was back alone with Bella. Bella was a very unsettled baby and appeared to be in pain. She slept no longer than twenty minutes at a time. Any effort at packing for the impending move was difficult, as I was constantly trying to soothe her miserable cries. I was getting very little sleep and was an exhausted zombie. My eldest and younger sisters, both experienced mothers, kindly left their own families and arrived at Bourke to help me for a weekend. I was relieved and grateful to see them, and they soon sent me to bed to get some much-needed sleep while they took full responsibility for Bella. After making up beds for themselves in the lounge room, they closed the door and confidently prepared for a slumber party with their new niece. Bella's baby book reads, 'First sleepover, you were a little bitch.' Months later, we discovered Bella was lactose intolerant, and with a change in diet, she was soon a 'normal' baby.

Finally, the house was finished; well, it wasn't exactly finished, but we could certainly move in. Dave came to town, and in between cuddles with Bella, he loaded most of my packed boxes and furniture and returned to the property. I was to follow in my car the next day with the last of my belongings. Overnight, torrential rain fell. With ninety percent of my furniture gone and the unsealed road to the property now closed, I felt tired and beaten. With Bella, I drove four hours in the opposite direction to Dubbo, to my younger sister's home. After an unsettled but restful week, the rain finally stopped, and the roads dried. The expected flood had arrived, but the road was still passable, however the water was rising, and soon, the Warrego River water would cut the road. Dave and I rendezvoused in Bourke at my almost empty home. Grateful to be back together, we placed the bed mattress on the floor of the empty room, and as we dozed off, I thought that my last night in Bourke was just like my first. However, this time, I had a gorgeous husband next to me, and a precious baby sandwiched between us.

We woke to more rain! Seriously frustrated, Dave said, 'Let's just go.' After quickly phoning my twin and buying food and baby supplies, I tentatively followed Dave's ute west out of town. Inexperienced at driving on a wet, unsealed road, I struggled to keep the car and trailer on the road and avoid getting bogged. As the mud flicked up and the loaded vehicle slipped left and right, I slowly followed my husband's muddy tracks as John Denver and I sang *Sunshine on My Shoulders*. We finally arrived at the river, only thirty kilometres from the property entrance, but due to the relentless rain, the water had risen quicker than expected, cutting access to the main road completely. We were now forced to take a much longer alternative muddy route, and I prayed that road was still passable. Six-week-old Bella was hungry and crying, and I had no way to warm a bottle for her. What should have taken two hours took eight. Finally, at 1 am, with relief and a little apprehension, I bumped over the stock grid and followed Dave's taillights through the property entrance. As I weaved along the entrance, fringed with tall mulga trees, I thought after eighteen months of marriage, we were now together as a family. The distance between my twin and me continued to expand.

We still had no flooring, blinds, or air-conditioning. A satellite dish was yet to be installed to allow the TV to work, and we could not get a commercial radio signal in the house. A telephone was not yet connected, and there was no mobile service or internet back then. Many station homes had UHF radios to communicate, but we didn't even have one of those. As a concerned first-time mum, I was acutely aware that we had no means of communication if there was an illness or accident. The world literally could have ended, and we would have been oblivious. Our closest neighbour was a half-hour car drive away, and each night, as I dozed off to sleep listening to the sound of frogs croaking, I felt dreadfully isolated.

Within days, I had all the mud-splattered boxes unpacked and the inside of the house comfortably set up. With that job completed, I sat and nursed Bella, staring at her endearing face while I listened to flocks of chattering cockatoos fly by. I discovered that bushmen are never home before dark. I would have to share him with the land. David's parents owned four properties, and much of the work seemed to be done at the other three. The summer temperature rarely went below forty degrees, often reaching the maximum on the temperature gauge, fifty degrees. Our water came from an underground bore, and when the cold water came out of the tap, it was hotter than the hot water. I had to run a bath for Bella in the middle of the day so that it had several hours to cool. We had no close line, so I strung the washing over the wire fence. There was no lawn or house verandah, and preventing mud from entering the home was a challenge.

The mailbox was seven kilometres from the house. I learned that the mail truck arrived twice a week, on Wednesdays and Saturdays, and the mailman, for a fee, would bring not only our mail but any other essential items we needed from town. The only problem was we needed a phone to order these items. If it rained and the roads were closed, there was no mail delivery, and we went without. I would have to buy baby formula in batches of six or eight cans at a time. One weekly item delivered was The Land newspaper, which I understood was Dave's version of the bible.

Each evening, after a simple meal, we would settle on the couch. Although we couldn't watch free-to-air TV, I did own a VHS recorder; however, we only had two VHS tapes, our wedding video and the movie Titanic. Every single night, I nursed Bella while Dave and I watched Jack and Rose. I genuinely thought Bella's first words would be, 'I'm the king of the world.' Finally, our telephone was connected. The first phone call I made was to Jacki. It was the longest we had gone without speaking, and it was an enjoyable, lengthy catch-up.

The La Nina weather pattern continued, and there were countless violent storms. Our windows were still bare, so many nights we silently watched magnificent lightning flashes shooting through the sky as the storms rumbled past, the thunder musically rolling off the nearby hills. Some of these storms resulted in lengthy blackouts, which was a problem as we didn't have a generator. The only way I could warm Bella's bottle was to start the BBQ and boil water in a billy. At 3 am, this process wasn't fun. Soon, Bella's bottles became known as billy bottles.

Weeks after arriving, it was shearing time, and Dave's parents decided the shearers would stay in the original historic homestead next to our house. This meant I would have to cook breakfast and dinner for the shearing team. With a newborn baby, I found it easier to have the shearers eat in my home rather than I go to them. On the first night, the entire team was seated around my dining table. I was washing up when one of the shearers with a smile on his face said, 'You know him, Kylie, don't you?' indicating another shearer seated at the table.

I grinned and said, 'Yes.'

He replied, 'How?'

I said, 'How is between me and him.'

All the shearers burst out laughing. The last time I served him a meal, he was in a prison cell. My life was shifting in ways I had never expected.

The deadly snakes were active and out in numbers, so at first, I was hesitant to leave the house unless Dave was home. Eventually, feeling locked in, I started to venture outdoors, and pushing Bella in the pram, went for short walks. As my confidence grew, I walked further, but often, the pram got bogged, either in mud or sandy soil, or it got a flat tyre from the burs. Later, I replace my beautiful pram with a much more robust 4WD style pram with solid-filled tyres. One day, while pushing the pram, I walked past a trailer with four sheep in it, and I stopped to show Bella. That night, I asked Dave about the sheep. He casually replied, 'Oh, they're killers.' I love meat, but I could not look a sheep in the eye and eat it later; I would rather it just appear in the freezer, preferably with a pink stamp. The next day, when Dave was away working, I opened the trailer cage and watched as the sheep scattered to the wind. Later, Dave came home and was about to do the deed when I confessed that I had set them free. Sheep meat continued to appear in the freezer; we just didn't discuss it.

Soon, boredom set in. If possible, I would jump in the dusty farm ute and nursing Bella go to work with Dave. I learned that a good bra was essential to travel on the network of rough farm roads. Dave asked me if I could help him jump-start his old Mercedes Benz prime mover, which had a flat battery. Eagar, to be of use, I sat in the old Toyota ute and laid Bella safely on the passenger's seat. Dave hooked up the tow rope and climbed into the cabin of the large truck. I started the ute and eased it forward until I could feel the slack on the rope stiffen, before I put increased pressure on the accelerator and felt the weight of the large semi start to move behind me. I increased my speed, and soon I heard the truck's engine kick in, its big motor revving at my rear, so I stopped. Suddenly, there was a violent bang at the rear, and the ute, which forcibly jerked forward before the rope stiffened again and jerked the ute backward, before the ute finally stopped when it hit the now-stopped truck.

Suffering whiplash, I quickly scooped up Bella, who had been brutally thrown off the seat and was now lying face down, screaming on the car floor mat. Thankfully, Bella was not seriously harmed. Dave had failed to tell me the ancient truck didn't have brakes, and I was supposed to keep rolling slowly forward until the truck stopped. Over the years, I have recognised that Dave's instructions are always limited; he just presumes I understand the rest. I wasn't sure I was happy with my new unqualified Jillaroo role.

I made contact with a caring neighbour, Cheryl, who lived an hour's drive away. She had two young children and was generous with advice and information. She told me about the Royal Flying Doctor Medical Clinics (RFDS) held at the small Queensland town of Hungerford, sixty kilometres further west. The RFDS was established in 1928 by Reverend John Flynn. It is an air medical service that provides emergency and primary health care to people in rural and remote Australia. The RFDS could be phoned in emergencies and held monthly clinics at various locations. Cheryl also told me about the Bush Children's Mobile Playgroup, which was often held on the same day as the RFDS clinics. Three experienced bush ladies who lived on nearby properties, Iris, Norah, and Elaine, phoned me and welcomed me to the district. All three had raised children on the land, and they were full of helpful information and country wisdom. Norah would often say comments like, 'In my day, Kylie, we didn't have fridges,' or 'In my day, Kylie, we didn't have air-conditioning.'

Quite frankly, I was happy to be living in the present day. I wanted every luxury I could get and gratefully let the older generation win the hard life award. Norah and Iris convinced me to become a member of the Country Women's Association (CWA), I laughed, remembering my parents met at a CWA dance. The ladies also convinced me to join the small local Bush Fire Brigade. However, I didn't give a thought to the fact that one day, I might actually have to fight a fire. Over the past twenty years, I have helped fight several fires, some of which were on our property.

I attended my first RFDS clinic, followed by a mobile playgroup. I was very fortunate that, at the time, many young families lived within a seventy-kilometres radius of Hungerford. The ladies were all very welcoming. Some had always lived here, but some, like me, had given up careers to move to the bush. There was a large group of young children, and Bella happily watched them. One lady was fortunate to have fraternal twins who had been born after successful IVF treatment. After the RFDS clinic and playgroup, I learned that all the women headed to the one pub in town for afternoon refreshments, which often lasted into the evening. For most, this monthly tradition was our only face-to-face contact with other women, and a visit to Hungerford became my monthly ritual.

After six months, all my leave entitlements were finished, and we had to make the enormous decision of whether I should return to work or resign. I knew this decision would shape my future. I was concerned about losing my career and financial independence, but I felt fortunate that I would have the opportunity to be a 'sort of' stay-at-home mum. I was reminded of the hardships my parents had endured on our childhood farm and did not want to repeat history. However, I wanted to see my husband daily, not weekly. If only the property was closer to Bourke, I could have both.

With trepidation, I handed in my resignation to the patrol commander, and soon afterwards, I was invited to Bourke for a police farewell. After, as I drove back to the property, I knew that as a police officer, I had been hit, kicked, punched, spat at, risked my life, attended numerous traumatic incidences, worked long irregular hours, missed many family events, and dedicated thirteen years to my career. It was over, just like that. I felt I was just a number!

Now that I would be remaining permanently at the property, I knew if I was not only going to survive but also thrive on the land, I had to learn to be resilient and adapt. I would have to do all my learning on the job. I had another whole new language to learn: weaners, steers, up the wing, strainers, and bore run. I started to ask Dave questions and wanted to learn.

Finally, our flooring was laid, a TV satellite dish was installed, and air conditioning was fitted. I was very grateful for them, but now it was winter, and we didn't have heating. Without heating or blinds, the house was freezing, so we cuddled with Bella on the lounge under blankets at night to keep warm. I watched large numbers of alien-looking bugs attracted to the house lights splatter the glass windows and found it fascinating that a new little swarm of creatures arrived every night. Eventually, Dave and I purchased blinds and a wood heater. At last, I was fortunate to have a very comfortable home.

Dave and I had settled well into our delayed married life, and soon, I had lived on the property for twelve months. Every day rolled into the next, and it was very easy to forget what date or day of the week it was. Once, I spent all day trying to ring a store in Bourke, eventually reporting their phone number as faulty, only to discover later it was a Sunday and the store was closed. Dave's parents bought a fifth and sixth property, and there was even more work to be done! Dave was a typical resourceful bushman and would perform many tasks such as stock work, fencing, laying pipe, welding, installing troughs, mechanical repairs, or grading roads. I learned that the extensive farm rubbish tip was Dave's version of a hardware store. He would often rummage through the tip, looking for an old pipe fitting or other items that could be improvised for some purpose.

Dave and I were excited when we found out we were expecting our second baby. Just prior to the birth, we discovered the baby was in the breech position, and I was told I would have to travel away to give birth. We decided to go to Sydney, where I would have my twin's support (as she had just returned there). Dave had been working hard and was exhausted when we left to start the lengthy drive to Sydney. Three hours into the trip, he collided with not one, but six kangaroos, damaging the headlight, indicators, and panel work. Thankfully, the car was still driveable, and we swapped drivers. Dave slept, while I continued to drive as my swollen belly rubbed the steering wheel, my vision impaired with only one headlight. Many hours later, we stopped at a service station in the Blue Mountains an hour from Sydney, and I took Bella to the bathroom. Bella was just the perfect height to walk under the electric hand dryer, and her movement set it off. She jumped, having no idea what it was, so I demonstrated how it was used, which fascinated her. This reminded me of how isolated our life truly was. Rested, Dave took over driving; however, he was very inexperienced at city driving, and many cars aggressively tooted their car horns at him in frustration. Dave would give the driver a friendly country wave and would joke that they were all just saying 'gidday'. We arrived at a cabin park in Emu Plains, not far from Jacki's home. Bella, only nineteen months old, had had limited contact with other people, but she felt completely comfortable in the company of my twin and her young cousins.

After being wheeled into the theatre, the doctor was soon in deep conversation with Dave, discussing caesareans on sheep. He offered Dave the opportunity to stand up and watch. As I lay hidden by a medical sheet, I thought, 'Hello, don't forget me down here.' Baby Harrison arrived very cold and was quickly taken to the special care nursery. Harry suffered from jaundice but, unlike Bella, had no problems with milk, and my twin shared the breast milk experience with me. Dave certainly would not have coped without my twin's support while I was in the hospital. She was amazing! While I was in Sydney, I reunited with all my police friends and our cousins, Lyn and Joan. Lyn's husband had an executive position with the company Toy World, and they generously brought us boxes and boxes of new toys. Their loving kindness reminded me of how their parents, Kell and Marie, had helped my mother all those years ago.

Soon we climbed into our smashed-up vehicle, and with two small children, shopping, new toys, second-hand clothes from my twin, many farm tools, and a wheelbarrow strapped to the roof, I felt we resembled the Beverly Hillbillies as we left the smog and traffic behind. I was still very sore and tender from the surgery and now had to travel the eleven-hour trip home, painfully feeling every bump along the way. I was envious of mums who lived close to medical facilities.

Once home and often alone, I struggled with the medical advice that would have improved my recovery, such as resting and not lifting anything heavier than my baby. With Dave out in the paddocks, Bella and Harry needed care, the mail needed collecting, washing had to be done, farm animals had to be fed, and I still had to cook every meal. Over the years, there were many times after a long day or during an illness that I wished I could order takeaway, but my waistline has probably thanked me for not being able to do so.

I was slowly adapting to life on a cattle and sheep station, although there was always something new to learn. I had taken for granted the high rainfall and abundant grasses, but since Harry's birth, the clouds appeared to run out of rain. I was about to experience my first drought. The grasses died off, leaving a blank canvas of dirt; the water tanks became small pools of mud, and the dust storms were endless. We were grateful to have some underground water fed from the Great Artesian Basin. Dave, under a lot of pressure to keep the stock alive, spent hours pushing down mulga trees with the bulldozer so starving cattle had something to eat. This is done with careful consideration to the environment, with only small sections knocked over at a time. Mulga regrowth from both seeding and resprouting is vigorous, and revegetation occurs quite quickly.

One day, wanting to be of use, I asked if he could teach me how to drive the bulldozer. As usual, his instructions were limited, I felt like I was driving an Army Tank, but slowly it started rolling forward and I pushed over my first tree. Looking back over my shoulder, I could see Dave and the kids following me in the ute.

Dave was proudly smiling at me, which increased my confidence. Wack! A tree branch hit the side of my head, and I felt blood fall from my ear. I quickly lost interest in the machine and happily let Dave resume the work.

The drought was reported in the media as the one in a 100-year drought; I was happy to have the other ninety-nine years. The dust storms were constant and horrendous and would seep into the home and cover everything with a thin layer of red dirt. I have always had OCD tendencies and was exhausted trying to keep a clean house. With the financial pressures, the heat, the dust, the isolation, and the death, it was hard to stay positive. Each day, as the hot morning sun continued to fill the clear blue sky, I would look at Dave's face and wish I could erase his stress. I would try to lift his spirits, and on other days he would raise mine. I had a little film camera and captured every high and low on the property. I had taken a photo of our windmill, standing in a thick dust storm, with its blades barely visible. I entered it in a photography competition, and I was delighted when I was awarded a small prize. I have a dedicated 'property' photo album, and my photos are a good reminder of how good things can be when times are favourable and vice versa.

Daily life was stressful, and I still wanted to help in some way, so after putting baby car seats in a ute, Dave gave us a job he thought we could manage. Our new job was to put out lick blocks, hard blocks of minerals, along with molasses, a liquid sugar, both of which help starving cattle. We also checked any dams for bogged stock. Once, I spotted a calf sunken to its eyes, with its nostrils protruding above the quicksand-style mud; gasping for air, it was alive. There was no way I had the strength to get it out, so as the kids watched on, I dragged a thick log down the bank, sloshed into the mud, and wedged the log under its chin. I cleared the mud from around its face before rushing to find Dave, who was bulldozing in the next paddock. Dave pulled the weakened calf to safety with a rope and vehicle. I cleaned it and helped it stand. That little fellow survived, but despite every effort, some did not.

Another day, we were all in one vehicle when I spotted a weak cow who had fallen down and was very ill, a black menacing crow pecking her eyes as she lay. I jumped out of the car and sat protecting the cow while Dave returned home to get the gun. I stroked the cow's head as she pitifully looked at me and told her that I was sorry and that we would soon stop her sufferring. A blood-filled tear fell from her eye. I burst into tears, and together we cried. Most graziers care deeply about the environment and the health and well-being of their stock. Without both, there is no income. Shortly afterwards, although not medically confirmed, I know I sadly suffered and early miscarriage.

Jacki and I continued to speak regularly and shared all our news, good and bad. Her life was not without its challenges. As she lived in a high rainfall area, I found it very hard to be sympathetic when she complained that she couldn't dry her washing. How different would our lives and the environment be if we could control the rain-filled clouds? During one of our daily phone conversations, she told me how she had recently been doing canteen duty at her daughter's school and needed to drop something off at the school administration block. As she walked into the building, a group of parents were seated, waiting for new kindergarten interviews. She spotted a man sitting amongst the group, who gave her a stunned look as he watched her pass. As my twin left the building, she suddenly fathomed who it was: my long-lost former love, Ben, looking slightly different with a short haircut. I wonder if he knew it was Jacki or thought it was me? It's a small world. She moved shortly afterwards, so she didn't see him again.

Wildlife naturally stops breeding in drought, and their in-built awareness fascinated me. The only thing that seemed to be breeding in the drought was us, as we were expecting another baby. The daily struggles continued as my waistline expanded. When my labour commenced, I had another unpleasant drive, as we bounced to Bourke on a road that hadn't been graded for some time. I discovered this baby was in the posterior position, and I silently wished for a larger hospital that offered epidurals. At one point, I prayed to God to take me. Finally, I was given a shot of pethidine; the effects are how I imagine heaven will feel. I was told if the baby wasn't born by sunrise, I would have to be flown out to a larger centre by the RFDS for an emergency caesarean. I did not want another caesarean; it was too hard recovering on the property without help. Meanwhile, Bella and Harry, who were being cared for by a visiting relative, became distressed at being away from us. Dave was assured our baby would be a while yet, so he drove the five kilometres to comfort them. In the short time he was away, I gave birth to a gorgeous baby girl, Adelaide, who arrived silently with the umbilical cord around her neck. I anxiously said another silent prayer before I heard her cries. Dave and I were devastated he missed the birth. With three beautiful children under three and a half, I was now never bored, and we soon got into a comfortable routine while property work continued.

At last, the rain came, and I emotionally watched as Dave held Harry into the sky to witness his first sight of rain. I kept watching as Harry finally learnt the joy of jumping in puddles and playing in the mud. Within a short time, the soil was covered with small green sprouts, proof of nature's resilience. The rain also brought lots of deadly snakes, with twenty-six browns visiting the house yard over one summer. I had to watch our small children constantly. For the next several years we appreciated some good weather patterns, and with green grass, full dams, and fat cattle, we decided to slip off to sunny Queensland for a much-needed holiday. Our sheltered bush kids were amazed as we explored the tourist areas, and I was stunned when Bella asked what the lights on the sticks were; she was referring to streetlights.

With things improving, I occasionally packed the kids up and drove 550 kilometres to Dubbo for specialist medical appointments or to meet with the accountant. My father was living in Dubbo, so I would always visit. Despite his behaviour in my teenage years, I still loved him and wanted my children to have some memories of their Poppy. I was grateful that my younger sister always provided a bed and good company. In only two or three days, I would do six months' worth of shopping, not only for clothing for my growing children, but also for pipe fittings, mechanical parts, garden hoses and groceries. I always shopped like a doomsday prepper, as I was never sure when I would be back near a supermarket. It was tricky with three small children in tow. Once, I had a bad pap smear result and was referred to a gynaecologist. I was lying with my legs in the air, the doctor saying, 'Now just relax,' as I rocked Adelaide in the pram with one hand and held Harry's hand with the other.

Bella hung onto the pram.

Although we live in different environments, Jacki and I had many identical medical complaints. Once, Jacki and I coincidently had mammograms days apart, where we were both notified of suspicious lumps. Within two weeks Jacki had an appointment arranged for her, at a special clinic for six to eight call-back patients. She was met by a counsellor, and then taken into a room for a second mammogram, which was immediately followed by an ultrasound. The counsellor instantly discussed her negative result.

I received a phone call from the doctor before I had to book myself in for an ultrasound appointment, which was to be four weeks later, in Dubbo. While waiting, my anxiety levels were on overdrive, and I even started telling Dave my final wishes. I thought of my maternal grandmother's premature death. Finally, I travelled hours away and walked into a very clinical waiting room before having an ultrasound. Afterwards, I was told I would need a biopsy, so I went to another clinical-looking room, waiting some time before a stressed doctor with no bedside manner rushed in. He was frustrated when, after several painful jabs with the needle, he was struggling to get a sample and said, 'I think I got it,' before rushing back out. Upset, I drove all the way home and had to wait another nerve-wracking week before I was finally given the all-clear.

There have been occasions when I have been unable to get a medical appointment to have stitches removed, so I have sat in our local vet clinic, surrounded by my fellow patients barking and meowing around me, while my girlfriend, Charlotte, a vet, removed them. Medical care in the bush is not equal.

For me, it had taken time to adjust to station life; however, our children knew no different; life on the land was their world. All three of my children were best mates. If I went out working with Dave, all three kids would be involved or close by, creating their own healthy fun. My children were my companions and friends, and we did just about everything together. We worked or explored the property, and they learned about the environment. Living remotely, they did miss out on some things, but they also gained so much. I was grateful to have shared every day of their young lives with them, and now it was time they learned some more.

The distance between home and school was too great to enable our children to attend mainstream schooling. Over the next several years, our three children were enrolled in Distance Education (DE), also known as School of the Air, or School by Correspondence. Through the biggest school in the state, students complete an identical school curriculum to their peers in normal schools; they just had to do it from home. Distance Education is not home schooling, where there is more flexibility regarding what and how the children learn. Distance Education replaced the Blackfriars Correspondence school that my mother had undergone for a short time as a child. Dave had also undergone several years of correspondence school in his early years before he attended a Catholic boarding school in Sydney.

When a child is enrolled in Distance Education, the student is allocated a teacher, and the student's schoolwork is posted out in bulk once a term in big green bags. Each school day I would be required to teach the kids, and at the end of the week post their work back to the school centre. The students also had to record some activities on a tape recorder, which was returned with the schoolwork. The allocated schoolteacher then marked the work before returning the schoolwork in the post. I was provided with a computer, and the students had to do several lessons a week with their class teacher over satellite. The computer system had just replaced an old-school radio system. Through the computer, the student was able to see their teacher. Satellite lessons are comparable to the now popular Zoom lessons.

If property work such as mustering or shearing was on, if the children were sick, away for school-related activities, or if we had to attend medical or business appointments, the kids were required to catch up on their schoolwork over the weekends or at night. My children were enrolled in the Bourke Walgett Distance Education Centre. At the time, roughly thirty students were enrolled at our centre, including two sets of unidentical twins. I was now an unqualified teacher.

Reef

I had resigned from the Police, but my husband was still working in 'the job', so I still felt connected to the Police in a weird way. While at home caring for our children one day, my husband unexpectedly arrived home covered in blood. Scott told me, after a phone call from the distressed officer was received at the station, he and another policeman had raced to the house, but when they arrived, he had already shot himself with his police gun. He was still alive but very sadly died shortly after. His suicide impacted our home life, as suicide does in many homes. We both had investigated many suicides in the Police, but this was different. We had interacted regularly with this man, and so we were intimately affected by his death. Scott's blood-soaked shirt, which I washed, confirmed this.

I had to contribute to support our family and worked in a few odd jobs to fill in time and make some extra income. I applied to work with the Corrective Services as a court security officer at the Coffs Harbour Court House, and started work there on a casual basis a few months after my resignation from the Police.

Ironically, I actually had to work back at the police station, as the office of the Corrective Services was attached to the cell complex and charge room inside the Police station. I wore an almost identical uniform with a different patch on my sleeves. The full-time correctional officers transferred the prisoners in prison vans from the correctional facilities to the cell complex, and we would process the prisoners and escort them to court, guarding them during their proceedings. If an individual was sent to jail, we escorted them to the cells, searched them and completed the paperwork. I was appreciated, the work wasn't difficult, the pay was good, and the staff were great fun. We had lots of laughs. I enjoyed sitting in court, analysing the proceedings, watching all the players in action, and dissecting the court cases.

Each shift, I would watch a police officer be cross-examined and saw how he/she was being led up the garden path by the defence. It was interesting watching my former Coffs Harbour police colleagues give evidence, and I quickly worked out who the more competent investigator was, as any oversights in an investigation would almost certainly be identified by the defence. Some of the cocky officers were very nervous in the witness box, and it showed. The skill of an experienced or inexperienced police officer is emphasised in court proceedings. Working this job helped me understand that each participant in the courtroom had a role to play. Up until this point in time, I had a very narrow point of view, which weighed heavily in favour of the Police.

Walking around the court complex, I became familiar with a lot of the solicitors and the court staff. One of the local solicitors would often joke with me and say, 'I don't know why they have you working here. What would 'you' do if one of the inmates played up?' I would give him a bit of cheek back and the banter continued over many months.

One day I was in the foyer of the court house, and he said the same thing to me again. I decided that day I would show him what I could do. With one quick sweep of my leg and a push on his shoulders in the right direction, the solicitor's paperwork went flying. He was face down in his suit in front of an entire waiting room of people, including Police, criminals on bail, onlookers and other solicitors. I was holding his arm up behind his back, his wrist bent in a submissive position and I was resting my knee on his back. The entire waiting room cheered and clapped. I whispered in his ear, 'That's why they have me here.'

From that day on, the solicitor would walk pass me very quickly laugh and say out loud, 'Don't go near her. She's dangerous.'

We did have prisoners that would go off like firecrackers, and some of them were big, strong, and determined. I am not arrogant enough to believe I am as strong as a male. We were taught different techniques to assist in controlling people in custody, and I never underestimate the power of 'word'. Talking to the inmates often helped. Inside the courtrooms and along the corridors where we used to walk the inmates to court, we had emergency buttons in case we needed help. When this button was activated, an alarm went off in the Corrective Services office as well as the Police Station, and staff would come running from everywhere. When judges were finalising a sentence, I learnt to look for triggers by the inmates. Their breathing would get quicker and heavier; they would rock slightly and become fidgety. Inmates were generally not handcuffed in the courtroom, so if a jail term was looking likely, on occasions, some thought taking a chance on a dash for freedom was worth it. We would try to get the prisoner out of the courtroom quickly. There are enormous personal pressures within the court with the offender's home, their assets, their own personal relationships and even their liberty in jeopardy. We would often have the inmates and their families yelling out last-minute messages to each other, and a victim's family would not miss the final opportunity to yell abuse at the inmate, which would result in the offender's family turning on the victim and their family. It's a highly charged emotional situation.

When a fresh custody arrived at the cell complex, they had to be stripped and searched. Over the years, in both the Police and the corrective services, I was required to search hundreds of people. Contrary to popular belief, it's not something officers generally like doing, but it's a procedure that is required to protect us and the inmates from themselves. It's also done to detect any possible evidence hidden in the various crevices of the human body. When we strip-searched a female, we required them to squat on the ground, as this position would sometimes 'release' evidence hidden in an area usually reserved to nurture and protect unborn children. One inmate I searched had three credit cards, jewellery and some marijuana hidden inside her.

The anal passage of males and females was another special place an inmate would conceal objects. I cannot describe any one particular human body I remember searching as we all look pretty much the same naked, just a few tweaks and twerks in different places.

Female officers were not required to strip search a male offender, but we would give them a 'pat down' and run our hands over their bodies to check for hidden weapons or evidence. There were times when we did this that the males would get an erection. They delighted in this and tried to embarrass us. There were different strategies we used to release that erection very quickly.

I continued to work in the corrective services, but to supplement my income, I obtained my private investigator's licence. I started working assisting another private investigator on jobs around Coffs Harbour, and soon, I was working my own jobs. A company contracted me to follow a man who had a third-party personal injury claim. He had recorded in his claim that he was unable to walk without the aid of crutches. I followed the man in my car to a popular beach reserve and watched him walking and swimming without his crutches having a great time, splashing around in the water. I needed to get footage of him, but there was nowhere I could conceal my camera. Surveillance equipment over the years has become a lot smaller and more discreet than what was available in those days. I made a quick call to my babysitter and had her bring my two daughters down to meet me. I placed my daughters in my line of sight to the man, and instead of a loving mother recording her children, I was filming the man swimming and running in the shallow water without the use of the crutches. The insurance claim was a fraud and was subsequently knocked back.

I quickly became known for doing investigations on infidelity cases and picked up work in this area. At the start of an investigation, I would meet a female client in a place like a coffee shop for an initial consultation. An observer would see two friends meeting up for coffee. Often, the female had a strong belief that her husband was having an affair, but she wouldn't know with whom. The women wanted to know if it was love or just sex. Other times it was just suspicion, but not often.

Doing surveillance is very difficult with only one person. When surveillance is carried out by the Police, it is often done with a team of people in multiple cars or on foot, moving forward and back to avoid 'getting made' or detected. Most private investigators are lucky if they can have two cars following someone; this comes down to cost and what the client is prepared to pay. It is difficult for some clients to conceal money from their partner to pay for the investigation. I would sit with the client and try to get a detailed routine of the person in an attempt to reduce the surveillance hours required by speculating about when I thought the husband had the best opportunity to engage in infidelity.

I followed one man who worked as a rep to a housing estate that was comprised of small acreage blocks. It was late in the afternoon, and there was very little cover. So, I went home, got up at four in the morning and drove back to the area. The cheating husband's vehicle was still parked at the house where I last saw him. I parked my car well away from the house and walked closer. I crawled like a crab through long, wet, dewy grass like an army commando and got myself in a position close enough to film the suspect. I lay in the cold grass for hours, but the wait was worth it. My intuition was correct, and I filmed the unsuspecting husband walking out of his lover's house. As he left, he gave her a long, passionate kiss on the front steps of the home. Case closed.

There are occasions when doing private investigation work on your own can be very dangerous. Most police officers worked in pairs, and there was always backup not far away. Police called off at jobs to the radio operators. If we were off the air for too long, the radio operator did a 'radio check' or 'welfare check' to make sure all was good, and nothing untoward had happened to us. A private investigator generally has no backup; in country areas, we were lucky to have a phone signal.

I had to investigate an alleged stolen vehicle case out the back of the township of Woolgoolga. I was aware before I left that I might not have phone signal in that area and said to my husband that if I didn't come back by lunchtime, something had happened to me. I gave him the address where I would be. He was the only person I could rely on to check on my welfare. I arrived at the isolated address and noticed that the house looked more like a shanty in the middle of the bush. When I parked, two big Rottweiler dogs charged at the car and jumped against the side doors, leaving scratch marks. My initial thought was that I would have to do my own insurance claim if they didn't get off my car soon. There was no way I was going to get out of the car until the owner arrived. I honked my car horn to get the insured's attention. I'm sure she was aware of what was happening and allowed the scene to take place in an attempt to intimidate me. Eventually, she came and restrained the dogs.

I had an initial look around, but I couldn't see anyone else there. The insured told me she was at the property on her own. The shanty was a dilapidated shack that was almost uninhabitable. I used a computer and a small tape recorder when conducting an interview and had to set up somewhere. Under a torn canvas awning, there was an old card table that had various car parts scattered on top, and the insured cleared the table by swiping her arm across it, which resulted in the car parts falling into the dirt. The Rottweilers kept a watchful eye on their owner and were sniffing me and giving me gentle nudges. The insured gave the two dogs big chunks of frozen mince to distract them but threw them straight at my feet. The dogs licked and chewed the mince like big lions for the entire interview, and I dared not move my feet in case they thought I was going to take their meal.

The interview went on for about an hour, and it was obvious to me quite quickly that the insurance claim was a fraud. The insured would have been aware of this by the direction in which my questions flowed and her inability to answer the questions I asked. While the interview was taking place, a man came out of the bush behind me, and it was quite obvious he was on drugs. He initiated a disjointed conversation about the insurance claim and a wallet that he had lost. He then proceeded to pick up the card table and toss it across the yard. I managed to quickly grab my laptop just before the table went flying. Both of us tried to calm him, and I could tell the insured was just as frightened as me; even the big dogs had now cowered and moved away. This was not a good sign. I just wanted to get out of there quickly, but I needed the insured to sign the statement, and I needed to inspect the vehicle that had been towed to their home after the alleged theft.

I quickly had the insured sign the document and examined the motor vehicle with the man pacing up and down behind me. If this had been a police job, one officer would have kept an eye on the man so neither officer's back was exposed to the agitated male. When I examined the vehicle, there was a wheel missing, and there were lots of cobwebs both in the car and around the engine that had allegedly been driven only a few weeks earlier. The driver's side window was supposed to have been smashed during the theft, but there was no sign of glass inside the car. The dogs were barking, and the man was screaming out random sentences. I took some photos and left the chaotic scene as quickly as possible. On inspection of the location where the car was alleged to have been stolen, I found lots of glass on the roadway, which meant the window had been smashed from inside the car, which would not have occurred if the car had been stolen the way the insured had reported. The insurance claim would be refused. These types of jobs had started to rattle me, and I was grateful to walk back into the safety of my own home.

Scott and I were thrilled to get pregnant for a third time, and we had no reason to think we would have any problems with this pregnancy. I was healthy and at thirty years of age, still relatively young. I knew that as soon as the corrective services found out I was pregnant, I would have some issues with my employment. There was no where I could be transferred, so I decided to keep the pregnancy a secret from work. I confided in another female court security officer, and she gave me a bigger uniform to wear. As the courthouse always had the air conditioner on, I was able to wear a big jumper to hide my growing stomach. I had all the routine blood work done and gave it no further thought.

At twenty-one weeks pregnant, I was at work at Correctives Services when the boss told me that there was a doctor on the phone for me. Confused, I took the phone that was located in a communal area, which was also the office. While I was speaking with the doctor, all my colleagues were sitting next to me. I had no privacy to take the call. The doctor told me that the blood work had come back, indicating a high risk of Down syndrome in the baby, and he wanted to see me straight away. Stunned, I hung up the phone and burst into tears. My male workmates didn't know what to say and were shocked to discover I was actually pregnant. I left work immediately and went straight to see the doctor. I discussed the blood work and asked the doctor if I could see the results. He obviously wasn't expecting me to ask to see them, as when I looked at the results, he had written the word 'Shit' with three exclamation marks after it. When I saw this, I immediately knew the seriousness of the situation.

The doctor had made an emergency appointment for me to have an amniocentesis in Sydney the next day. I would have to fly to Sydney first thing in the morning. The doctor discussed termination and said if my husband and I wanted to terminate the pregnancy, we would have to make up our minds before the results came back, which would take four weeks. Our decision was time-sensitive. Termination is illegal after a certain stage, and due to the advanced stage of my pregnancy, they would have to fudge my dates as it was. The phone call, medical tests and information were given to me within a whirlwind hour. I hadn't even had a chance to speak to my husband. Airfares were very expensive in those days, so I had to fly to Sydney on my own, and Scott stayed with our daughters.

Once home, the days slowly ticked by, and all we could do was wait. I was sent to a genetic counsellor to discuss my options. My boss at Correctional Services let me continue to work, which was as much a shock to me as it was to everyone else. I bought myself a blue sleeveless dress and wore a large male corrective services shirt under it so the patches on my uniform were still visible. The short sleeves came down to my elbows, and I worked until a few weeks before her birth. My workmates kept me out of harm's way, and I have to say most of the inmates were really nice to me and would often ask when the baby was due, etc. I wondered if the sight of a pregnant woman softened them a bit.

There were a lot of 'discussions' going on in our house. When the results came through four weeks later, we still hadn't made up our minds about whether to terminate or not. It's not easy when the parents have conflicting views. The results showed our baby did not have Down syndrome. I had emotionally disconnected from our baby as a form of self-preservation, so when I was asked if I wanted to know the sex of the baby, I said yes. I needed to fall in love with her all over again.

We had another daughter, and she was born on 11 September. Our eldest daughter started school four months later, and while I was sitting on a bench seat inside the school, I started talking to another mother who was also holding a small baby, who was facing away from me. I asked the mother what date her baby was born, and she told me her daughter was born on 11 September at the same small hospital as my daughter. I laughed and said it was the same date as my daughter's birth, and the mother turned her daughter around to show me. The beautiful baby girl had Down syndrome. I felt a shiver go through me and got goosebumps all over my body.

Scott was still working in the detectives' office and became involved in a job of conspiracy to murder, in which a man had attempted to contract a hitman to have his gay motorbike lover killed by having him run off the Dorrigo mountains. An informant of Scott's told him about the hit, and Scott arranged for a team of undercover Police to come up from Sydney, with one of the undercover detectives posing as the alleged hitman. Registered informants are people who are registered with a police handler and periodically provide intelligence to the Police for some sort of reward. Most informants are criminals themselves and associate on the fringe of criminal organisations.

Undercover Police are very discreet while doing their jobs, particularly in a small town. We were friends with the detective in charge of the undercover section, so we invited his team around to our house for dinner, as it would be better than eating in a motel room. When Kylie did undercover work, she had worked with most of these men. The men coordinated an operation, and the scene was set for the job to take place the next day. The operation went well, and a male was charged with conspiracy to murder, with Scott, the officer in charge of the case.

A few months later, we received word that an informant had come forward to say that the male offender, who was now in gaol, was so pissed off with being set up by the Police that in prison, he had attempted to contract another hitman to kill Scott. Police, corrections officers and members of the legal fraternity are often threatened with insults and threats of harm against themselves and their families. Mostly, we just brush it off as part of the job, as most crooks don't have the financial means or the fortitude to carry out their threats. However, on this occasion, we were told that the offender had sold his house to pay for the hit. This put Scott and our very young family at risk. This was the first time in my life I was really frightened for my family.

The Police were asked to keep an eye on our house and called in and checked on us regularly. One night, two uniformed police officers called in to check on me while Scott was away for work and arrived right at dinner time. They provided great support and helped me out with feeding and bathing of my three children under four, giving me a bit of self-assurance. I lay awake in our bed many nights, wondering how I would be able to protect three small children.

The witness protection section had talks with Scott, but for many reasons, we decided to stay in our home. During this time, Scott was mowing the front lawn when he saw a male sitting in a car not far from our house. He continued to mow the lawn but kept one eye on the man. The male got out of his car and slowly started to walk towards Scott, reaching inside his jacket pocket. Scott turned the mower off and started to walk backwards to our house, where I was with the girls. He told me he thought he was about to be shot on the front lawn with us inside. As it turned out, the man was looking for directions.

The male offender was charged with conspiracy to murder Scott, but the charge was later no billed due to the Department of Public

Prosecutions concern with the credibility of the key witness, who had his own extensive criminal history. However, the offender was convicted of the original conspiracy to murder charge and spent many years in jail.

This incident was the final nail in the coffin for Scott, and after some advice, he decided he would start studying law on a part-time basis. I was about to become a single mother, as I did not see my husband much for the next four years. He spent many hours studying in our old, detached garage with our big old dog lying on his feet to keep him warm in winter. At the time, our children were ten weeks old, two years old, and four years old. As we only had a small house, this was the most peaceful place to study.

Scott resigned from the Police and started studying full-time. He also got his private inquiry licence and worked in a pub at night. I kept working casually and looked after the girls. Life was busy; we didn't have much money, but we were happy. This happiness ended when we received terrible news that Scott's fifty-eight-year-old mother had terminal bowel cancer. The same week of her diagnosis, my father was hospitalised after having a massive heart attack.

We decided we would move back to Sydney to give Scott's family the emotional support they needed. Within a whirlwind three weeks, and in between having travelled hundreds of kilometres to visit both our sick parents, we had rented out our home and were headed back to live in Sydney. On the day we arrived, the removalist was unloading our furniture when our youngest daughter, who had been unwell, started to fit. She was ill with gastroenteritis, was severely dehydrated and almost died. She was admitted to the hospital for several days. The next day, our beloved dog was run over and killed. We were being tested. We were in for a few hard years, but we were lucky as we moved into a lovely little street, and these people became our friends. Kylie's husband called it McHappy Street, as our neighbours were so friendly.

The corrective services transferred me to the Penrith Court Complex, and I started work there as soon as we arrived in Sydney. The work was exactly the same as in Coffs Harbour, but they had substantially more inmates each day, and the cell complex under the courthouse was extensive. It wasn't unheard of to have anywhere from fifty to 100 inmates in the mini-gaol complex. Each cell had a TV hidden behind security screens so the inmates couldn't damage them. Some of the large holding cells housed between ten and twenty prisoners. The TVs were linked to the same system as the TV in our staff meal room. So whatever programme we had on the TV in the meal room was the same programme broadcast on the TVs in the cells.

On 11 September 2001, our youngest daughter turned three. We had a quiet birthday dinner at our house with Scott's parents, with his mother's health deteriorating. We went to bed that night and woke up to the September 11 attacks in America. Like most people, we were saddened and shocked by what was happening and couldn't stop watching the continuous TV footage of the events unfolding.

I had to work that day in corrective services, and when I arrived at the court complex, all the staff were equally shocked by what had happened in America. In between escorting inmates to court, we were watching the TV with continued interest. Our inmates had a habit of watching the controversial American reality program The Jerry Springer Show, which aired every weekday at midday. On a 'normal' day, we would tune our meal room TV to Jerry Springer so the inmates could watch the show. Soon after midday, we heard the inmates yell, 'Jerry, Jerry, Jerry.' It was obvious that the inmates wanted us to change the channel so they could watch The Jerry Springer Show. They had no interest in watching the unfolding day of unprecedented shock and suffering that was live on television. Watching two people attack each other because someone slept with someone's sister was far more interesting to the mostly low IQ of your standard inmate. Obviously, every channel was airing the September 11 attacks, so Jerry had to wait.

During the collapse of the Twin Towers, forty-six twins lost a twin sibling. The actual name of the towers is quite symbolic. I wonder if the remaining tower would have retained the name' twin tower' if only one building had fallen, with the identical buildings no longer being a pair, 'twins'.

Scott graduated from university, and we moved to the Central Coast where he could work as a lawyer in a large law firm. However, we were still close enough to visit Scott's family, who were just a couple of hours' drive away. We now had another move under our belt.

Palm Trees
and Gum Leaves

Beef

Day one of preschool arrived! There was no school bell, so I tentatively sat at the kitchen table with Bella and said, 'Okay, I suppose we should start.' It felt somewhat surreal.

Bella was eager, mature, and easy to teach. The hard part was wrangling two younger children who were as active as a pair of runaway calves. Harry and Adelaide wanted to be included in 'school', and I realised involving all three kids with arts and crafts activities was easier. Despite my best efforts, glitter ended up in unimaginable places, and I learned that there seriously should be a licence for hot glue guns. I would lay the wet creative artworks and paintings on my bedroom floor to safely dry. One day, I walked into the bedroom and discovered red kitty cat prints all over my bedding, carpet, and Bella's wet artwork. Shortly afterwards, we built a dedicated school building. Within years, all three children were enrolled in school.

Our schoolroom was set up like a typical school classroom. The amount of schoolwork increased each year, and although I was not initially proficient with technology, I soon learned. The kids often had to make a short movie for a school unit, and all family members would need to get involved. Over the years, I had some Oscar-winning performances, with roles such as a fearsome bushranger, once, Dave played the Pope.

Each school term, all the distance education children would meet for several days at the school centre in Bourke or on a designated family's property out of town. The children completed school activities with their peers, and had assessments with their teachers. I met many other western parents, mostly mothers who had also travelled long distances to attend, their cars packed to the brim with camping gear and excited kids, including toddlers and babies. All the mothers got on very well, supported each other, and cooked all the meals during the camps. With alcohol secreted in travel coffee cups, sitting in paddocks or shearing sheds, we also held P and F meetings. For several years, I filled the role of P & F President.

Harry was 'school resistant', and I silently wished I still had my police handcuffs. He was also a handful out of the classroom, was frustrated by some things, was a very fussy eater and insisted on routines. He would have many meltdowns, some of which were difficult to control. We decided to take him to the Flying Doctor for a check-up. We were referred to a Paediatrician, which was followed by a trip to see a Psychologist, which resulted in a diagnosis of autism. At first, we were gutted, and it took some time to come to terms with it. I then recognised that his diagnosis gave me the answers to many questions concerning his behaviour. It wasn't my fault or bad parenting; equally, it wasn't his fault.

I was also very aware that there were many children worse off.

I busied myself reading every book and website relating to autism that I could find. There is no exact cause for autism; however, there is a solid link to genetics. A twin study showed that when one identical twin is affected by autism, the other twin is highly likely to be affected. However, identical twins can have slightly different genetics that occur in the early stages of embryonic development, which can explain why one twin may be affected and not the other. I don't know how or why our son was born with it; all I know is, he was.

We were told about a facility, Royal Far West, in Sydney, that offered specialist medical services for country kids, so we attended, and Harry underwent comprehensive screening and assessments. The doctors confirmed his diagnosis, along with a diagnosis of obsessive-compulsive disorder and attention deficit disorder. We worked with the Royal Far West team for many years, travelling the lengthy distance to Sydney every six months for week-long visits. I was trained to complete Harry's OT and speech therapy back at the property, which added to my already extensive list of jobs. On one visit, Royal Far West officially launched a new mobile medical van that could drive to rural areas with specialists on board. As a patient, Harry was selected to walk on a stage and meet with the then Governor-General, Quinton Bryce. I was very nervous and not sure how Harry would react. Sure, enough to the amusement of the extensive media gathering, when she bent to kiss him, he screwed up his face, yelled, 'Yuk,' and jumped back, all captured by the laughing media. I shrunk deeply into my chair.

If Harry had been enrolled in a mainstream school, he would have been eligible for a teacher's aide and had assistance with his school programs. None of this was available for distance education students unless they were diagnosed with an intellectual disability. I decided to complete a TAFE Teacher's Aide Certificate through distance learning, which I thought might help. As a family, we had many challenges, but with patience, understanding, hard work, and medical intervention, our loving young man thrived and he is now living a regular life in every way.

As the kids got older, they started sports, and I became a swimming and athletics coach. We would set up markers on the airstrip and use sticks to train for the relay, the kids would use rocks for shot put, or I would set up bed mattresses with a piece of electric conduit for high jump. Long jump was practiced in a dry creek bed. The kids were reasonable at sports, and if they were placed in a race, we had to travel away to compete at the next level of competition. I unashamedly admit that after a few years, I silently prayed they might trip and fall, so we didn't have another long and expensive car drive. Unfortunately, they didn't trip and fall, and we attended many regional athletics and swimming carnivals. We travelled over two thousand kilometres to Sydney, three times for state athletics, for one eleven- or twelve-second race. In one three-week period alone, we travelled 4662 kilometres for school events. A common joke amongst parents was that instead of School of the Air, it should be called School of the Road.

Jacki and I made contact most days, and she heard all our news, good and bad. Despite our very different lives, we giggled when we discovered 'magical' twin things had occurred. I once woke with severe left shoulder pain, which continued for days. At the time, my twin was holidaying in New Zealand, so we had not spoken. When Jacki returned and made contact, I found out that while she was on holiday, she had been blow-drying her hair and somehow managed to tear ligaments, and had painfully dislocated her left shoulder. The injury was so severe it later required surgery.

One night, I woke panting after experiencing a very disturbing dream where dark-skinned people were being brutally slaughtered. The following morning, my twin phoned, and during our conversation, she told me about a violent movie, *Hotel Rwanda*, that she had watched the previous night. Despite the extreme distance between us, these sorts of small 'twin' things have commonly continued throughout our lives.

Although resigning from the police, I continued to be subpoenaed to appear in court for old investigations. These court appearances meant a three-to-four-day trip to Bourke, Dubbo, or even Sydney, which was frustrating. While I attended court, there was no one to teach the kids, and they would get behind with their schoolwork. If they remained on the property, Dave's jobs were limited to those he could do safely with three children in tow. If the kids came with me, there was no one to look after them while I was in the courtroom giving evidence. I remember once having to leave them seated alone in the foyer of the Dubbo Court complex, which was not an ideal or safe location.

Many of the cases were historical sexual assaults, as offenders were now being identified thanks to modern DNA technology. People have often asked, 'What if the suspect has an identical twin with the same DNA?' In a standard DNA test, only a tiny fraction of the DNA code is analysed, enough to differentiate between two average people, but not identical twins. Still, there are some minor differences in twins DNA. As DNA technology continues to improve, there might be a few nervous twins enjoying their last days of freedom.

To my surprise, Dave's parents decided to retire and worked out a sale where we purchased three properties from them. We now had a combined total of 100,000 acres of land to manage, which gave us independence but also debt, and our bank balance often looked like a drunk blowfly losing altitude. I was now responsible for the office side of things. It was a small business and was no different to any other small business in a town or city. I had no bookkeeping skills, and with minimal help, I had to set up a books program, learn to reconcile accounts, pay all the bills, keep stock records, and set up biosecurity plans and chemical records.

Trying to juggle bookwork, along with teaching and caring for children and working on the property, was an enormous job. My life was not unique and was repeated on every surrounding property. Women on the land are forced to fill many roles, and I was no different. I had days when it all felt overwhelming, and obviously, I couldn't slip around to a girlfriend's house for a coffee, so I would go for a walk in the bush, occasionally letting a few tears fall. When I sat in nature, I felt more connected to God and hoped he had time to listen to my prayers.

We were returning to drought, but Dave and I were eager for our first independent shearing. We had to save costs, so I was given two jobs: cook for the shearing team and press the wool. I cooked as much as possible leading up to shearing and helped muster the sheep and prepare the shed. Of course, the kids were all involved.

When shearing started, I woke well before the sun and cooked breakfast. Dave would take this food to the shed. I prepared morning and afternoon smoko and lunch and drove thirty kilometres to the shearing shed. Once there, I would wash up the breakfast dishes before going into the shed to press the wool. When sheep are shorn, the wool is put into wool bins according to its quality and grade. The wool from each bin is lifted by hand and thrown into a wool bag sitting inside a wool press machine. Now and then, I pressed a lever on the wool press, and the wool was squashed and compacted. The bale was sealed and labelled once the bag reached a set weight. Throughout the day, I stopped to serve the meals and continued pressing wool all afternoon.

Surrounded by shearers, the kids soon learned that there were words we classed as 'shed words' and could not be repeated. I also had to supervise the kids who were supposed to be doing schoolwork on the shearing shed floor. When the shearers knocked off, the shorn sheep had to be processed. One job was to earmark lambs. I was a novice, and Dave said, 'Ewes are marked in the right ear, weathers in the left. An easy way to remember, females are always right.' At the end of the day, I would leave pre-prepared evening meals for the shearers before taking the kids home, cook their dinner, bath them, put them to bed , and then cook all the food for the next day. During the three weeks of shearing, I had a surprise offer: one of the females from the shearing team offered to have a threesome with Dave and me. I politely declined, telling her I didn't have the energy for sex with either one man or one woman, let alone both.

Our three properties were quite run down and required lots of work; erecting some decent fencing was the first priority. It would take years to renew or replace them all, so we started with the worst fence and, little by little, tried to improve a fence line at a time. One job I immensely enjoyed was tying on the wire. This is when I connected the fence wire to the metal posts. At every post, I would have to tie five or six pieces of wire, and as I squatted up and down, the exercise was brilliant. I could not wear the fencing gloves that Dave provided as they were too large, so I always went without. If there was lots of barbed wire in the fence, by the time each day finished, my hands looked like they had been attacked by a cat with schizophrenia.

We found out about a government scheme that would give us some financial assistance to employ a nanny to help supervise the kids when they were not in our classroom or while I was out working on one of the properties. I posted an advertisement and began sifting through the applicants' resumes. Most only wished for a twelve-month position and were often young school leavers. I was reminded of my governess experience back in 1986. If I felt someone might be a good fit for our family, I requested they come for a trial period.

The hit television series McLeod's Daughters had recently started. In it, two sisters run their family's cattle station and have some very good-looking young neighbours. Many romanticised that our life was similar to the popular series, so the first thing I told applicants was that our cattle and sheep station was nothing like what was seen on TV, and most of our neighbours were over fifty years old.

Over the next six years, we had some interesting applicants. One lady arrived for a trial period carrying ice hockey equipment. Another had recently been a victim in an armed robbery, and explained through tears that she thought coming to our property would be a way to forget her trauma. We had much more success with some other lovely young ladies who stayed for twelve months or longer. Having someone else live permanently with our family came with different challenges, but for six years, I was extremely grateful for the help and company.

The Catholic priests from Bourke wanted to hold services for isolated families, so several times a year, we had a church service at either our property or one nearby. On one of these visits to our property we were the only ones in attendance, so two priests held mass in our lounge room for just our little family. After mass, we sat for lunch, and one of the priests commented that Harry needed a brother and that we should have more children. I looked across at Harry hanging upside down over the lounge and had to keep myself from bursting out laughing. As the kids were getting older, they needed to start their Catholic Sacraments, so now I had another job, religion teacher. The kids were sent workbooks that, over several months, they worked through on the weekends. Later, we drove to Bourke to attend the official sacraments held in the church.

When we bounced the two hours over the corrugated dusty road to Bourke, we often went on a weekday so we could conduct business or go to the open shops, which meant we rarely attended weekend church in town. Often, when I went to Bourke, a person would pass and say, 'How many kids do you have now,' or 'When are you going back to the cops?' When my kids asked me later who the person was, I often replied, 'Oh, I locked them up years ago.'

Recently, a lady stopped me to ask how she could get compensation for a historic incident that I previously investigated. I grew accustomed to being known locally as a police officer or a former police officer.

Our children all mastered basic driving skills by the age of four, and they drove the fourteen-kilometre round trip to drop off or collect the mail. Their motorbikes were fitted with training wheels, and the kids would help muster stock from a very young age. It didn't take long before the kids' motorbike skills overtook my basic skills, and unceremoniously, I was only included if absolutely needed. Even then, after several falls, I was put on a four-wheel bike.

Another shearing commenced, and the whole family was involved in the muster, including Dave's dad, Bruce, who had arrived to give us a hand. The sheep were in a paddock that was split down the centre by a creek. The plan was for Bruce to muster one side of the creek while the kids and I mustered the other side. Harry and Bella were on their own motorbikes, and I doubled up with Adelaide. Dave was in the aeroplane spotting the sheep from the air, directing us where to go over the UHF radio. Gradually, we got the two mobs of sheep together and were walking them slowly on parallel sides of the bank. Things were going smoothly when Dave's dad said over the UHF radio,

'You are not going to believe this; fish are falling from the sky. It's raining fish.'

The kids and I all looked up at the blue sky and back at each other. 'I think Grandad is losing his marbles.'

A short while later, there was a break in the creek, and we joined up the two mobs of sheep. Bruce rode over to us, pulled out some newspaper and unwrapped it, saying, 'I knew you wouldn't believe me. Have a look!' Sure enough, Bruce had a good handful of small fish, about fifteen centimetres in length. The kids and I were amazed and confused. Shortly afterwards, Dave landed the plane and joined us on his motorbike to complete the muster. Apparently, when Dave was in the air, a massive flock of pelicans flew close to the plane. We believe that while in flight, a pelican dumped its food stashed in its bill pouch, and as the fish fell, they just happened to land on top of Bruce.

After the sheep are mustered, they must be drafted. The sheep are run through a race and separated according to sex and age. As any bush woman can testify, drafting sheep with your husband often results in many 'shed words' being yelled at each other. I think if you can survive a day drafting sheep, you are doing well, as it certainly can bring out the worst of the best couples.

Drought-funded courses were offered through Technical and Further Education for graziers and farmers who were experiencing drought. They were self-paced and could be completed from home, so I decided to complete a Certificate III in Agriculture. I finished the course quickly, so I continued studying and completed a Diploma in Rural Business. As I was already time-poor, I had to get up very early each day and study before my family woke. While the drought stubbornly continued, I attended a locally held ladies' drought-funded writing and photography workshop. This fired up my creative spark, and soon, I was taking photos of anything moving or sitting still. As the battle to keep stock alive continued, I captured many heartbreaking scenes with my camera.

In times of drought, many animals that give birth to twins abandon one, leaving it alone to die. If we found these abandoned babies early enough, we would bring them home and bottle-feed them. We had a lot of success and always had a poddy sheep, goat or calf around the house. These poddies were lovely to photograph; they gave me a glimmer of hope despite the harshest of conditions. Along with poddies, we also had several sheep dogs. I got a Kelpie pup, who I named Jacki, after my twin. I took great delight in yelling, 'Jacki, sit,' 'Jacki, come behind,' or 'Jacki, come here.' As it turned out, Jacki did not display any working dog traits and only wanted cuddles, so she became a house dog.

Woman's Day magazine asked to interview us about families affected by drought. Shortly afterwards, we were asked to be involved in a drought story for the TV show 60 Minutes. Peter Overton arrived by helicopter with a film crew and spent several days with our family. Not long after the 60 Minutes interview, we were asked to do another interview with Paul Lockyer from ABC TV. Tragically, he was killed in a helicopter accident in 2011.

Finally, the heavens opened, and not only did the rain soak the thirsty soil, but it drowned it, causing an enormous flood. Due to the large volume of water, we soon had our very own island, minus the palm trees, and were completely isolated for six weeks. My water views were better than Jacki's. Along with many neighbours, we relied on emergency food deliveries. There were so many planes and helicopters flying in the area we could have had our own control tower. During the flood, Dave was out moving cattle and saving sheep from drowning while I taught the kids and tried to celebrate my milestone fortieth birthday. As we were marooned, I did not receive any cards or gifts. I sadly sat and ate a Vegemite sandwich and thought of my twin. On that day, she sat in restaurants and was spoilt by friends and family. Briefly, I wished I was living her life.

60 Minutes wanted to capture the contrast between the drought story and the flood. Just after my birthday, Tara Brown and the 60 Minute crew helicoptered in, bringing our mail and some essential supplies, and stayed for almost a week. During the week it was Tara's birthday, along with the pilot's, so my children cooked us all a joint birthday cake, and we celebrated with our minimal rations. The entire crew was terrific.

Days after the media crew left, the power dropped out, and remained out for three long days. We were thankful for our relatively new generator that kept our precious food supplies fresh; however, we had not been able to get any fuel deliveries for weeks due to the flood, and our fuel supplies were running low. Usually, our fuel is delivered in bulk every two to three months. To keep the generator running, we were forced to drain fuel from all the motorbikes.

Soon, the water subsided, and lush grasses grew. I am continually amazed by the environment and its ability to return to life after years of debilitating drought. Good seasons often bring plagues, and we have experienced many. I despise mice plagues, and thanks to Dave's good building, we never had a mouse inside the house; however, we had hundreds outside. I have also experienced locust plagues, caterpillar plagues, and, my favourite, budgie plagues.

With a continued good season, we decided, or knew, we all needed a breakaway. My family had only had a couple of minor holidays in twelve years, so we decided for a generous Christmas gift to book a holiday for the family to Fiji. A few weeks later, Dave quickly flew our small plane to Orange for maintenance work while I stayed and finalised the packing. The following day, I was to drive the 670 kilometres to Orange with the kids and collect Dave en route to Sydney. That night, torrential rain fell. Of course, we were happy for the rain, but it always seemed to fall when I really didn't want it, and when I did want it, it just stopped! The unsealed road out was impassable, and Dave couldn't fly home due to the poor visibility. To complicate things further, Fiji was experiencing a severe weather event. After several dramas with our insurance, I managed to postpone the holiday. Dave eventually arrived home to his disappointed family.

Six weeks later, Fiji had recovered, we had recovered, and we packed for the second time. Of course, overnight, it started to rain again, and we received more flooding. Frustrated, we packed the car and quite dangerously drove through floodwater, then continued the long drive to Sydney before flying to the holiday island. We had a brilliant time once we convinced Dave to ditch the Akubra hat and boots. In swimmers and sundresses, we stood out amongst the other tourists; our tan lines stopped abruptly at the sleeve mark of our T-shirts. Our holiday week went way too fast!

The weeks turned to months, the months into years, and with each new year, the children were getting older. It was time to select a boarding school for them. Although Catholic, we decided on Calrossy Anglican School at Tamworth, 770 kilometres from the property. Suddenly, it was time for Bella to start boarding school, so with school name labels sewn on clothes, we sombrely drove nine hours to Tamworth. Although I knew we had done all we could to prepare Bella, I was broken-hearted as I watched my thirteen-year-old daughter bravely enter this extremely foreign environment. Many of the schoolgirls in her year knew each other from primary school, and as they were assembled, they gathered like noisy flocks of budgies in little friendship groups. As parents were ushered from the room, I glanced back over my shoulder, and my heart tightened as I watched our brave daughter seated all alone at the side of the room. As a twin, I had never had to experience that feeling of childhood loneliness, as Jacki was always close by, giving me a sense of confidence and support. We drove to a motel, and Dave and Harry sat solemnly while Adelaide and I cried a river of tears. That night, I drove past the school to feel close to our young daughter. Driving home, I felt like a sad cow that had had her calf taken from her, and for me, the whole experience was horrific.

Pleasingly, Bella adjusted brilliantly to mainstream school and boarding life, but it took longer for the rest of us. Soon, it was Harry's turn to attend boarding school. Harry was excited to go, and although he would miss the land, he was keen to have boys to hang out and play footy with. Again, with sadness and apprehension, we waved goodbye, but we felt comforted knowing that this time Bella was close by. Harry thrived! I had time at home alone with Adelaide, and I was grateful to have some individual time with her. As the youngest, I felt she was sometimes overshadowed by her elder siblings. Suddenly, it was time for our baby to leave, and her drop-off was just as difficult. As we tearily drove home, I thought, for thirteen years, I was their full-time teacher, and they not only kept me very busy, in and out of the classroom but were my company and friends.

Dave also lost his musterers and his mates out in the paddock. Jacki's youngest daughter left for university the same year, so my twin and I were both now empty nesters, but as my daughter was only thirteen years old, I felt I was a 'premmie' empty nester. Suddenly, our school social life ended, and things became too quiet. I eagerly looked forward to my nightly phone catch-ups with the kids.

Another birthday arrived. I woke early, excited for my special day, wondering what gift Dave had bought me. One year, he gave me a wheelbarrow while on the same day, Jacki received tickets for an overseas holiday. As young children, Jacki and I complained about receiving identical gifts; however, I would have been happy to get identical gifts now! The phone rang, and I enthusiastically grabbed it, thinking it would be Jacki ringing for our birthdays, 'Hello.'

It was my father's partner on the line, who abruptly said, 'Your father has died.'

'What?' my mind raced to process the words. Our father was suffering from cancer, but the last time I saw him, only weeks earlier, he had looked remarkably well. With a sinking heart, as the tears fell, I phoned my twin and told her of our father's death. Through my sisters, I found out that our father died alone, during the night, and that his body was removed from the house before any of us were told. Two of my sisters only lived five minutes away! There are 365 days in the year; I wish he didn't die on my birthday, on 'our' birthday. I felt a downpour of emotions.

Arriving in Dubbo, I met with all my sisters. We had no say or control in my father's funeral, which infuriated me. Our father's body was to be delivered to the chapel an hour before the service, and as he had died alone, we did not want him arriving at the chapel without his family. My sisters and I arranged to be there, and together, we walked the coffin in.

We stood in an emotional but silent group. I hugged my twin. A curtain surrounding the coffin, customarily used for cremations, suddenly closed around the coffin and us. No one had pressed the button. Gee, was his spirit here? The service commenced and there was a brief time for reflection. A song chosen by our father's partner started playing. As I listened, I thought, this is not what our father would have wanted. I sat there feeling annoyed, when a second CD player with outdoor speakers started playing a Slim Dusty song, one our father would have loved. I couldn't help but smile. I spoke with the funeral staff later; the music was not supposed to be played, and no one had been in the backroom to press play. They were as bewildered as us. It was all a bit eery.

Soon, we arrived back home, and over the coming months I felt my grief come in waves. I tried to bury my bad childhood memories, and as I looked through old photographs, I let memories of the good times flood me. I had never accepted my father's abusive actions; however, before his death, I had forgiven him. Gradually, my grief lessened, the sun rose each morning, and life continued.

Bookwork and household jobs are chores that are never completed, so with this, along with helping Dave with property work, I was busy. However, I now had some spare time with our children away at school. I started teaching myself the guitar and had more time to take photographs. My photography taught me that even in drought, beauty is everywhere. I just had to really look for it. There is something magical about sitting in the quietness of the bush, witnessing a kaleidoscope of colours as the sun heads to bed, or watching animals live their lives in their natural habitat. As I gained confidence with photography, I decided to start a photography business that might provide a small off-farm income. I needed to find a business name, so I picked the two things I love: Land and Life. I still have my little business today, and I take a wide variety of photos, covering media and marketing, websites, family and newborn sessions, and even the occasional wedding. I get so much enjoyment from capturing and preserving my client's memories.

I have taken so many photos of my children that they have laughingly suggested they will take legal action if I take any more. The house was very quiet without the kids, and counting down the weeks until they came home for their leave breaks was a constant pastime. I am unsure who was more excited when they arrived home, them or us. They always had a long bus journey, followed by a two-hour car drive, so they were always pleased to walk in the door, and we all treasured our brief family time together.

Over the years, we have had many visitors arrive for a sabbatical in the bush; most just want to experience our way of life, explore the bush, or go hunting. In 2016, I was excited when the kids arrived home for the Easter break. Hours later, we had visitors arrive for the weekend: a relative and two teenage boys. They dumped their bags and left for a hunt. As it was Good Friday, I set about making our customary Good Friday tuna casserole; obviously, we find it hard to have fresh fish.

Our visitor's car suddenly returned, and one of the visitors came rushing in shouting, 'There's been an accident. A pig got him.'

As a result of my police days, my mind sharpened, and I could block out noise and the panic surrounding me. Over the years, I have come across quite a few car accidents on our isolated roads and have had to help an injured person. I calmly reached up for our small first aid box. Dave had gone to investigate and came running in. 'It's bad. He's going to bleed to death.' My husband often panics in emergencies, and I thought it was probably just a tiny cut. It was dark by now, so I picked up a torch and calmly walked out.

The injured boy was lying in the ute tray with a t-shirt wrapped around his upper thigh. As I climbed into the back of the tray, I was told the injury under the t-shirt was severe. I looked around the t-shirt bandage using my torch and could not see blood seeping through, which was a good sign. However, a considerable amount of blood was pooling in the tray of the ute. I started to look over the rest of the boy's leg for other wounds, and as I lifted his leg to look underneath, I was instantly shot in the chest with blood. I could see a wound behind the boy's knee, and I watched as the blood pulsed out like a water pistol being pumped. I am certainly not a medical professional, but I was pretty sure the bore's tusk had pierced an artery. Shit, this was bad, really bad! I clasped my bare hand over the wound and applied pressure, raising his leg over my shoulder, and asked my family for a bundle of bandages and the cordless phone. The visitors were understandably rattled and wanted to drive straight to town.

Knowing how far that was, and knowing how severe the injury was, I said, 'No.' I wanted to speak to a professional before we made any decisions; perhaps we could meet the ambulance halfway. While keeping the boy's leg high over my shoulder, I quickly washed the wound and applied a pad, then one bandage, then another, then another, then another. I kept his leg on my shoulder and pressed firmly over the bandages. As I did this, I could tell the boy was going into shock, so I confidently reassured him, although inwardly, I was feeling unsettled. Dave wasn't relaxed, so I sent him to get a pillow and a blanket.

I dialled the emergency phone number and spoke with ambulance control, explaining the injury in detail. After several discussions, they informed me that the only ambulance in the entire Bourke District had been sent to an emergency at Enngonia. The next option was the Royal Flying Doctor Service (RFDS), but the closest night airstrip was sixty kilometres further west.

Due to the seriousness of the injury, they set up a three-way conversation with a 000 supervisor, a doctor, and me. I was told in no uncertain terms that we could not leave the property until I was instructed. The 000-operator tried to organise a police vehicle to help out, but they were all busy. As I was using our only phone and there was no mobile service, 000 staff contacted the boy's parents to inform them of the accident and find out his blood type. We were instructed to drive slowly to the RFDS airstrip at Hungerford in Queensland. They wanted to time our arrival with the arrival of the RFDS plane. We were to take two vehicles, so if the boy started to bleed out on route, the other vehicle could drive to Hungerford, collect the doctor and bring him or her to the boy. I glanced at my children, who were casually standing near the ute, not panicking and helping where needed. I wondered, had they all seen too much in their short lifetimes?

Finally, we were given the green light to head off. Dave drove very slowly while I remained seated in the back of the ute, with the boy's leg balanced above my shoulder. As we approached the airstrip, I could see the plane's lights on the horizon; it was timed perfectly as planned. I was secretly relieved when they landed. The doctor jumped in the ute and asked if the blood through the ute tray was from the pig.

'No, it's the boy's!'

The Doctor unwrapped the bandages and was instantly shot in the chest with blood. The boy was flown to a Sydney hospital and immediately taken to surgery. We arrived back home to our kids at 5 am. I was told I saved his life.

Life on the land was never dull. There was always something that needed attention and an enormous amount of work to be done. Each day, as the sun rose, I wasn't sure what the new day was going to bring.

Reef

Soon after yet another move, Scott's mother passed away at the age of sixty-one. I finished work with the Corrective Services and went to TAFE to enhance my secretarial and computer skills, as we planned to open our own criminal law practice in the future. After Scott completed another year with a smaller law firm, we were ready to start our own business. We did heaps of research and travelled up and down the north coast, deciding where we would settle. It wasn't long before we knew we should return to Coffs Harbour. We had moved twelve times in ten years with our young family and lived quite a migratory lifestyle. My twin had established firm roots in her red soil while we had been living like grains of sand on a windy beach, moving from place to place, changing the girls' schools on three occasions, finding suitable preschools, a doctor, dentist, mechanics, etc. We thought traversing back to Coffs was the easiest move for us and our children. The girls returned to the same school they had started at, and our eldest daughter had the rest of that year to reconnect with her friends before starting high school. We were going home.

We had only been back in town a few days when ghosts of the past confronted Scott. He had gone to Woolworths to buy groceries, and as he walked up the aisle, he came face-to-face with the man who had been charged with conspiracy to murder. He had since completed his sentence and was now out of jail. After a brief standoff in the isle, the male dropped his shopping basket and took off in the other direction. He wasn't so brave when face-to-face with Scott.

We packed up our little family a few months later and headed to the beach. We had hauled all the towels and umbrellas down to the beach, and just before we settled on a spot to set up for the day, Scott turned to me and said, 'We're leaving.'

I didn't know why, but I knew there was a reason. I didn't question him and rounded up the girls who were now whinging and complaining about having to leave when we had only just arrived. When we returned to the car, Scott told me he had seen the same crook on the beach. We didn't want our children identified by the man, so we went to another beach for the day.

Country police have to deal with running into former criminals quite a bit, and in fact, I had had an incident years earlier when I was in the corrective services. Prison inmates call all female corrections officers' Miss'. I was walking up the shopping mall at Coffs Harbour, pushing my youngest daughter in a pram. A former inmate recognised me and said, 'G'day, Miss, is this your baby?' I didn't recognise him, as we had hundreds of inmates processed through the cell system, but because he called me Miss, I knew he was a former inmate. My little blonde-haired baby was about six months old and gave him a lovely toothless smile while sitting in her pram. Our youngest daughter was born with a birthmark on her face that wraps around her eye and descends down her cheek. It wasn't the same as my strawberry birthmark, but a different type called a pigmented birthmark. The birthmark is brown and becomes more obvious when exposed to the sun, or if she is unwell and pale. Without any warning, the inmate licked his thumb and tried to wipe the birthmark off her face, and simultaneously said to me, 'Aww, Miss, she's got food on her face.' It happened in seconds.

I was horrified and took off running with her to a nearby chemist. I had completed many medical documents when processing inmates and was well aware that infectious diseases are common in correctional institutions. My immediate concern was my baby might get hepatitis, as this is a common disease within the prison system. Once inside the chemist, I grabbed anything on the shelf that I thought would disinfect her face. In rambling, stunted words, I managed to relay something to the chemist's assistant. She could work out what had happened, and we cleaned my baby with a suitable product. It was obvious that my life would always interact with criminals, but I didn't want my kids exposed.

I didn't see Kylie very much during these years as working with a family, moving about and starting a business put obstacles in our attempts to see each other. She was busy with her own young family. The phone was our only connection. Before online shopping was introduced, I was Kylie's personal shopper. She would send me a cheque with an extensive list of things for me to buy. The list would include things like four size 0 Bonds singlets, pyjamas for the kids, a can opener, a set of sheets, a sprinkler, etc. Once the cheque cleared, I bought the products, boxed up the purchases and sent them back to Kylie. She appreciated what I did, and always made sure there was enough money left for me to go to a coffee shop and have a little treat when I had finished, even though she didn't have much money to spare. I did this for her a couple of times a year until the introduction of online shopping, something both our husbands have grown to hate. Kylie's husband calls it easy buy, hard to pay!

We managed to catch up every few years in person, and on one such occasion, we organised to have a weekend with our families. While there, we decided to do some shopping in a huge centre. We had six small children, so we took them to a play area. I went shopping first, and Kylie watched the cousins have some rare playtime together, and then we swapped over. Later that night, we showed each other our purchases and discovered that we had been to the same shop and had bought identical doona covers. The staff must have been very confused. We laughed as this happens a lot to us. We often buy the same birthday card for a relative. Kylie doesn't get much choice out where she lives, but I have an abundant choice of cards from many different shops and sometimes still manage to select the same card.

On the rare occasions Kylie and I do manage a catch-up and we are out and about walking around, I forget I'm a twin. In my head, it's just Kyl and me. But inevitably, people stare at us. Initially, I think, shit is my fly undone, or do I have toilet paper hanging off my shoe? Then it dawns on me, oh the twin thing. Sometimes people ask us, 'Are you sisters, or twins?'.

We often reply, 'Both.'

We have noticed when we are together, out at a pub or bar, we often get, 'hit on'. We don't think we are particularly pretty, just ordinary-looking women with 'lots of personality', but men seem to notice us when we are together, and some sickos are hopeful we want a menage a trois with them, one recently even licking his lips to get our attention. If twins were to have a sexual relationship with each other in a group setting, it would be incest. We both have happy marriages, and we are definitely not interested.

My girls continued their schooling and were active in school life, playing sports on weekends, involved in lots of extracurricular activities after school, and had lots of friends in their lives. They were all doing well in school, and our business was going well. I did my obligatory duty at the school working the canteen roster, being class parent and volunteering as a teacher's aide. I was on the committee for the school fete, sat on bench at basketball and drove enthusiastic kids away to sport on weekends. I organised birthday parties and cooked cupcakes for fundraisers. I went to dinner with visiting barristers and accompanied Scott to judge's dinners. I was lucky to be self-employed and could do my work when it suited me. I would schedule work appointments around my kids' activities and get up at 4am to do my reports before my children woke. I was living a normal, busy family life in which I didn't have a minute in the day for myself.

The day-to-day rigours of life were exhausting, and we decided we needed a holiday. We booked to go to Fiji, with the first half of our holiday to be spent on a forty-berth boat. As we cruised out, suddenly, I was experiencing deja vu. Just like my last boating experience in Fiji, we sailed straight into a storm and a five-foot swell. I was seasick immediately and regretted having the buffet lunch at the dock just before our departure. I couldn't move from my bed, apart from a wobbled walk to the bathroom every five minutes, where I would vomit and wet my pants simultaneously. Lying on the bed I watched the waves swirl around the port hole like a front loader washing machine. At one point, I managed to get up and check on the girls in the cabin next door. They were all sitting happily on a bed playing the card game Uno. I didn't need to worry about them. Two days later, the seas calmed, and I left the cabin to meet my unsuspecting fellow travellers who didn't know I existed. They thought my husband was a single dad on a trip away with his daughters. My family had forgotten to mention me. We had a lovely holiday, but I avoided swaying hammocks for the rest of the trip.

This holiday gave our children a glimpse of life outside Australia. The high school our kids attended had many opportunities for students to travel overseas. We told the girls they could each go on one trip that we would pay for, as long as they saved up for their own spending money. All our girls had part-time jobs during high school. Our eldest daughter chose to go to America and lived with a Mormon family for a week as part of the experience. Our middle daughter went to Europe and was able to indulge in history, one of her passions. Our youngest daughter went to Africa and volunteered at the sister school that our school fundraised for. Their chosen trips reflected their different personalities and these experiences made them more resilient people.

A few years later, we took the girls to America for three weeks and had Christmas in Las Vegas. After Las Vegas we headed to San Francisco, a favourite of mine. We did an organised tour on this cool open-air bus. During the tour, we went through an area called the Tenderloins. The Tenderloins is known as one of the most dangerous locations in San Francisco. It has a high number of homeless people and a bit of a drug culture surrounding it. The tour operator warned us not to venture into that area. We had a fabulous day weaving in and out and up and down the many charming streets, looking at the sights and the beautiful architecture.

The next day, after breakfast, we decided to separate, with Scott exploring the city on his own while I took the girls shopping. Our tour guide from the previous day pointed out a shopping strip with quirky shops with no multi-national brands. We thought that would be a great place to shop. We got out our trusty city map and found where we needed to head. I thought we could just walk there as it didn't look that far, as the crow flies. Within two blocks, I noticed we had stumbled into an area that didn't look safe. There were dilapidated buildings, old lounges on the footpath and rubbish scattered everywhere on the streets. There was a woman dressed like a typical movie prostitute screaming at someone, and there were a lot of homeless people hanging around.

I looked at the map again, and it was very obvious we were tourists. One of the girls said to me that she felt scared. I was trying to blend in and look like a local. The girls and I, who all have long blonde hair, looked like preppy Californians in our colourful holiday attire. We stood out. I said to the girls, 'Just act confident. We will be okay,' although I was having trouble convincing myself that we would be alright. As we rounded a corner, all these desperate faces turned around and looked in our direction simultaneously. There were about 200 homeless men lined up to get a free meal. They kept their eyes fixed in our direction and appeared to have forgotten about the meal they were waiting for. I said to the girls, 'Quick, turnaround,' and we quickly headed up the hill. This wasn't as easy as it sounds, as the streets in San Francisco are really steep. As luck would have it, a taxi passed an intersection near us. I let out a whistle to get his attention, and he screamed to a halt. All my whistle practice as a young girl came in handy. The first thing the driver said to us in an alarmed tone was, 'What are you doing here?'

I said, 'Is it not safe here?'

He said, 'You're in the Tenderloins.'

Not good parenting on my part!

That afternoon, when we met up with Scott, I noticed he had broken blood vessels on his face, and his eyes were red, puffy and swollen. The girls and I were excited to tell Scott about our 'near-death experience'. We told him we had an amazing story, and he said, 'So do I.'

When he left us, he walked around the city exploring and ended up in the Chinatown area. This is something Scott enjoys doing in most countries, as he loves a big bowl of soup. He walked into a restaurant, sat down and ordered. While he was waiting for the soup, he noticed two Chinese gentlemen talking and looking in his direction. They spoke to the lady running the restaurant in Mandarin, and she looked at Scott and replied to them. He was the only customer in the restaurant at the time. When the piping hot soup arrived, Scott wolfed down the meal. He has always been a fast eater and has a special 'talent' for eating hot food fast. He finished the soup, paid and walked out.

As soon as he got outside onto the street his head started to spin, and he felt like he was having trouble walking. He had a sudden, unexplained change of consciousness. He had been drugged. The Chinese men in the restaurant didn't know he would eat so quickly, and more than likely were trying to weaken their unsuspecting victim so they could rob him. Had he eaten slowly, he would have collapsed inside the restaurant. He knew that he had to get the soup up really quickly, so he stuck his fingers down his throat and made himself vomit violently. He had to use street rubbish to wipe his face. He had vomited so violently all the capillaries on his face had burst and made his eyes swollen. He ended up crawling on his hands and knees up the street with the San Francisco community stepping over him. From their perspective, he was just another homeless man.

Eventually he was able to get some water and had to rest for ages before he could make his way back to the hotel. We decided we should stick together for the rest to the trip. Travel is an adventure, but there is nothing like heading home. Home provides a refuge, most of the time!

Sawtell is a satellite city of Coffs Harbour. Sawtell has a subtropical feel about it; the summers are warm and humid, and the winters are short and cool. We do experience high rainfall, with most of our rain falling between late summer and early autumn. On occasions over the years we have experienced flash flooding, when it is sudden, and we have little warning it's coming. Flash flooding occurs as a result of very heavy rain.

On the 31st of March 2009, we experienced relentless rain that kept falling in sheets. I collected the girls from school and dropped my eldest daughter at work at Woolworths in Coffs Harbour. While I was driving home, the heavy rain obscured my vision, and I had to lean forward and squint my eyes to see the road. The gutters on the road were filling up quickly, and the drive back home was slow and dangerous. We had to change our normal route, as roadways were already underwater and flooded. As soon as we were safely home, I regretted making my daughter go to work.

Unfortunately, the high tide collided with the heavy rain. The rain didn't let up, and the local rivers and the surrounding creeks were filling up fast. Our daughter rang to let me know they had closed the Woolworths. She had been working at the checkout, but within minutes, she was standing in water. She waded outside and was now standing in water up to her knees. She looked across the street and spotted her dad, who was also working in town, had just moved his car to higher ground and was now coming to rescue her. He took her back to his office, which was on the second floor, and they both got out of their drenched clothes and put on suit jackets that my husband always kept at the office. They were at least warm and dry. They watched from his office windows as cars floated down the flooded street.

Having done insurance work as a private investigator, I was aware of the fine print in insurance policies regarding flooding. The estuary behind our house started to fill, and I decided we needed to move our furniture and belongings to our second storey. Within an hour, my youngest two daughters and I moved all our belongings, including every kitchen product, apart from the white goods like the fridge and the heavier items like lounges and TV cabinets, to the second storey. I then put a stake in the backyard to keep a watchful eye on the water level. All the males in the estate were at work and stuck in town, so some of the neighbours needed a hand. Once I helped them, I got the younger girls some dinner and put them to bed. There was nothing more I could do but wait. The only sound I could hear was the heavy rain thrashing on the tin roof, and it did not let up for hours. I had an eerie feeling of impending doom. I couldn't sleep and was worried about Scott and our daughter, so I decided to distract myself by ironing and listened to the ongoing radio updates in relation to the flooding on our local station. Our house might flood, but the ironing would be up to date!

The power had gone out in town, and Scott was lucky to find a Chinese restaurant open. As they were cooking with gas, he could get himself and our daughter some dinner. Late that night, the rain eased, and as is typical with flash flooding and the tides, the water subsided as quickly as it rose. They made it home at about two am, wet and tired, having had to weave their way through the flooded streets, going backwards and forwards on closed roads to get home.

The next day, the area was declared a natural disaster, and many people spent the night in evacuation shelters. School children had slept in schools all night, and many people remained stranded in flooded areas for days. Hundreds of homes and businesses were flooded. We were saved, as the sandbank at the mouth of the ocean gave way under pressure, and the water in Bonville Creek drained out to sea as quickly as it would if I let out a plug in a bath. We received 440 millimetres of rain in twenty-four hours. This type of weather event is not one that my twin sister has to deal with. They have their own issues with the weather. Kylie's reaction to rain is also very different from my own. She looks at rain like liquid gold, whereas I see it as pure inconvenience.

I have only made the arduous journey to Kylie's property a few times. My girls find it a real eye-opener when we go there and feel that they are being punished for having no mobile phone coverage to stay connected with their friends on social media. My husband, on the other hand, is happy that his work mobile is pleasantly silent, with no mobile towers for kilometres. I struggle with being unable to go to the shops and grab ingredients for a dinner that I decided to cook that morning, and I miss the convenience of chemists and restaurants and ducking to the shop the minute I need something. However, I still love getting out there and helping out once every five years or so.

Kylie had to have an operation, so my mum, two of my daughters, and I went to the property to give her a hand. I had to drive eight hours to Dubbo on day one, collecting my mother on the way. After an overnight stay, we picked up the patient who had been discharged from the hospital. It had rained quite a bit, and we were unsure if we would be able to get to the property on the dirt roads, but we headed off anyway. We decided that our mum would drive my car with my daughters, and I drove Kylie's manual 4WD. I hadn't driven a manual car for many years; this would be interesting! Although Kylie was drugged up to her eyeballs, she still managed to point out that I was riding the clutch. The jerking motion of the car created pressure on the seatbelt resting on my twin's fresh stomach wound. She undid her seatbelt and thought she would risk the fine. Thank God we were out on the open road quickly, and once I was in fifth gear, the car drive was far smoother.

After an hour or so, we drove through a small town with a petrol station selling beer. Kylie thought she would grab a six-pack. The alcohol combined with the Endone was sure to make this difficult drive more comfortable for her. An hour or so later, I decided I might join her and had one beer myself. It wasn't illegal to drink and drive, just not to be drunk and drive. It was nice to relax, catch up with Kylie, and chat in person for a change.

After some time, Kylie needed to go to the toilet, and she picked the only rest stop with a waiting highway patrol car concealed behind some shrubs. I knew I wasn't over the limit but didn't want to tempt fate, so I quickly put my beer out of sight. Our mother pulled in behind us and decided to start a conversation with the highway patrol cop. Thankfully, Kylie managed to get rid of him by saying she had to go to the toilet. There was no toilet there, so she would have to do a bush wee. He left quickly.

Once in Bourke, we all got into the 4WD and left my car at Bourke, as it would not be roadworthy on the rough dirt roads. We bought some groceries to take out to the property. Mum and I had planned all the meals for the week and bought all the ingredients we needed. The 'skilful' employee at the IGA secured the boxed groceries to the roof racks for us as the car was full of our luggage and the shopping my twin had purchased before her surgery. I had no idea how to tie a good knot, and Kylie couldn't reach up in her condition.

We left the township of Bourke and started the last leg of the journey well after lunch. I quickly ground my way to fifth gear and accelerated to 110 on the last bit of tarred road. Not long afterwards, out of the corner of my eye, something caught my attention in the rear vision mirror, and I noticed that all our groceries were blowing off the roof. The helpful shop assistant was as useless at tying knots as I was. We pulled over and had to walk along the road and collect all the scattered groceries hundreds of metres behind us.

After quite a long time, Kylie, who was in a lot of pain, grew impatient and told us to leave the rest. Mum and I weren't going to leave any ingredients, and we spent some time looking for sanitary items that one of my daughters would need that week. It wasn't like we would be able to run to a chemist. Remarkably, the only item broken was a bag of flour, and by some miracle, a large glass bottle of olive oil was the only item still sitting on the roof.

We secured the groceries by me holding the rope taut and throwing the rope over the roof of the car. Kylie would tie off the load by balancing on the opposite side of the car, and then I would run around and hold the rope taut again. She then slowly got down and went to the other side of the car, and we repeated the process. I had visions of the surgeon's handiwork tearing open inside her. Once we were satisfied, we headed off, and thankfully, the ropes held the groceries in place.

We drove on a few kilometres of tar road, and just before we came to the start of the dirt section, we came across a big yellow 'closed road' sign. These roads are normally pretty rough, and I always recommend putting on a good bra for the drive, but today, the road was covered in thick, sticky mud. There had been too much rain.

Usually, Kylie would never drive on a closed road as this can cut up the road surface, but we needed to get her home. I had some last-minute instructions: 'Don't stall, or we will sink in the black mud.' My heart was racing, and as soon as we left the security of the tar, the car soon had a mind of its own. It slid back and forth along the roadway, the car sometimes sliding sideways, and I had to try to turn the car the right way. The steering wheel was spinning in all directions.

My twin sister was frustrated and was yelling at me to follow the tracks made by other cars that had braved the mud before us. I could see so many tracks and didn't know which ones to follow. They all looked the same to me. I was driving really slowly and was cautious not to slide off the main road and down into the table drains on either side of the road. If I did, we would almost certainly get bogged.

My girls would generally think this was fun, but they knew if we got bogged, we would be sleeping in the car for the night, and this was not an option for me, my mum or my city girls. We are glampers, not campers. There were times when Kylie would put the car into gear for me as I needed both hands on the steering wheel. I had a huge headache from concentrating, and every now and then, Mum would reach from the back of the car and give me a reassuring pat on the shoulder. I inched my way along, and after what felt like hours, we ended up on a better section of the road. I thought the worst was over until we reached a condemned bridge that sat ten-odd metres off the ground.

The local council had made a road that ran down the side of the bridge into the creek bed and back up the other side, but this was impassable due to the height of the water in the creek from the recent rain. We had no other option; we had to go across the bridge. We sat in the idling car and assessed the situation. Kylie said we should be right and just to drive slowly. I was concerned as the car was heavy with all our gear, including the groceries we had bought, and I started to wish we had left them scattered on the side of the road. I told my girls to wind down their windows and undo their seatbelts in case the bridge collapsed into the water below and they got trapped in the car. I held my breath as we inched our way along really slowly. The only sound I could hear in the car was the engine and my pounding headache. We made it. We eventually arrived at the property late at night after dodging another hazard: kangaroos. It was a long day.

Reflecting on our stay, I understood that I had had the same surgery as Kylie a few years earlier, and I was lucky to stay in a private hospital for a week. My husband drove me home on a tarred road. It took fifteen minutes. We hired a cleaner for six weeks. That was it! It was a much simpler process.

People often ask Kylie and I about our medical history, intrigued. It's interesting that they feel comfortable asking a twin about her private medical history, and I'm certain they wouldn't ask a singleton the same question. If one twin gets an illness, will the other twin get the same illness?

Much research has been done to see how specific diseases affect the body, and a lot of research has been conducted with the help of twins. How much does the environment influence our illnesses, and how much of a role does our genetics play? For example, studies have revealed that smokers have an increased risk of bone fractures. So, because my sister smokes, and I don't, according to research, she should have more fractures than me. It has been discovered that leukemias can originate before birth. Twins who both contracted leukemia were studied, and it was revealed that one twin started their leukaemia in the womb, and the leukaemia spread to the other twin through blood vessels in a shared placenta. The location where the fertilised egg implants in the womb is random, but some locations are more favourable for growth, so if twins are fertilised in different areas of the womb, this chance encounter could create a healthier embryo or a healthier twin.

We are as perplexed as anyone when our twin occurrences happen. I'm sure even science would be stretched to explain the extraordinary coincidences that have sometimes occurred in our lives. My sister and I had three births each. We were only close together for one of those births, Kylie's son. We had spent a lot of time together the week before and after his birth, as Kylie had travelled to have her caesarean in a bigger hospital, and I could help her. On day three after his birth, I woke to very swollen breasts and discovered that my milk had come in. I wasn't pregnant and hadn't breastfed for three years. This only occurred with the birth of Harry. I had so much milk I could squirt milk across a room like an old dairy cow. I did have a bit of fun and breastfed Harry, as he was the closest thing to a son I was likely to get, but my bras didn't fit that well for a week or so.

When we were about three years of age, one of us walked into the house with a bleeding left nostril. While mum was cleaning up that twin, the other twin walked into the house with a bleeding nose, also out of the left nostril only. Was this a twin thing, or, out of mum's sight, had we swung at each other and socked each other in the face, causing the nose bleeds? The bleeding noses would then be an environmental factor. We have both had lots of skin cancers, but we believe our complexions, the harsh Australian environments we live in, and lifestyle choices over the years have caused this. If we had been singleton's, we would have more than likely developed skin cancers, and it has nothing to do with the fact that we are twins.

My girls finished school. Our eldest daughter went to university and graduated as a teacher, working in a small town not far from where my life began. Our two younger daughters graduated as lawyers, and we are often at the end of their developing argument and persuasion skills. We are lucky to have one teacher in the family who can balance our conversations. Her conversations reflect on the innocence of children and bring us back to reality with a touch of humour. The family refer to her as the Disney Princess because she would rather not know about all the unpleasantness in this world. However, she has ended up teaching in a small country town with low socio-economic households and a high Aboriginal population, so without knowing it, she still sees the daily struggles and hardships many Australians face.

As the girls have now finished their education, we have more opportunities to travel. Travelling always involves something unexpected and unplanned. Often, when we travel, somehow, we come across an incident where a person has died. In Malta, a tourist drowned while scuba diving at the beach we had gone to for the day, and we were there when they dragged the body onto the shore. In Bali, a man had a heart attack on the beach, and we stood five metres from him while the unskilled Balinese staff tried to get a defibrillator going. Other tourists who were medically qualified took over, but it was too late, and the man passed away. In Vietnam, a tourist had been killed, and his body was lying motionless on the roadway, with a hundred or so locals standing around observing the death of yet another tourist who died in a scooter accident. Our taxi stopped within two metres of his lifeless body, and I looked into his vacant, open eyes, staring into the abyss.

I think we are more observant because of our careers. It's instinctive, and I do have a meerkat personality. There's an old saying: once a cop, always a cop. However, we found that while in the Police there is an abundance of support within the police family, once we left, we were viewed a bit like the divorced brother in-law. We weren't always loved or remembered by our ex-family members, especially when we ended up working in a criminal law practice. Many people asked us how we could have a business that defended criminals after being police officers. They stopped asking if one of their kids got into trouble after doing something stupid. We live by the motto that they are not bad people, just good people who make bad choices. Most of our clients are just ordinary people who have made a split-second, thoughtless decision.

When we travel to underdeveloped countries, I try to do some sort of community service or donate food or goods to an organisation. During the Easter period in 2016, we travelled to Vietnam with some friends, and I was keen to do some community work while I was there. I spoke with the hotel concierge and inquired if there were any orphanages in the area, and she told me there was one not far from the hotel. We arranged for her to take us to the orphanage the next day. The men went off to watch Aussie football that was being aired in a local bar.

We pooled our money and caught a taxi to a large, bustling market to buy goods to take with us. We bought large bags of rice, nappies, baby formula, treats for the children and other essential items that we were told were needed. The staff member from the hotel did a great job of bartering with the locals to get us a good price.

The orphanage was situated up a small, unremarkable dirt laneway that many tourists drove past every day in their search for leather goods or a cheap tailored suit they could wear to their white-collar jobs without any knowledge of the tiny inhabitants laying in the many cots only a few hundred metres away. We walked into the immaculate, tiled-floor building to the sight of many cots squashed side by side, with one baby in each cot. The babies ranged in age from newborns to about sixteen months old and were either lying or standing with small, pleading eyes watching us. Some even had freshly tied umbilical cords.

Our Vietnamese staff member interpreted for us, and we asked how to help. Before we arrived, we honestly believed we would be cleaning or washing. The orphanage staff said the best thing we could do to help was cuddle the babies. The only problem we had was trying to decide which baby to nurse. My friends and I separated and allocated ourselves an area so we could try to give every baby some much-needed human affection.

The babies all appeared happy and healthy, and my top priority was to divide my time evenly between each baby. Some babies as young as four months old clung to me so tightly in an attempt to remain connected with me. They would have hung on if I was game to let go, even at that young age. Some of the babies reached out to me while I passed their cots, with their little hands opening and closing in non-verbal infant sign language, asking me to pick them up. We sat on the floor holding two babies at a time and sang nursery rhymes to them while their little companions watched from their cots and kept a curious eye on the unfamiliar intruders in their home.

The calm Vietnamese staff reassured us that the babies were all clean and appeared to be well looked after. When the day was over, we left the orphanage with heavy hearts and with the promise to return to spend some more time with a new group of abandoned souls. That very same weekend back in Australia, Kylie had her own remarkable life-changing experience, although very different from mine.

In Australia, the daily grind of work is only balanced for us by the central goal of travelling, and working towards having yet another experience in another country. A new adventure is never far away, and seeking out the extraordinary, expanding my knowledge, eating different foods and meeting people worldwide has become a part of me.

Pilgrimage

Beef

We were entering a whole new version of drought, with Australia experiencing the most extreme and prolonged drought in our country's history. I didn't know it then, but this drought would last for many years, the longest and hardest I had experienced. I was grateful the kids were away at school and didn't have to witness it first-hand. Even at the start, I found this drought harder to deal with than any before, and as the months continued, I had to force myself to stay mentally strong. Droughts decrease the quality of life for our stock, our plant life, and us! Our happiness was controlled by the weather. I did love my life and felt that living on the land had so many advantages, but as I did a mental audit, I felt the bad was starting to overshadow the good. Despite my strong appearance, I felt like a bush flower slowly wilting.

I am a clean freak, but during droughts, I put in extra effort to maintain a dust-free house and keep a little lawn alive, creating a small oasis to come home to after working out in depressing dusty paddocks. I had spent several days washing down the house, cleaning the windows, and tidying the yard, and I was exhausted but satisfied. Without warning, a savage dust storm hit; everything inside and outside the home, including me, was blanketed with thick red dirt, and all my hard work was rapidly undone. I burst into tears. After having a good cry, I made a cuppa and calmed myself down before I walked to the bathroom. I glanced at myself in the mirror and stopped! I could see snail-like tracks down my weathered face where the tears had dried in the dirt, and instantly, I burst into tears again. I felt trampled.

Days later, I woke early, deciding to do the ironing. I turned on the TV, and a movie, The Way, which I hadn't seen before, was just starting. Fixated on the film, and totally out of character, I stopped ironing and just sat still and watched. The movie was about a man, Daniel, played by Emilio Estevez, who travelled to France intending to walk a 799-kilometre pilgrim route called the Camino de Santiago. Early on in the movie, during a storm in the French Pyrenees, Daniel died. His father, an American ophthalmologist named Doctor Avery, played by Martin Sheen, is notified of Daniel's death and travels to France to collect his body. Once Doctor Avery arrives in France, he has a change of heart, arranges for his son's body to be cremated, and decides, while grieving and unprepared, to walk the Camino Frances carrying the remains of his son. In the movie's early stages, Doctor Avery meets three other pilgrims, all very different characters, and they form a Camino family, and while walking together they face many experiences as a group and individually along the way.

The movie was very thought-provoking and had a powerful effect on me. Interested, I googled the Camino and discovered that the

Camino de Santiago, known in English as the Way of Saint James, is a 1000-year-old pilgrimage route leading to the shrine of the apostle Saint James at the Cathedral at Santiago de Compostela in Galicia, north-west of Spain. In the Middle Ages, many thousands of pilgrims per year made their way to Santiago.

I couldn't stop thinking about the movie for the next few days. Two weeks later, as I walked inside for lunch, the TV was on, and I was shocked to see a documentary about the Camino just starting. After never reading or hearing about the Camino before, I felt twice in two weeks was too coincidental. Some people believe a person is called or receives a sign to walk the Camino. For reasons I couldn't explain, I felt like a magnet being pulled to metal. I had to do it, but realistically, the idea was impossible.

I discussed the Camino with Dave and asked if he would ever consider walking it with me. He laughed; he did not find the idea of walking across Spain appealing. Later, on the phone, I told Jacki the story, and without hesitation, she suggested we walk it in two years for our fiftieth birthday. Absolutely! I strongly hoped the drought would be over before then, and what a way to celebrate our milestone birthday and reconnect with my twin after all these years apart. Despite our current hardship, Dave supported me wholeheartedly. Like me, I am sure he thought, or hoped, flooding rains would arrive soon. Dave had flown to America in his mid-twenties and had journeyed around the country for six months, and he understood my wish to experience the wonders of overseas travel. I told my three teenage children my plans; they knew I would do it, but all doubted I would make it.

Operation Camino commenced, which was a brilliant diversion from the dispiriting drought. There are many Camino routes all leading to Santiago, but I wanted to walk the same route as they had in the movie, the popular French path, starting at the foothills of the Pyrenees in St. Jean Pied de Port and finishing at the Cathedral in Santiago. I set a goal to save every bit of my photography business income, thereby not adding any further financial strain to our limited farm budget. Without this income, it really would have been impossible for me to go.

If I was going to walk 799 kilometres and survive, between ongoing property work, family matters, issues that come with a drought, and attending photography bookings, I had to get fit, so eight months out, I started to train. Four weeks before our scheduled departure, I woke one morning with a very painful knee, resulting in a nine-hour drive to have an MRI. I discovered I had a grade four chondromalacia, basically no cartilage. I made an urgent physio appointment. The physio gave me some good news: if I stayed off my leg for the next month, took medication, did daily physio, and bought a special knee brace, she felt I could walk the Camino. She emphasised it would hurt a lot, but I could do it.

The skies remained cloudless, and everyone in my community was struggling. We were struggling, and I felt guilty and selfish because I was about to jump on a plane, travel overseas, and walk for weeks. I was anxious about my husband's mental health and safety during my impending absence. He would have no physical contact with anyone for weeks. Our kids were all at boarding school but still needed me. Bella was soon to sit her final exams, and my knee was very painful. I started questioning my decision and discussed my qualms with Dave, who was selfless and encouraging. Jacki's position in life was very different from mine, and she was fortunate to have no obstacles.

One month later, I put the crutches against the wall, and Dave and I drove 550 kilometres to our closest airport for my first flight to Sydney, where I met Jacki. We had lunch with one of the Dubbo girls, Lisa. She generously gave us bracelets to wear on our walk; mine appropriately had a Saint Christopher medal attached. We flew to Dubai, caught a connecting flight to Madrid, and then caught our last flight, finally arriving at Biarritz in France, where we collapsed in bed.

We arranged a private car transfer to Saint Jean de Port the following morning. Our French-speaking driver unexpectedly arrived with Kenny Rogers music blaring in the car. I was expecting something like the French Can Can music. I laughed and couldn't help but think of our father and our car trips as a child. We started the journey, but it wasn't long before my twin and I had a conversation with our eyes, as we realised our French driver was lost. Half an hour later, this was confirmed when we drove past the motel where we had spent the previous night.

Finally, our driver appeared to find his way, which we had secretly confirmed, thanks to Google Maps. The little car sped along an open road and soon approached an S-bend when a car travelling in the opposite direction suddenly pulled across in front of us. Our driver locked up the brakes, our seatbelts jerked, and our bodies stiffened as our car slid sidewards towards the other vehicle. I found a new meaning for the French word Oui (wee). All shaken, we recovered slightly before our driver cautiously continued, and we arrived at our pre-booked accommodation at Saint Jean de Port. Relieved, we dragged our bags into the motel, and although I did not speak French, it was apparent the lady in charge was uptight. After our near-death car experience, and despite not knowing what caused the lady's cranky demeanour, I was pleased to be alive to hear her grumbles. After two years of planning and four days of travelling, I was finally here!

We decided to explore the picturesque medieval town bustling with pilgrims. We went to a restaurant and overheard a welcoming Aussie accent at a neighbouring table. We met fellow pilgrims Eugenia, Zoran, and their daughter Holly. Over a drink, they told us where to locate the Pilgrim's Office. I didn't even know there was one! Walking along a cobbled street, I giggled when a Dutchman suddenly appeared in front of me and said in a wonderful accent, 'Hello'. I swear he was an identical clone of the Dutchman in the movie The Way, which started this whole adventure in the first place. We returned to our happy hostess and prepared for the following day. As part of our 'reconnecting' and for some fun, my twin and I decided to wear matching clothes, which we had not done since early childhood. I phoned Dave, who wished me luck. Unbeknown to me, my husband and children were all running bets on whether I would make it.

Early the next day, suffering jetlag, Jacki and I walked out of Saint Jean Pied de Port and commenced our Camino adventure. I think physically, mentally and spiritually, I was one of the most unprepared pilgrims ever in history to walk the Camino. Our research warned us that on day one, a twenty-eight-kilometre walk from St. Jean de Port to Roncesvalles would reach an elevation of 1200 meters and it would take seven to nine hours. It was said to be one of the most challenging physical days along the entire Camino. Reading this and doing it were very different experiences.

We eagerly walked out of town on a cool, overcast morning and headed up a 'little hill' that soon turned into a mountain, part of the Pyrenees. Only a kilometre in, I was struggling for breath, and my knee painfully ached. I was thankful for the sizeable supportive knee brace hidden under my clothes. As we continued to climb, the air got cooler, and of course, it started to rain. We had been waiting for rain at home for years; I wasn't sure I welcomed it now.

Soon, I knew my sister had had the advantage of both time and hills to train on, and the gap between us expanded. I desperately tried to get my breathing into a rhythm. The only thought in my head was, What the hell was I thinking? Fellow pilgrims were spread out kilometres in front and behind me and were climbing, all with varying abilities. After about five kilometres, I had to stop for a minute and have a break. I stood there and noticed a lady about the same age as me also resting. I didn't have to tell her I was struggling; my physical appearance gave it away. With a Canadian accent, this kind lady smiled and said, 'It's your Camino, do it at your own pace.'

I gratefully thanked her and struggled on. The rain was getting heavier, and my sister was out of sight. I caught the look many pilgrims gave me as they passed me on their way up. They glanced at me and then glanced again, followed by a concerned, 'Are you alright?' Unbeknown to me, the rain had made my mascara run, so besides erratic breathing, the black that surrounded my eyes was illuminated by my bright red face, making me look even more unwell.

As I approached the edge of Orison, our first rest stop only eight kilometres in, I spotted my twin, who, frustrated with my mountain climbing abilities, had come back looking for me. As she approached, she suggested I wipe my eyes. I don't wear makeup daily, so I don't know why I did that day. I followed my sister into an albergue, fell into a chair, and gratefully received the hot cup of tea she handed me. The room was packed with wet, cold pilgrims excitedly talking in a variety of languages. At our table were the Aussies we had met the day before. After a brief rest, my twin said, 'Let's go.' I didn't want to leave the warmth of the building; I had just arrived and was envious that my twin had rested longer.

The next steep walking section had a sealed road, for which I was grateful. As I struggled on, I couldn't help but hum the song, I Will Walk Five Hundred Miles, a hit by the Scottish twin brothers, The Proclaimers. The rain got heavier, and visibility was poor. Somewhere surrounding me were supposed to be great views, but thanks to a thick blanket of fog, I couldn't see more than a few metres ahead. I wasn't sure where all the other pilgrims that I had seen at Orison were; all I could see was Jacki walking meters ahead of me. Suddenly, I spotted something emerging from the fog. What was that? Pigs! We stopped, swinging our walking poles for protection as three large pigs snorted at our feet. Shit, what do we do now? We were trying to shoo them away when I spotted two other pilgrims emerge from the fog behind us. The pigs turned their attention to them, and completely un-pilgrim-like, we took off and left the men to the pigs.

The temperature plummeted, and the rain was unrelenting as we climbed and climbed. I was sure if we climbed any higher, I seriously would meet God himself. As I was behind my twin, I started to think I was not walking in Saint James's footsteps but in Jacki James's footsteps. We rounded a bend, and here, high in the mountains, were several pilgrims crowded around a mobile food van. I'd reached heaven! We ordered a steaming hot cup of tea, and while standing in the pouring rain, I gratefully swallowed. I could feel the warmth of the tea travel through my cold body. I took off my boots and poured out the few millimetres of rainwater they were carrying, and I knew Dave would appreciate those millimetres more than I did. Reluctantly, I walked on.

We arrived at the 1100-meter level, where a little hut, an emergency shelter built for pilgrims, had a small wood fire burning. That day many pilgrims took turns huddling inside for a few minutes, and here we met back up with our Australian friends. Holly, a teenager, was very cold, so Jacki kindly handed over her gloves to help keep Holly's freezing fingers warm. Hopefully, this gave us good God credits after abandoning the pilgrims with the pigs. We left the tar road and walked along a woodland path before crossing a cattle grid. I was oblivious that we had left France and entered Spain.

I started the slippery, wet descent through a dark, damp beechwood forest. The gap between my sister and I lessened a little as I lifted my feet through the ankle-deep mud. A short while later, I spotted a fellow pilgrim pinned to the wet ground with a pushbike on top of her; she wasn't moving. As I approached, I could see she was so exhausted that she didn't have the strength to lift the bike off herself. I helped her up and checked she was okay, then continued to plod through what resembled Shreks Swamp.

I met an Irishman who had stepped off the main walking track to go to the toilet. He slipped in the wet and, with his backpack on, stumbled several meters down a muddy embankment. He had severely sprained his ankle, but full of Irish cheer and, I suspect, some alcoholic medicine, he limped on. The heavy rain continued, and I felt the temperature drop further. Finally, late in the afternoon, I emerged shell-shocked from the forest and arrived at our destination, Roncesvalles.

Like a sheep, I confidently followed groups of pilgrims ahead of me as they walked into a building, the Monastery Albergue, where many wet, cold pilgrims were lining up to book a bed. I joined the cue, but I couldn't spot my twin. Eventually, I was at the head of the line, and as I shivered, I explained I had a booking, only to discover I was at the wrong building altogether. Finally, I found our motel, which felt like a heated palace. Jacki was not there and had gone to yet another building. She finally found our accommodation, meeting me in the foyer. We both enjoyed very long hot showers in our toasty, warm room. Ahh, bliss! We were grateful for the heaters we used to dry our walking clothes. Later, we had a delicious meal before attending a neighbouring church, where a pilgrim mass was held, and we were all blessed. I was grateful as I felt I was going to need all the blessings I could get.

Exhausted, I went off to sleep, thinking an island holiday might have been a better option. Only 771 kilometres to go!

Despite climbing to the outskirts of heaven the previous day and waking sore all over, I was well-rested and excited to start the new day's walk. I stood outside the building, taking in the scenery, when Jacki rushed out, marched past me, and started walking. I called her name, and she looked back at me as I pointed in the opposite direction. I thought of the fable, The Hare and the Tortoise. Laughing, she turned and we headed off.

It was drizzling rain, but my stiff leg muscles loosened gradually, and I enjoyed the walk on flatter terrain. Sometimes, as I walked past a fellow pilgrim, yes, I did pass some; I would smile and say the Camino greeting, 'Buen Camino' (meaning good way), but instead of replying 'Buen Camino', they looked at me strangely. I could tell they were thinking, didn't you pass me five minutes ago? I had to readjust to this sort of twin confusion, which I had been accustomed to as a child.

Camino gossip travelled fast. We were told about a young Irish lady who had been rescued on the treacherous Pyrenees Mountain the previous day and had been hospitalised, suffering hypothermia. With around 300,000 people walking the Camino every year, there were inevitably some deaths. Most were due to being hit by a motor vehicle or suffering a heart attack. In the Middle Ages, it was said if a pilgrim died whilst on a pilgrimage, they would bypass purgatory and go straight to heaven. Tragically, four pilgrims died during the period Jacki and I walked the Camino. I was grateful to survive day two. That night, we stayed at a motel where a scene from The Way had been filmed. Over a meal, we met four Canadian ladies, including the one who had encouraged me on day one.

Our daily pilgrimage continued, and we arrived at our first Spanish city, beautiful Pamplona. The city is filled with narrow, cobbled streets and ancient buildings overflowing with colour, all oozing with history. As I took photos in the square, I couldn't help but feel an overwhelming sense of gratitude. I had never dreamt I would have the opportunity to travel to Europe, and here I was in Spain in this magnificent city square, surrounded by beautiful historic buildings. It was surreal. I felt so privileged. I told my twin how I felt, and she said, 'Oh, that's right, you haven't seen a European city before.' Her reply reminded me of our contrasting adult lives.

Each pilgrim walks their own pace and distance, so I could meet someone and only chat for a few minutes or a few hours, or perhaps walk together for a day, but then never see each other again. We found a connection with some pilgrims who were walking similar daily distances to us, and our Camino family developed. It consisted of Jordan, Kyl, Christina, Rex, Jose, and Diana, all from various locations in the USA. We also continued to run into Ken and Alyssa, and Jane, from England, David from Argentina, Emmett from Ireland, and Italian sisters, Ester and Rosanna.

Understandably, my knee was sore, but unexpectedly, for the first week, my hips and thighs were also extremely painful, and I was soon walking like a robot. Kyl suggested I adjust my backpack and helped me do this. As my twin had purchased my pack and posted it to me, mine had never been fitted correctly for my body. I didn't even know there was a correct way to carry one. I also had two walking poles with me, and again, I had never been shown or learned that there was a right height at which they should be positioned. I was using the poles like two walking canes. Rex adjusted them, and I was amazed at the difference this made. Thanks to Kyl and Rex, within a few days, the pain in my hips and thighs disappeared, and soon, I was walking quite well and keeping up with our pack.

Frustratingly each day Jacki would wash and blow dry her hair, and apply makeup, before putting a hat or beanie on her head. As I watched and waited, I felt it was unnecessary and a complete waste of time; a ponytail did the job. I found that each morning Jacki was always very impatient to start the day. I genuinely couldn't see the problem with waiting an extra five minutes, and I wanted to walk at my pace, not hers. Particularly early on, I noticed she preferred to talk to someone as she walked. She needed people. I was, and am, very comfortable with my own company. I was conscious that we still needed to reach our destination at the end of each day, but I didn't want my Camino to be a race, and with my sore knee, it couldn't be. With no hills to train on and a bad knee, I struggled to climb the many hills and often fell behind when our group ascended. Jordan gave me some hill tips and told me to squeeze my glute muscles as I climbed. I thought I'd just be the rear guard and protect us from the pigs.

Jacki constantly worried about me if she was too far ahead; however, she didn't need to. I was pleased to make my own friends, I felt safe, and I reminded her that I would catch up eventually. I did increase speed descending hills or on the flatter paths, and the gap between us always lessoned until the next hill. When I look back at all my photos, my twin's backside is in many of them, so overall she was never too far ahead. Over the weeks, Jacki and I eventually established a comfortable Camino routine that suited us both.

Although I spoke with Dave daily, gradually, I selfishly stopped thinking about home and just concentrated on myself and each new day. Most of the paths weaved through rural areas and into small Spanish villages that had magnificent churches or cathedrals, and occasionally, we would stop and say a prayer. Besides gaining some spiritual enlightenment, I found sitting in church was a great chance to rest my aching body. In the first few weeks, many of the surrounding paddocks were filled with bright red poppies, and as I plodded along admiring their beauty, I couldn't help but think about all those who served and died in wars, including many of my ancestors. I picked a poppy and put it in my headband and did this every day until the poppies disappeared.

Like two sore-footed cows, we hobbled into the city of Burgos. My injuries consisted of a large blister on my heel, half a toenail missing, what I thought were shin splints but may have been self-diagnosed tendonitis, and, due to perspiration and heat, blisters under my knee brace that accompanied not one, but now two very sore knees. I was supposed to be doing this walk to rejuvenate!

My twin was equally suffering. The artistic view from our accommodation window was the magnificent, ancient Cathedral of Saint Mary of Burgos, founded in 1221. We walked through it, admiring its amazing architecture, artifacts, and history before attending a pilgrim's mass. I found the cities alive and exciting; however, I preferred to walk along the comforting country paths.

After leaving the city of Burgos, we arrived at a small village for the night, and I decided to explore. I hobbled up a street and smiled at an older man who approached me and started speaking Spanish. The man implied to wait and walked away. Jacki joined me while he was gone. He returned, carrying a little basket covered in a tea towel, and indicated that we should follow him. Confused, we trailed behind him as he walked us to the side of a hill, where there was a row of padlocked historic wooden doors. With medieval keys, he unlocked a door and directed us to enter. We are only five foot two tall, and this man came up to our shoulders, so I felt pretty confident that we could tackle him if needed.

Hesitantly, we entered, and I was amazed to discover it was a wine cellar full of ancient dusty bottles. The older man lifted the tea towel; the basket contained a bottle opener and wine glasses. We watched as he enthusiastically opened a dusty bottle of red and poured us a glass each. I have never been a wine drinker, but as he stood with a gratified smile, I attempted to show my appreciation and thought I'd just gulp it down, and that would be it. This approach didn't work. As soon as my glass emptied, he poured some more. I felt somewhat guilty as I don't think I fully appreciated what I assumed was a good drop. The scene was even funnier as this older man's trouser zipper was down the whole time. Thanking him, we returned a little tipsy to our accommodation.

We soon started to walk the much harsher 200-kilometre Meseta section. This section has an enormous sky, is scorching hot, is very flat with open fields, has little shade, and limited infrastructure. It was just like home. I loved it! I happily walked along, my steps in a comfortable rhythm with my walking poles.

Since arriving in Spain, my stomach had disagreed with Spanish pilgrim food. Most days, I was timing my loo stops well; however, one day along the Meseta, surrounded by very flat open wheat fields, the urge came quickly, too quickly. I needed to go, and I had to be fast as there were pilgrims ahead and approaching from behind. Living in the country, I was used to bush loos, but at home, I only had to worry about a cow watching me. I ran into the paddock, and with my backpack still on, dropped my pants and, balancing carefully, did my business. Unfortunately, a strong wind was blowing, and my business was more like a liquid. The wind caught it and blew it all over my shoes. Shit! Literally shit. I was forced to walk in dirty shoes until the next town, where I could finally clean myself up.

That night after a shower, we met up with Jane from England and David from Argentina. While some cool beers rehydrated us, David slunk off and returned with a generous gift for each of us, a necklace with a wooden-style cross. How thoughtful and kind! He explained these are meant to protect a pilgrim from illness. I certainly needed that!

The days continued, and we reached Carrion de los Condes. Our accommodation was a beautiful, restored eleventh-century monastery with piped music playing. After settling into our room, we attended an albergue where we heard there were singing nuns. Here, straight from The Sound of Music, were four beautiful young nuns, one with a guitar. We joined our fellow pilgrims from all over the world and were asked to introduce ourselves individually and, if we wished to, state our reason for undertaking this pilgrimage. Each pilgrim took their turn. Some were walking for hope, guidance, inspiration, transformation, for fitness. Some were grieving, commemorating, forgetting, forgiving, praying, or just walking for fun. We sang along with the nuns who had voices of angels, and I'm not sure why, but this room felt filled with love and had a peaceful aura, and my eyes filled with tears. The nuns gave us all coloured paper stars to remind us to look up, that they were praying for us, and for us to remember God's love. That night, I phoned Dave and told him that I thought I might become a nun.

Early one morning, our village departure was blocked thanks to an agitated donkey. While trying to come up with a safe solution to navigate it, we met Bill, a middle-aged priest from Boston. As a group, we safely moved around the donkey, left the village, and were soon walking together in a peaceful rhythm. When walking, pilgrims often talk about issues that are not easy to talk about at home. Bill was considering leaving the priesthood so he could marry his childhood sweetheart, who had recently reappeared in his life.

As I waited for a farmer to muster his sheep across the road, I thought of Dave; we were Jack and Rose. Of course, like any honest couple, we have had relationship challenges, but for twenty years, we have worked through them and become a strong team.

I knew Dave would love the Camino experience and thought one day I would enjoy walking it with him. I understood that walking the Camino with Dave would be a very different experience to walking it with my twin.

Jacki, Bill and I stopped for a much-needed rest, huddling under the one tree that provided shade and respite from the heat, and shared our packed food. The simple pleasures! With Bill, we celebrated when we reached what the Spanish consider the official halfway point.

We arrived at the unappealing town, Mansilla de las Mulas, with the town's electronic temperature gauge reading forty-two degrees. Disappointingly, our accommodation was basic; our room had ripped blinds and was above a noisy bar. Jacki and I were not looking forward to our night. After some essential jobs, we returned to our simple accommodation and discovered that the bar was now closed and the area quiet. The owners, a beautiful family, took one look at my feet and rushed off, returning with a bowl filled with iced water before they served a lovingly prepared meal. I was reminded not to judge a book by its cover. I was amazed when the Spanish people would apologise for not speaking English, as I felt we should have been apologising to them for not knowing at least a little Spanish; it was their country, after all. Despite thousands of pilgrims invading their country, clicking walking poles through their peaceful villages, they displayed true Christian values.

Each new day brought new challenges, surprises, and delights. We had a few unintentional detours but soon were helped back onto the correct path. We met some fellow Aussies, Caitlin and Glen, and thoroughly enjoyed their company. Sometimes I meet a couple and know they are meant to be together; I felt they were like two brolgas, and would be mates for life. As a group, we arrived at Astorga, where later, running late for a pilgrim's mass, we rushed into a church and quickly sat. Beautiful singing filled the small church, and I thought it was a recording. When the service was over, I turned to leave, and was in awe when I spotted a large group of traditionally dressed nuns standing behind an ancient, black-caged barrier. I was unaware that the church was attached to a strict convent. That night, with the great company of Rex and Jose, we had a beautiful meal, which they insisted on paying for. We still owe them a meal in return.

On day twenty-nine, we climbed up towards the village of O'Cebreriro. The mountain was steep and wet, and the path was covered with fifteen centimetres of cow dung, which made it difficult for my shoes to grip the slippery surface. There was a fork in the path; unbeknown to me, Jacki had walked to the right. I went to the left. This fork reminded me of how our lives had changed. While walking, I thought about my twin and our fifty-year relationship. I am not sure why nature or God made two of me. I do know that despite being an identical twin, I am not a puppet; pulling her string doesn't make my leg move. We were very similar as young girls, but we had grown in different directions, had our own individual hopes and dreams, and were now unique in both looks and personality. Rightfully, we are our own spirits. Jacki and I have had many different experiences throughout life, and our responses have shaped our individual personalities in many ways.

Twins are often sought after for research as they offer scientists a unique opportunity and provide a valuable source of information for health and psychological research. Their unique relationship allows researchers to pull apart and examine genetic and environmental influences. In 1937, a German, Josef Mengele, joined the Institute for Hereditary Biology and Racial Hygiene in Frankfurt, where he worked as an assistant for a German geneticist who had a particular interest in researching twins. During World War Two, Mengele transferred to Auschwitz, a German Nazi concentration camp, because he wished to continue his experiments on twins. Although in his earlier life, Mengele's twin experiments had been legitimate, his work in Auschwitz-Birkenau was not. He abandoned all medical ethics and research protocols and began conducting horrific and inhumane medical experiments on an estimated three thousand sets of twins, many of them innocent young children. The twins were cruelly and unwillingly exposed to disease, disfigurement, and torture under the guise of medical research.

Today, twin experiments continue to unlock a new understanding of nature and nurture, and twins are in such high demand by scientists that at an annual twins fair held in Twinsburg, Ohio, USA, scientists set up booths hoping to attract twins to their studies. The studies show that although identical twins have the same genes and look strikingly similar, they can develop slight differences through their environment, and these differences can commence in the womb. One twin may grow a few inches taller than the other, or one twin may have a distinctively different weight or facial feature. So, through these twin experiments, researchers can find out with more certainty how the environment interacts with genes and how it affects a person's health and appearance.

When we were small, and still referred to as two white mice, our mother registered us with the Australian Twin Registry, and agreed for us to participate in various approved twin studies that were being conducted at a Brisbane University. These studies involved completing lengthy surveys, and as young children, we did not understand what we were participating in. However, in our early adult life, my twin and I both started to feel like lab mice and were uncomfortable answering very personal questions. We unanimously agreed to stop our participation in the medical research. However, as we have aged, I can see the importance of these studies.

When at an altitude of 1300 meters, I arrived in O'Cebreriro, a small village with traditional Celtic Mountain dwellings that predate the Romans. I caught up with Jacki and our friend Diana, and we attended a pilgrims' mass at a ninth-century church. The presiding priest was young and spoke English. He selected people from different languages to read, and I was chosen to represent English-speaking pilgrims. As I was seated behind the priest, for the second time along the Camino, for reasons I can't explain, I felt a sudden inner warmth. I felt peace, I felt loved, and I had to take deep breaths so I didn't cry. I was feeling the Camino's power. At the end of the moving church service, the priest handed us all a little rock painted with the Camino yellow guide arrow, to remind us of our journey. I treasure this!

The following day, as we walked in the pouring rain and thick fog, we met a gorgeous group of Spanish teenagers, one of whom had fallen and hurt herself. We offered help, and they laughed when I told them my children were devoutly running bets on me. We walked on together, and I thought of my three perfect kids. They were all growing into beautiful adults with good ethics and morals. They are sixth-generation graziers; life on the land was engraved in their DNA. Knowing they were about to start their adult lives, I was satisfied Dave and I had done all we could to prepare them for the adult world. Soon, they would branch off and make their own life memories. I understood I couldn't be involved in all of them, but I knew I would be part of some.

My pilgrimage continued, and as I walked through a forest filled with natural beauty, we approached the village of Arzua. I started to cross a very pretty, ancient bridge, and saw a hill ahead, and let out a sigh. A soft, meditating voice said, 'The hill will wait; cool your tired feet.' I turned to see a Japanese man sitting on the side of the bridge, gently smiling at me. He had a mystical and peaceful aura that radiated from him. I looked down over the bridge and saw a clear stream; the sun glittered light off the gently flowing water. It was surrounded by emerald green grass and large shading trees. A few pilgrims were dotted on either bank, sunning themselves. Yes! I convinced Jacki to stop. We walked down to the water's edge and dropped our heavy backpacks before removing our hot shoes. We paddled into the brisk, cool water, which felt soothing on our sore and battered feet. Afterwards, I dropped onto the soft grass, the sun's rays caressing my face, and the beauty of the scenery left me speechless. We ate bread, and I pilgrim-watched. It was glorious! I noticed a young man cautiously walk into the edge of the water, and I was a little concerned as this fellow with Down syndrome appeared alone. After a short time, another young man arrived, took his hand, and together they paddled into the gently flowing water. They stood together, laughing and splashing. As I watched, I was reminded of what makes me genuinely content: the simple things: my family, love, laughter, nature, and my twin.

Very few Australians were walking the Camino at the same time as us; however, I think we managed to find them all. On our second last day, we met Cherie and Laura from Brisbane. Together, as we walked, we came upon a pilgrim's bar that had custom-made pilgrims' beer. Despite it being 10 am, we felt as Aussies we should stop and just have one or two! We sat happily chatting, drinking in the sunshine, and as I listened to their Aussie accents my thoughts were drawn to home. Eventually, a little tipsy we walked on. That night, due to the location of our accommodation, we were separated from our Camino family, and as Jacki and I ate our 'last supper' together, I felt confused. I was dreadfully missing my family but relishing my Camino experience, truly not wanting it to end.

Our last day arrived, and we woke very early and started walking in the dark. Looking up at the stars shining brightly, I though, they were 'almost' as beautiful as the stars at Bourke. We arrived on the outskirts of Santiago, walked into a small church, and lit a candle. As William Shakespeare said, *'We came into the world like sister and sister, and now let's go hand in hand, not one before the other,'* With this in mind, we walked side by side the last few kilometres to the magnificent Cathedral of Saint James. Euphoria filled me as I gently touched the cathedral wall. I had made it!

We sat together in the symbolic Plaza do Obradoiro, a courtyard square, outside the Cathedral where pilgrims have ritually stood for hundreds of years. I felt a mixture of emotions as I witnessed fellow pilgrims celebrate the completion of their Camino journey. We attended the Pilgrims Office, and received our Compostela's, a certificate to confirm we had walked the Camino. These have been issued to pilgrims since the ninth century.

The following day, Jacki, Diana, and I attended the popular pilgrims' mass at the Cathedral. I thought, for the past thirty-six days, over the 799-kilometre pilgrimage, my twin and I had struggled, laughed, cried, and rejoiced. We had gotten lost and found our way. We had fought and made up, and supported and encouraged each other. We walked alone. We walked together. We walked in groups, and we met wonderful new people. Our accommodation was varied, from beautiful monasteries to private homes and everything in between. Nature ensured we experienced all weather types while trekking over mountains, through vineyards, forests, small towns, large cities, crops, and open plains, all different but all equally beautiful. Like the scenery, the walking paths changed regularly. Some had rough rocks, hard to walk on; some were steep and difficult to climb; some were soft grass, fringed with flowers, so pretty and beautiful. What a remarkable experience! I sat in quiet reflection.

Life has a natural unpredictability and my first fifty years had certainly been filled with moments of elation, and challenges.

Each of the highs and lows has offered a lesson, teaching me to cherish the fleeting beauty of happiness and to find strength amidst adversity. This has helped me to navigate my journey with more appreciation, and through it all, my twin, my clone, has always been by my side, sometimes from a distance, but always there.

I arrived back to the bush and my fantastic family. The stubborn drought had continued, still sucking the life out of anything living. However, my spirit was lifted, my energy had been re-mustered, and I felt like a wild bush flower that had been watered. As I adjusted back to 'everyday' routine, I went for a walk through the bush. I looked down and noticed some emu tracks in the bare red dirt. These footprints, resembling a Camino guide arrow, served as a poignant reminder that my pilgrimage was far from over. I realized that as I continued to live my life, I would keep leaving my footprints in the red dirt, while my twin would leave hers in the beach sand. I wondered, what would the next fifty years bring?

As I continued to stroll, I thought back to the twin's story about the one spare life jacket and wondered at this point in my life who I would give the one life jacket to, my husband or my twin? It didn't matter; we had no water anyway.

Reef

When I get home from a holiday, washing is my number one priority, followed by a marathon phone call with my twin sister to exchange all our news. Talking about travel is a delicate situation when talking to anyone, as I don't want to sound pretentious, and I have to gauge my audience. I'm mindful that Kylie would love to go to some of the countries I have travelled to, and on occasions, I dumb down the holiday, so I'm not gloating about my new experiences, especially if it's somewhere she has dreamed about visiting.

During yet another long conversation on the phone with Kylie in 2016, she casually told me about a movie she had seen called, The Way, on 'some walk' in Spain. I filed it away with other random topics we have had in our numerous disjointed conversations. A few weeks later, she rang and told me to quickly turn on the TV. There was a documentary about the same walk she had seen about 'that' movie. Watching the documentary, I immediately felt a compelling allure to complete this pilgrimage, the Camino. After an unusually brief conversation with my twin, we decided we would do the walk to celebrate our fiftieth birthdays—two years away. My decision was made without any consultation with my husband.

I researched the walk, which is loosely described as the Camino, and I found there was plenty of information out there. The more I researched the Camino, the more I was intrigued. I don't think many of our family and friends thought we would actually do the walk, but I knew, with the utmost certainty, that I would complete the walk with Kylie. I wanted to; we needed to do this walk together. It was time we spent some time alone without the distraction of family, work, and life.

I found a company that would do most of the organising for us and decided we would book our accommodation each night in hotels, BBs and rural houses. On the Camino, we discovered that pre-booking our accommodation was an advantage, but could also be a disadvantage. Once we paid for the flights and paid our non-refundable deposit for the accommodation, we knew that there was no turning back. Much to both our husband's frustrations, our daily phone calls increased to a minimum of two a day while the organising took place.

I spent a lot of time researching the equipment we would need, and as the date of our departure grew closer, I started to buy our gear. Kylie, living out where she does, obviously had trouble getting her own equipment, so for practical reasons and convenience, I bought her gear as well. It took me a bit longer to get my backpack fitted as I also had to get Kylie's fitted; we are almost the same height. When I bought a rain jacket, I just bought two. For the first time in decades, we would be dressing the same as twins. Buying shoes on the Camino is the most important purchase a pilgrim makes, and being identical twins, we have the same shoe size. The research I conducted on footwear was extensive, and we still didn't get it quite right. I spent so much time researching equipment that I really didn't spend any time thinking about the walk. I had no idea what to expect emotionally and had no preconceived ideas about what I wanted to achieve on the walk, except to spend some quality time with my twin sister and finish.

As the date drew nearer, I was starting to wonder if I was going to have to be the 'parent' on the trip. Kylie had only been on one short holiday overseas to Fiji and was asking a lot of questions. Flights, money, and other things like transport were left to me to organise. I had never travelled overseas without my husband, so it was a bit daunting. I felt a responsibility on my shoulders to get us there and back again.

I started training for the walk, taking small hikes on the north coast, and my few kilometres turned into ten when I had the time. Scott enjoys bush walking, and it was great to be able to do some training with him. But I knew on the Camino I would be walking day after day for weeks. I needed to up my game, so my husband and I organised a hike with some friends to Mt Warning, which is located on the far north coast of New South Wales. I wondered if the name of the mountain had any significance. This hike is an 8.8-kilometre, grade four trail with an elevation of 1156 metres, and this hike provided me with an epiphany. Was this what the Camino was going to be like? I was aware that on day one of the Camino, we would be walking twenty-four kilometres at an altitude of 1400 metres over the Pyrenees mountains. This sudden realisation made me both determined and frightened at the same time.

We arrived in France full of enthusiasm, and even though it was a drab, overcast day, I couldn't ignore the electric energy in the atmosphere of the small ancient town of St Jean de Port. I looked at Kylie, who was carrying a recent injury, with great frustration. Her training had commenced far too late and had resulted in a knee injury. To be fair, it was much easier for me to train living where I do, and I have also had dodgy knees most of my adult life. It's probably a genetic fault, and we haven't treated our bodies kindly over the years. Both our bodies have started showing evidence of the active life we have lived, and I wish, in the past, I had treated my body more like a Southern Belle sitting on a veranda drinking iced tea. Well, okay, maybe alcohol. I had no idea how my twin was going to finish the walk, and she had almost pulled out of the trip three weeks before, adding to my frustration. There was no doubt about it, day one on the Camino was going to be difficult.

We went to the Pilgrims Office where we registered for the Camino and had our first stamp placed on our pilgrims' passports which was confirmation that we were there, and our pilgrimage had commenced. The pilgrim's passport is a document and a way to accredit the completion of the pilgrimage. It is stamped each day along the path at various locations. The pilgrim's office sounded like a beehive buzzing with the sounds of different accents from fellow pilgrims, who were also registering their intentions to start this well-known pilgrimage.

Adrenaline-fuelled, we headed out of town. Kylie was walking quite slowly, and after all the planning and anticipation, I just wanted to take off and get into it. Walking with her on day one was like trying to Christmas shop with a toddler, where I tried to rush ahead, but they forced me to slow down, whinging because they were tired and over it. I was conscious that we had decided to do this walk together and to spend some much-needed time reconnecting as twins, and I had an obligation not to leave my sister.

If I am honest, I was also frightened that I actually might get lost if I walked ahead by myself and secretly liked the security she offered. I crept a few hundred metres ahead but also made sure Kylie was within my sight. The Pyrenees Mountains are the natural border between Spain and France, and this section of the Camino is where the very few people who die on the Camino are most likely to succumb. The only guidance we had were the odd blue Camino shell located in random places, indiscriminate yellow arrows pointing 'the way', and a guidebook. These navigation tools were our only compass to Santiago.

The scallop shell is a symbol of pilgrimage, and on the Camino, pilgrims display this symbol by securing a shell to their backpacks. The painted yellow arrows marked along the 799 kilometres are painted on rocks, roads and even the sides of houses. We soon discovered that a moment of inattention would more than likely make us miss the yellow arrows and subsequently get lost.

I walked among fellow pilgrims, passing some and watching others pull ahead and disappear. As I walked, I imagined what had brought these pilgrims on the same journey as us; we were a kaleidoscope of people and personalities. As I daydreamed, I developed a second wind, which made me walk like a general leading his soldiers into battle and put more distance than I wanted between Kylie and me. I had walked about eight kilometres and reached the township of Orrison. This was a great place to have our first break.

Exhausted, I walked into a packed café filled with pilgrims and ordered lunch for Kylie and me, thinking she wouldn't be that far behind me. I waited and waited and waited. I was worried something had happened to her, and my anxiety was building the longer I sat there. I couldn't relax, and although people were talking to me, I wasn't listening. I leapt from the table and asked some Australian pilgrims, who I had only met the day before, to look after my backpack containing all my hiking gear, my passport and money, and I ran back to find her. I would have never normally left my gear with random people, but fear overtook me, and all reasonable behaviour went out the window.

As I was running, I was asking any pilgrim I saw, 'Have you seen another lady that looks like me?' They must have thought I was suffering from hypothermia. Let's face it: How many twins our age walk around dressed the same way? I only ran about a kilometre back when I found her walking, happily chatting to other pilgrims, oblivious to the fact that I was so worried about her. She didn't know what all the fuss was about. I almost killed her! I then panicked; I had left my backpack with strangers and ran all the way back to the restaurant, and gratefully found my bag safely where I had left it. My Fitbit recorded two more kilometres to my day than my twin's.

After a quick lunch we gathered our belongings and slowly, ever so slowly, climbed the mountain. We still had sixteen kilometres to go. The weather started to close in, with fog shrouding us and heavy rain providing a spiritual cleansing. We had lost sight of most pilgrims who were walking much faster than us. Rain pelted our faces, and the water ran down our exercise tights, pooling in the bottom of our boots. Our rain jackets kept our torsos dry, but we hadn't thought to pack rain pants. The evening was drawing closer, and I was afraid we were going to get lost on the mountain. The fog curtained off the spectacular scenery and hid a famous statue of Mary from us. I was grateful I wouldn't have to face Mary while I was muttering unchristian words about how slowly Kylie was walking. It was a long day, a very long day!

It was obvious to me from early on the walk that I now lived my life very differently from my twin. I would get up early each morning and wanted to get going; used to living my life controlled by a clock. Kylie is an early riser but has a relaxed country personality. She would get up, have a smoke or two, and chat to other pilgrims passing by. She was happy to stop and have a yarn with whoever she came across. Don't get me wrong, I love a chat, but I couldn't understand why we couldn't talk and walk. Kylie has a better sense of humour than me. I am much more methodical and serious. Our environments have influenced our demeanour over the years. Country people often have to contend with flat tyres or emergencies like a broken bore and understand that, at times, visitors might be late. City people get irritated if someone doesn't make an appointment on time. As each kilometre passed and each new day presented itself, I learnt not to be so highly strung and relaxed into the walk, and my twin got better at being less distracted and moving a bit quicker. However, somehow, I always walked slightly ahead of her.

Whenever anyone in any relationship has extended time apart and then reconnects, there is a settling-in period, and this even includes identical twins. We did have the odd fight, and early on, on one particular day, she yelled at me because she wanted to stop for lunch. Frustrated, I took a deep breath, trying to control my temper. I looked around in the almost abandoned streets of the quaint Spanish village and screamed at her, "All the cafes and shops are shut; if you walk a bit quicker, we might get to a town before they close for siesta". We both walked without speaking for the next few hours.

As the days ticked by, we developed a routine, and our relationship became more comfortable again the more kilometres we put behind us. I knew for certain that Kylie was the only person I wanted to do the Camino with; I honestly can't think of one other person in the world I would want to do the walk with. I think we both wanted to have the same experience out of the Camino. It may sound strange, but we had to learn to compromise and be tolerant of each other all over again.

Our breakfast was included in our travel package, but we found out that if we waited around for our accommodation to provide us with breakfast, it delayed our departure and made the day far too long. If we left earlier, we would generally make our destination by about two or three in the afternoon and then have the opportunity to have a siesta before organising ourselves for the next day and do our washing. We would then explore our surroundings, attend a pilgrim's mass if there was one, and have dinner, either by ourselves or with fellow pilgrims. We decided to ask each accommodation to pack us a breakfast, and after walking four or five kilometres, we stopped mid-morning, ate our packed breakfasts and grabbed a drink at a local café. However, we had to ask them to stop putting meat on our baguettes, as we had no way to keep the packed meal cool. Our hot backpacks provided the perfect environment for cultivating salmonella.

Walking through the Navarre region, in the little town of Ayegui, we came across a wine fountain attached to a monastery. The Bodegas de Irache wine fountain was established in 1891. It is a free fountain that provides chilled red wine to the pilgrims and is thought to have been built to provide motivation for weary pilgrims. We don't usually drink wine, but it did motivate us. However, I secretly wished that Jesus had drunk beer at his last supper; then, perhaps there would have been a cold beer on tap instead of wine. We tasted the red wine, and it tasted quite nice and cooled our parched throats.

Pilgrims were lining up to fill their water bottles with the wine, but we didn't want to waste our precious water. We did have small bottle of juices that had been included in our breakfast packages, so we guzzled down our juice and then filled the bottles with red wine. While we were waiting for our turn to fill our bottles, another pilgrim lent her walking pole against a gate about six feet tall, designed with horizontal bars and spikes on top. Her pole fell through the locked gate onto a pathway a metre below, well out of arm's reach. She was devastated as these poles made walking so much easier on the body and helped us develop a walking pace. She stood there, not knowing how to get it. My resourceful country twin quickly lay down and extended the handle on her walking pole under the gate, using the wrist strap at the end of her pole to hook the lady's walking pole. It took a few attempts, but she eventually succeeded, and I lay down and grabbed the pole with my hand when it was within reach. Our walking poles continued to have many uses on the Camino.

The walk is something I cannot describe; it is unique in every way possible. Walking across a country slows everything down, and I felt like I was standing back watching the world in slow motion. This, in turn, enhanced all my senses. I noticed the smallest details. A huge snail crossed the path. The wheat fields rolled peacefully in the wind, reminding me of the ocean at home on a still day. I noticed the abundant colours nature had to offer. My feet walked on so many different types of terrain: old Roman roads, city streets, country roads, shale and through water. I gripped the handles of water fountains and reflected in church pews that have connected pilgrims with pilgrims over the centuries. I heard the crunch of my feet as I walked, accompanied by church bells ringing in the distance, traffic travelling past, voices from around the world, cows mooing and roosters crowing, prayer, wind through trees, and silence. I tasted beautiful food from all the different regions of Spain, and I smelled the salty sweat coming from my own body.

After hiking anywhere between twenty and thirty kilometres a day, sleep came easy on the Camino. We slept in a different place every night, apart from our two rest days when we stayed two nights. My sister and I slept in appropriately named 'twin' beds; they were always positioned so close together we might as well have slept in the same bed. Staying in this type of accommodation, I was grateful I was with Kylie and not a stranger. The accommodation was something that surprised us each day, as we had no idea what type of accommodation would be awaiting us. Sometimes, the accommodation was attached to an albergue, and we could mingle with our fellow pilgrims. Sometimes, a hotel was quite basic, with mould used to decorate the room. Other times, we would walk into a beautiful, serene monastery with the sound of monks singing Gregorian chants piped through the ancient sandstone walls. It was all part of the experience.

On occasions, we stayed in accommodation located off the main walking route. The instructions in our booking documents would tell us what we needed to do. We arrived in a little town called Villavante, and followed our instructions to ring a phone number on our arrival so someone would collect us. We sat outside a little shop, and I dialled the number. A person picked up the phone and didn't appear to speak any English. After a short time, he promptly hung up. We were concerned but also exhausted, so we decided to buy a cool drink and weigh up our options. For some reason, I actually didn't care, which is so far from my normal personality; I like to be in control. While we were sitting there relaxing, not really having a care in the world, it dawned on me that our booking company had given us the phone number of a Spanish contact in case of any emergencies or problems. I phoned the man and explained our predicament, and he said to leave it with him and that he would ring us back shortly. He rang us back and told us to walk to a bar up the road where we would be collected.

When we arrived at the accommodation, we discovered that the elderly father of our host had dementia, and he was the one who had answered the phone. The accommodation was an old mill that had been renovated into a BB, and cool water from a stream flowed under the building. It was a peaceful place to rest, and the older man insisted we all have a little kitten to cuddle while we ate cool fresh fruit and drank cold beer. The bonus was that a fellow pilgrim, a new friend of ours, Diana from America, was also staying at the accommodation, and we had an enjoyable evening hearing about her interesting life. Needless to say, it was an unexpected, lovely stay. After speaking with the host, we discovered that she was the mother of twin daughters and was very interested in hearing about our lives.

The best way to hydrate on the Camino was to drink as much as we could at night. I admit that the beverage wasn't always water. This made us go to the toilet more than normal during the night, and one of the biggest challenges I faced was finding the toilet and toilet roll holder in the dead of night in the various accommodations we stayed in. The light switches were even harder to locate. Kylie and I got plenty of bruises on our shins from running into furniture in the middle of the night.

We woke each day and had no idea what experiences we would encounter. Our only expectation was walking from one destination to the other, and this unknown was part of the allure of the trail. One day, I was pacing along doing a reasonable speed, as both of us had improved our fitness as the weeks went along. Walking became a natural act. My heavy backpack now felt like an extension of my body, and I hardly knew it was on my back. I actually felt weird when I wasn't wearing it.

I was walking on a narrow path with thick foliage growing on either side when I rounded a bend and came face to face with a bull. Spain is known for the running of the bulls, but that is not what I came to Spain for. Kylie, as usual, was further behind me, and I stood at a distance and weighed up my options. Having had little experience dealing with bulls I was now regretting walking ahead of my grazier twin. The standoff lasted several minutes until I grew impatient and yelled, 'Move, shoo, go,' while waving my walking pole at it. The bull did not move and continued to have a stare off with me. Where was Crocodile Dundee when I needed him? Frustrated, I found somewhere to sit while keeping a watchful eye on the stubborn bull and waited. Surely another pilgrim or Kylie wasn't that far behind me? After some time, a pilgrim came bounding along without a care in the world. He looked at me and then looked at the bull. He yelled at the bull, and I realised the man was a Spaniard. The bull moved. Ahhhh, the bull needed to be spoken to in Spanish. I would remember that if it happened again, but I hoped it wouldn't.

Generally, we found our way pretty easily if we were attentive. We only got lost on two occasions, and thankfully we were walking closely together both times. The first time was leaving the city of Pamplona. Looking for the pilgrims symbols was difficult in the cities as we were easily distracted; there was much to see and the streets were busy. As we headed out of the city, we were following both Camino symbols and other pilgrims. We were pretty sure we were on the right path and could see the wind turbines on the mountains ahead of us that were marked in our guidebook. Kylie and I both took lots of photos on the Camino and as we left the city, we saw a beautiful park and crossed the street to photograph it.

When we crossed the street, distracted, we didn't notice that the pilgrims ahead of us had turned left, so we kept walking straight. After about a kilometre, we became conscious that we hadn't seen a pilgrim or a Camino symbol for a while. We stopped and obviously looked lost. A Spaniard approached us and tugged at my backpack to get my attention. Startled, I swung around thinking I was being pickpocketed and noticed that the stranger was pointing back in the direction we had just come from. He said the word 'forest' and pointed straight ahead and then to the right. We understood he meant we should turn right at the park. We had become quite good at using broken English and primitive sign language as a means of communication. Unfortunately, we had just gained an extra two kilometres for the day, but we were grateful to our Camino angel.

The second time we got lost was walking near the town of Granon. We had left the town and saw some pilgrims quite far ahead. We had started to talk to another pilgrim and hadn't looked for a symbol or sign, relying on the navigation skills of the pilgrims walking ahead of us. We were walking past a farmhouse when we heard a man yelling at us in Spanish. We didn't know if we had done something wrong and looked around, confused. We had no idea what he was saying, but the yelling was actually an animated conversation trying to let us know that we had gone the wrong way. The pilgrims ahead of us were now out of sight and too far ahead for us to let them know. We turned back the way we had come, discovering that the old farmer had fetched his bicycle and was following us to ensure we got on the correct path. We had to collect a few other pilgrims who had, in turn, followed us. We got to an intersection, and the old man pointed the correct way. The Camino marker had fallen into a ditch, which was why we missed it. My only regret that day was not thinking about trying to stand the heavy marker back upright so other pilgrims wouldn't get lost.

We started to get a reputation on the Camino and were identified as the Aussie Twins. We even got a text from an Australian pilgrim family that had done a shorter walk due to time restraints. It read that while they were lining up to get their Compostela (Certificate of Completion) in Santiago, they had a conversation with an American pilgrim and told her that they were Australian. She said to them, 'Oh, have you met the Aussie Twins?' We had only been on the walk for two weeks and hoped we were being remembered for good reasons.

We did make an effort to meet people, and both of us had a little Australian flag that blew in the breeze attached to our backpacks. We were dressed the same, and we obviously stood out. We stopped at a café for a break one day, and a young pilgrim asked us if we would sign her wooden walking pole. She had decided to get noteworthy pilgrims she met along the way to sign her walking pole. We felt very honoured and left our mark with the words Camino Princesses and drew two identical stick figures next to it. The nickname came about because we stayed in hotels and BB's, not albergues like most pilgrims. We had brought with us little koalas and handed them out to pilgrims and local Spaniards we met along the walk, and this was one way that we connected with other pilgrims and the locals. We gave a little bit of Australia to pilgrims from all over the world.

Kylie's knee injury improved every day, and the building up of the muscle around her knee gave the injury more support. We both strapped our knees and wore knee guards on the more challenging days. Generally, we had good health for the entire walk apart from horrendous blisters, and in the last week, a bit of tendinitis. I was walking into a small village one afternoon, and my foot kept swinging in the wrong direction. Confused, I willed my foot to walk directly in front of me, but to my dismay, my foot swung out to the right. My research indicated I might have tendinitis. I Googled how to strap this injury, and to my astonishment, with ice and strapping, my leg healed quickly, but I kept it strapped for a few weeks. With all the research I put into our footwear, we didn't quite get it right.

We had been walking on one particularly hot day, passing many of the younger and generally fitter pilgrims, who were floundering in the heat. We were accustomed to the Australian heat; however, the English and Irish pilgrims were suffering. Kylie actually gave an English girl all of her water as she clearly was not doing well and had no water left. She knew I would share my water with her if she needed some. We spent a large part of that day encouraging pilgrims and offering care and support. Unbeknown to me, I had been developing blisters on my feet and hadn't felt a thing.

When I took my boots and socks off in the afternoon, I had blisters on my feet, some the size of an Australian fifty cent piece with blood inside them. The pain was horrible, and I had no idea how I was going to be able to put my swollen, very sore feet back in the hiking boots and walk another thirty kilometres the next day. This was one problem with pre-booking all our accommodation in advance.

The only solution was to try and find some hiking sandals. The town we were staying in for the night was small, and there wasn't much on offer. I couldn't find any hiking sandals, but I did find some thongs. After dressing the blisters, we headed off the next morning with me walking thirty kilometres, like an Australian Jesus, wearing white rubber thongs instead of brown leather sandals. The first day, my feet smiled with happiness as the air was colder, and the cool air was comforting on my feet. The day after that didn't turn out so well.

The heat started again, and the thongs created more blisters on the tops of my feet where the straps rubbed against my skin. After many stops to adjust dressings and strapping, I had no choice but to squeeze my swollen, sore feet back into my hiking boots. The boots felt a size too small.

Some days felt like war and peace, my body and mind in a constant conflict. The first half of a day we could be walking in an industrial area where there was lots of graffiti, and the second half we found ourselves walking in rolling hills blanketed with wild flowers. Some days I wanted to be close to my twin, and some days I wanted to be nowhere near her.

As we followed the path into Burgos there were two routes we could take; one route took us along a shaded river, and the other past the airport and into the city through kilometres of a very bland concrete industrial area in full sun. We were aware we needed to look out for the river route and had been warned it was easy to miss. Kylie and I walked together, as we always stayed close when heading into a city. She was also offering me some gentle support. Regrettably, we missed the river route and had to walk the dull route into the city. The heat was radiating off the concrete, and every step I took was deliberate and difficult. This was the fourteenth day of walking without a rest day. In hindsight, we should have had a rest day before. This was probably my hardest day on the Camino. I was hot, tired and sore.

As we got closer to the ancient city of Burgos, we could see two remarkable buildings in the distance. Sitting just above the skyline was the spire of the beautiful French gothic Cathedral, constructed in the twelfth century, and just ahead were the golden arches of a McDonalds, constructed this century. This was the only McDonalds we saw the entire walk. The significance of the McDonalds was that we knew that inside this fast-food outlet we could go to the toilet, eat, and most importantly, rest in air conditioning. We had no idea what we ordered as the menu was written in Spanish. We just pointed to one of the pictures and signed, 'Two'. I took my boots and socks off and let my bare feet rest on the cool, white floor tiles. Taking my shoes off in a restaurant is not my normal behaviour, but my current health dilemma was not normal either. We sat there for almost an hour and soaked up the cool air before I had to push my damaged feet back into my boots to walk to our hotel. We were grateful we had scheduled a rest day the following day, and our first priority was buying different shoes. That night I slept heavily with both my feet hanging over the end of the bed, without any linen touching my wounded feet.

There were days on the pilgrimage we remember for a significant reason, and walking to La Cruz de Ferro is one of them. At almost 1500 metres above sea level, this is the highest point on the Camino, and is marked by way of a tall pole with an ancient iron cross erected on top. The views were breathtaking, and the peaks of the mountains in the distance are decorated with snow throughout the year. There are many symbolic actions associated with the cross, but we focused on the story that carrying a small rock or pebble from our original destination and leaving it at the cross, is an act of releasing any sins we had committed or of letting go of a particular burden or worry we had carried throughout life; it is the start of a new beginning. It was interesting seeing the non-religious pilgrims perform this traditional ceremony with as much love and respect as the more devout pilgrims, and they appeared to walk away spiritually and emotionally uplifted. I thought the enormous mound of stones and rocks represented hundreds of years of love, sadness, faith, and, most importantly, hope.

Kylie brought a stone from her property that she collected with her husband, and I found a beautiful stone on Sawtell Beach with Scott. We carried our stones in our backpacks until we reached the Cruz de Ferro, and although we were both aware that we each had a stone, we hadn't seen each other's. When we placed our stones side by side under the ancient cross, we noticed that the stones sat perfectly together, with Kylie's stone wrapping around mine and fitting snugly like a piece of a jigsaw puzzle. Looking down at the stones, emotional from the significance of the whole ceremony, they looked strikingly similar to the x-ray of the two of us in our mother's womb, curling around each other for comfort and protection. We walked together side by side for the rest of this day, without talking. We didn't need to.

The last few days of the Camino walking was easy; we floated along in excitement with our fellow pilgrims. However, even though our fitness had improved, we started to walk slower, as we didn't want the experience to end. We had once again been 'just' Jack and Kyl for weeks. I was missing my family, but was enjoying having very little responsibility, and I knew once the walk was over, our lives would once again disconnect. Getting six weeks' leave from life was unlikely to happen again for a very long time.

Once we reached Santiago, we made plans to go to the pilgrims mass as it is regarded as one of the most memorable experiences on the Camino. The mass is a Roman Catholic service, and the difference between this and any other mass, is that pilgrims are blessed at the conclusion. The pilgrims who walked the Camino without religious motivation generally attended due to the significance of the experience. It was also a chance for the pilgrims scattered throughout the large city to assemble as a whole. The mass is generally well attended, and many pilgrims had to stand, even though it was an enormous cathedral.

With this in mind, I went to the Cathedral well before the mass and positioned myself in the front pew to the left of the altar. I was aware that if the huge botafumeiro swung, it would swing across this seating area. The botafumeiro is a fifty-three-kilogram incense burner that is swung on a giant rope. The one in Santiago is one of the largest in the world. The botafumeiro is swung with the aid of a large pulley and the pure strength of eight men, but it is not always swung. It is swung for special religious events or if a tourist group pays for the privilege.

I had arrived two hours before the mass and sat on the ancient wooden pew in the tranquil silence of the marvellous Cathedral. I had time to think. For me, the Camino was a bit like giving birth to my first child. Leading up to it, I was excited, but not sure what to expect. It commenced, and I experienced a lot of pain and discomfort, but through tears and laughter, I discovered my body was much more capable than I gave it credit for. The final push is where I was rewarded with a miracle, but in this case, it wasn't a baby, but the joy of reaching Santiago.

Daydreaming, I began thinking about the walk, my twin, our relationship, the different lives we lived, and our points of difference. I realised it didn't matter who was the bigger twin, who was the smarter twin, or the prettier twin. We are two women that happened to look the same. We have lived lives that both compliment and contrast one another, and that is okay. The love we have will continue to ricochet back and forth between us. Life is our pilgrimage, and the Camino arrows will continue to guide us and show us the way. Like on the Camino, we will sometimes walk together, and sometimes we will walk on our own.

Sitting in quiet reflection, I recognised that I have accepted that we now live very different lives, but living without my twin sister altogether is a concept I cannot bear to think about. I have been told that to lose a parent that is an identical twin, can be painfully difficult for the children and partner of the twin that has died. They have a constant reminder of their parent or spouse, in the deceased's twin sibling. A woman recently told me that her mother, an identical twin, had died when she was nine years of age. She said she has kept an up-to-date photo of her Aunt, the twin sibling of her late mother, on her fridge her entire life, as it gives her a constant reminder of what her mother would have looked like. To be 'twinless' is the term often used when your twin dies. Twins talk about never being able to celebrate birthdays again when their twin dies as they're just a reminder of their loss; it's a double-edged sword. Are you still a twin if your twin dies? I dread the day I might receive a phone call informing me that she has passed away. I cannot contemplate living a life without her; it's just too painful. I also know that if I go first, the pain and grief that I leave Kylie will be insurmountable. Sitting in the Cathedral and just thinking of the day that I might not have her in my life brought tears to my eyes, several rolling down my cheeks.

'My' twin arrived and slid silently into the pew beside me. No words needed to be said. We knew what the other was thinking. We sat reverently together in silence. As the church was filling, we saw the eight tiraboleiros (incense carriers) enter the Cathedral, and we knew the botafumerio would swing. We both instinctively grabbed each other's hands as the hum of the organ circulated.

The incense wafted over us giving us permission to gently release the chapters of our life that had been difficult and to inhale the vast amount of love radiating inside the granite walls of the huge Cathedral.

A few weeks later, back home in Sawtell, my feet still felt the aftereffects of the Camino. As I carefully lifted yet another blackened, damaged toenail from my toe, I smiled, thinking of Kylie. If I was on the Titanic and had to decide who I would give the only spare life jacket to, would it be my husband or twin sister? I guess I will never know unless I have to make that split-second decision. I do know, that if I gave the spare life jacket to my husband instead of Kylie, he would give it back to my twin sister anyway.

www.ingramcontent.com/pod-product-compliance
Lightning Source LLC
Chambersburg PA
CBHW061205070526
44583CB00025B/3119